TRANCE
FORMATION

Slaves to the rhythm. Willits, CA, August 2004. Photograph courtesy of Jon Ross (nephology.org).

TRANCE FORMATION

The Spiritual and Religious Dimensions of Global Rave Culture

ROBIN SYLVAN

Routledge
Taylor & Francis Group
New York   London

First published 2005
by Routledge
2 Park Square, Milton Park, Abingdon, Oxon OX14 4RN

Simultaneously published in the USA and Canada
by Routledge
711 Third Avenue, New York, NY 10017

Routledge is an imprint of the Taylor & Francis Group, an informa business

© 2005 by Taylor & Francis Group, LLC

International Standard Book Number-10: 0-415-97090-3 (Hardcover) 0-415-97091-1 (Softcover)
International Standard Book Number-13: 978-0-415-97090-7 (Hardcover) 978-0-415-97091-4 (Softcover)

Library of Congress Cataloging-in-Publication Data

Catalog record is available from the Library of Congress

Taylor & Francis Group
is the Academic Division of T&F Informa plc.

Visit the Taylor & Francis Web site at
http://www.taylorandfrancis.com

and the Routledge Web site at
http://www.routledge-ny.com

TABLE OF CONTENTS

ACKNOWLEDGMENTS

Doing research for this book has been an incredible experience; I have made great connections with so many cool people and been privileged to be able to attend many amazing events. Not only have I learned a great deal about the rave scene, but I myself have also been transformed in the process and my life has been immeasurably enriched. Working on this project has allowed me to integrate my professional, personal, and spiritual paths, and put them in the service of a greater good, and I am grateful for the opportunity. As I have traveled to various locations and tapped into different communities, I have come to see that this project, in some small way, is part of the next stage of new interconnections and networks developing in the larger rave culture. It is my deepest wish that this book can give something of value back to a scene that has given so much to me. Rave culture is such a powerful vehicle for people to connect with the sacred; may it continue to thrive and evolve and take things deeper.

I would like to thank James Romero and Dagny Thomas for initiating me into the rave scene in a good way. Thanks to James Frazier and Echo Mae for opening the door to the rave scene in the Northwest for me, and to Chrissie Wilson for doing the same thing for me in Los Angeles and Southern California. For their assistance and support, my thanks go to Isis and Osiris Indriya and Michael Manahan from the Oracle in Seattle; to Sobey Wing from Tribal Harmonix in Vancouver and the Sunshine Coast; and to Bobbi Gerlick and David Nugent in Bellingham, Washington. I would like also to thank Kevin Gervais and Manoj

Mathew in Portland, Oregon; Jason Keehn and John Kelley in Los Angeles; Irene Moessinger and Micky Remann in Germany; and Frasier Clarke, Jill Purce, Gregory Sams, Anja Saunders, and Rupert Sheldrake in London. To all of my friends and fellow travelers in the Rhythm Society—especially Shams Shirley, Natasha Singer, and Shannon Titus—I send my thanks; a big shout out goes to the whole San Francisco Bay Area rave community, and to all the great people and crews. Deep gratitude goes to all the producers and DJs who have provided music that continues to blow my mind and inspire me. Thanks as well to all of my good friends who have loved and supported me as I have worked on this project—especially Greg, Kara, and Patti, as well as James and Kyra. And, last but not least, thanks go to Spirit, which continues to manifest in new and powerful ways in this world and in my life. I dedicate this book to peace and unity on the planet.

PART I

THE WORLD OF RAVES
INTRODUCTION: THREE SCENES

Scene One

It is New Year's Eve 2001–2002 in the Mission District of San Francisco, a dicey neighborhood populated by street people picking through the detritus of discarded items left for garbage collection on the grungy sidewalks. In the midst of this gritty gray urban tableau, in front of the Episcopal Church of St. John the Evangelist, small groups of brightly dressed people congregate at the entrance, their colorful attire and vibrant energy standing out in stark contrast to the bleakness of the external environment. I am one of these people and, when I pass through the gate, friendly greeters welcome me with hugs as I enter into a completely different reality, the world of an all-night underground rave. This rave is called Alchemie and, according to what is written on my invitation, is conceived of as "a divine vessel for personal and global transformation through ceremony, dance, music, light, food and personal interaction." It is one of four seasonal raves put on each year by the Rhythm Society, a group of dedicated organizers who "come together in dance and celebration for primary religious experience, spiritual growth, and community."

I make my way through the courtyard to the church building itself, and the first thing I see upon entering the foyer is a large altar filled with an assortment of sacred objects. I step into the main room, which is normally

1

used as a sanctuary for church services, and the full impact of the rave environment overwhelms my senses. Incredibly loud, pounding, beat-driven electronic dance music is blasting from an enormous sound system at a volume that produces shock waves I can feel in my solar plexus and throughout the rest of my body. Innovative lighting fills every nook and cranny of the room in a variety of creative configurations, and one wall is completely taken up by huge projected video images morphing with state-of-the-art programming artistry. All of the pews have been cleared to the sides and the central area of the floor is already crowded with people dancing to the music. There are four distinct sizable altars in each of the cardinal directions, an area with massage tables and masseurs/masseuses, and an area of tables with food and beverages. At the perimeter, people have laid out cushions and blankets and personal items, and are sitting and lying together in various groupings, engaged in intimate interactions. As I search for a place to put down my own things, I run into a number of close friends, many of whom I have not seen since the last Rhythm Society event, and we greet each other warmly, sharing our excitement in anticipation of the night ahead of us.

At a certain point close to midnight, a person with a microphone calls the several hundred people to gather together and be seated for the opening ceremony. Welcomes and introductions are given, as well as an orientation to the church, the Rhythm Society, the space, and the scheduled sequence of events. Another person talks about the theme of alchemy, and the intention to create a sacred container for alchemical transformation from base elements to higher spiritual refinement. Another person calls in the four elements and the four directions, and yet another leads everyone in a guided meditation in which we draw energy up from the earth and down from the heavens into our bodies. Finally, we are given two small strips of paper—a white one, on which we are supposed to write down difficult issues we have been struggling with over the last period of time, to put in the fire in the courtyard to be burned, and a gold one, on which we are supposed to write down dreams we wish to call in over the next period of time, to be placed in an urn in the center of the main altar. We meditate on these two strips of paper and their meanings for us for a few minutes of silence, and this is brought to an end by the powerful reintroduction of uptempo electronic dance music. A palpable surge of energy fills the room as everyone jumps up and starts to dance enthusiastically, and the rave begins in earnest.

From this moment of midnight until the break of day after 7:00 A.M., participants dance to the continuously mixed, beat-heavy music, losing themselves in deep trance states as they merge into a unified field of sound, light, and motion. This intense experiential matrix of the dance floor is the central focus of the rave, the crucible in which powerful energies are activated, shaped, and transformed by both the dancers and the DJ, who leads them on a musical and spiritual journey. For long stretches of time, I dance in my own universe, experiencing transcendent peaks of joy and terrifying valleys of fear, working through personal issues of light and darkness. At other times, I am actively engaged with those dancing around me, interacting with gesture and movement; we acknowledge each other with eye contact, and let out shrieks of delight when the music carries us to a shared ecstatic high. This ongoing dance-floor experience is punctuated by occasional breaks to go to the bathroom, cool off, drink some water, eat some food, sit or lie down, and visit with friends. Over the course of the night, each person develops his or her own unique rhythm of oscillating between the high energy intensity of the dance floor and the more relaxed intimate atmosphere of the specially designed "chill" spaces. Although dancing is the primary activity of any rave, many people may also have their most profound experiences in quieter contexts off of the dance floor.

As the long hours of night give way to daybreak, light begins to illuminate the stained-glass windows and the music is brought to an end with one last uplifting anthem that leaves everyone smiling and happy. Acknowledgments and hugs are exchanged as music issues forth from the enormous church organ and people lie down on the floor to listen to the baroque intricacies of the Bach fugues. When the organ music finishes, we are brought together for a brief concluding ceremony that provides closure to the rave. Some people, like myself, begin to gather our belongings and get ready to go, saying goodbyes to old and new friends alike, while others busy themselves with the tasks of breaking down the equipment, cleaning the space, and putting the church back to its normal configuration. For those hard-core ravers who still haven't gotten enough, there will be an "after-party" in a different location when the breakdown is complete. I myself walk out into the morning air with a sense of satisfaction and fuzzy exhaustion, taking in the beauty of the new day. I find my car, drive home, and sleep until the afternoon. Although I am tired for days afterward, the rave has provided me with just the type of transformative experience I was looking for, and I enter the new year with a feeling of spiritual renewal that allows me to approach the next phase of time with fresh energy and vision.

Scene Two

It is Labor Day weekend 2002 in Nevada's Black Rock Desert, an ancient seabed that is one of the most desolate locations on the planet, a perfectly flat expanse where temperatures regularly exceed one hundred degrees and virtually no living thing grows. Nearly thirty thousand people are attending Burning Man, a weeklong festival of communion, revelry, and creative expression that culminates in the spectacular nocturnal burning of a forty-foot-tall wooden sculpture in the shape of a man. The gathering is laid out as a temporary city in a circle of "streets," with the Man himself as the central focal point, towering above everything. People live in elaborate theme camps they have created, which have a ramshackle, almost Third World quality that is counterbalanced by an astonishing display of creativity and high-tech wizardry. Because of the barren, two-dimensional nature of the desert landscape, anything that is constructed stands out in high relief against an empty backdrop, a blank canvas that is then filled with the vibrancy of the visionary mind. Indeed, any survey of the incredible proliferation of camps and installations reveals a mind-boggling array of artistic, conceptual, and technical expressions, forming a surrealistic tableau that feels like a waking dream. One is bound only by the limits of one's imagination, and these limits seem to be temporarily suspended out on "the playa" (the name is loosely based on the Spanish word for *beach*), as though the imagination has been exteriorized into a three-dimensional physical landscape where it is given form.

Yet these external forms, amazing as they are, are not even the main show; they are often mere backdrops for the humans that inhabit them. At Burning Man, the human body itself becomes another blank canvas on which to express creativity. In addition to widespread nudity, body painting, and outrageous clothing, there are amazing costumes on display, from eight-foot-tall satyrs to glowing machine men to aliens. And these costumes are usually not mere decorations, but are employed in all manner of performance that is constantly happening—dance, theater, ritual, music, and so on. These performances are also highly creative endeavors, ranging anywhere from original techno-operas to reconstructions of ancient

Sumerian ceremonies. Some performances function within the traditional performer/audience division, but more often than not, they break down the barriers between performer and audience and encourage audience participation. Such interactive engagement is one of the primary values espoused at Burning Man, expressed in the official aphorism "no observers, only participants." These intensive interactions can occur anytime and anyplace, not only at planned performances, but just as frequently in unplanned spontaneous circumstances. This spontaneous unfolding of intense experiences and interactions characterizes each individual's time at Burning Man. Although days are usually spent cowering in the shade, waiting for the heat to pass, evenings are spent wandering from camp to camp, never knowing what type of environment, performance, or interaction one might encounter.

Music is as much a part of Burning Man as visual art, and one can also wander from camp to camp with huge sound systems blasting electronic dance music of every variety, incredible decorations and lighting, and dance floors filled with dancers deep in trance. Although Burning Man is a multifaceted phenomenon that cannot be reduced to any one component or conceptual framework, the rave scene is clearly a very strong presence, not only in terms of the countless "mini-raves" going on and the large numbers of people involved, but also because the powerful experiential states, spirituality, sense of community, alternative/utopian values, and high-tech psychedelic aesthetic of raves are a perfect fit for the ethos of Burning Man. In fact, a few years ago, the rave contingent became so dominant that organizers felt that it threatened to take over the whole gathering, and so they discontinued the central rave after the burn and efforts were made to concentrate rave camps in one area. Nevertheless, rave culture continues to be an integral part of Burning Man, and there is a symbiotic relationship between the two phenomena.

This relationship is best illustrated by the activities the night of the burning of the Man, which is the culminating peak of the whole gathering. After days of intense adventures, wandering dispersed throughout the playa, the entire population assembles as a whole for the first time and the sense of anticipation and excitement is palpable and contagious. There is a long procession of a seemingly endless profusion of costumed performers and brilliantly decorated vehicles that moves slowly down the central boulevard to the cheers of the crowd toward the waiting Man, which glows with multicolored neon lights attached to its skeletal structure. The crowd gathers in an enormous circle around the Man, kept at a safe distance from danger, and begins to chant "Burn him, burn him!" The method by which the Man is set on fire differs from year to year, but it is always accompanied by a spectacular pyrotechnic display and a huge explosion that results in the Man going up in flames. Spontaneously, and as one, the crowd screams at the top of their lungs. It is impossible to convey the intensity of the moment and this intensity continues until the Man has burned long enough to lose its structural integrity and fall to the ground, which takes several minutes. The falling of the Man is another peak experience accompanied by a crescendo of screaming and then, as the crowd spills out onto the playa in all directions, what can best be described as total chaos breaks out as far as the eye can see. It is as though the final bonds of restraint have been broken and wild revelry ensues in thousands of manifestations, including dozens of raves going off in every direction. For many people, it is the best rave of the year, with the best DJs, sound systems, and visuals; the wildest, most dedicated crowd of dancers; and the most powerful experience on the dance floor. For myself, I went to the Illuminaughty camp and danced with friends to a series of incredible DJ sets and a live performance by the techno group Medicine Drum. The party continued all night into the next day, culminating with the pastel colors of the dawn and the spectacular desert sunrise, which provided an inspiring and memorable conclusion to the Burning Man experience.

Scene Three

It is the first Saturday afternoon of July 2000; in the central Tiergarten Park in Berlin, Germany, I am one of over a million people who have come to attend the Love Parade, the largest rave gathering of any in the world. As I exit the subway and begin to walk up the stairs to street level, I can already feel the ground shaking with the continuous pounding beat of incredibly loud electronic dance music. I emerge from the underground station into daylight and am immediately overwhelmed by the densely packed mass of people crowding the city streets. The vast majority of them are brightly dressed in all manner of rave clothing and paraphernalia, smiling and dancing to the music, which is blasting from countless sources at a volume of deafening proportions. I am still close to a mile away from the park and the actual parade itself, so after steeling myself, I begin slowly moving in that direction, pulled along in the flow of people.

Finally, after what seems like an eternity, I enter the park, its wide boulevards and wooded paths filled beyond capacity with ravers in full party mode. Several dozen large "floats," brightly decorated semi trucks with powerful sound systems, crawl up and down the boulevards through the crowds, each with DJs spinning electronic dance music and packed with gyrating dancers. All of the boulevards converge at a central circle, at the center of which stands the famous Victory Column—adorned with a triumphant angel at the top—that serves as ground zero for high-volume music, wild revelry, and a maximum density of people. Somehow I manage to reach this epicenter without getting crushed and take in the tableau. It is an ocean of humanity stretching endlessly outward in every direction as far as the eye can see, everyone smiling and moving to the insistent rhythms of the all-encompassing techno soundscape. The sheer scale is impossible to grasp, and yet the fact that so few people are injured every year is a testament to the palpable and pervasive feeling of goodwill, unity, and cooperation shared by everyone.

The partying continues unabated for hours into the evening. At a certain point, the floats come to a stop and all of the sound systems are linked by radio signal to a central stage, so that over a million people are now all dancing to the same music. It is undoubtedly the biggest party anywhere on the planet, and dancers are rewarded with a lineup of some of the world's best DJs spinning the best music and with hours of ecstatic trancedancing. Strangely, everything comes to an end at 10:00 P.M., a very early time by ravers' standards, a time at which most raves usually haven't even gotten started. There is, however, method in this madness. While many people have heard of the Love Parade, what most of them don't know is that the parade itself is just the tip of the iceberg, a pretext for dozens of raves occurring throughout the city in the days before and after. In effect, it is a raver's paradise for the hundreds of thousands of dedicated aficionados who have come from all over the planet, and they are the proverbial kids in the candy store, with an overwhelming variety of top-quality events to choose from. So, when the music shuts down at 10:00 P.M., most people go home to rest, perhaps take a nap, recharge, and get ready for a full night of raving. For myself, after dinner and a nap, I went to a club called the Tempodrom and danced all night under a big-top tent in a warehouse courtyard to the psychedelic trance music of DJ Goa Gil. (As his name implies, this particular style and scene of electronic dance music, known as Goa trance, got its start in Goa, India, and is strongly influenced by Hindu spirituality and iconography.) When I left at 6:00 A.M., happy and exhausted, the music was still going strong and the dance floor was packed.

Although these descriptions of events may seem strange and unusual to someone who has never attended a rave, in fact, thousands of people regularly engage in such activities every weekend in numerous locations across the planet. Since the mid-to-late 1980s, raves and the culture surrounding them have become a huge global phenomenon that has made an enormous impact not only on the lives of the people directly involved, but also on many aspects of larger mainstream popular culture. While most media accounts of raves sensationalize their negative features, emphasizing excesses of drug use and bacchanalian revelry, what goes unnoticed is perhaps their most important positive feature—their tremendous spiritual and religious power. For thousands of ravers worldwide, raves are one of their primary sources of spirituality and the closest thing they have to a religion. This is a theme that has emerged repeatedly in my research, and one that ravers have articulated again and again in my interviews with them:

> It's definitely a spiritual experience. And I never had any spirituality before, so this was my first time that I had ever experienced that.[1]

> I consider it to be a very spiritual experience. In fact, I can say that prior to doing that, my sense of spirituality was pretty weak, pretty undeveloped, pretty dormant in me. . . . I definitely felt a very strong sense of spirituality. . . . At that point in my life, things really transformed in me. I really started feeling like I had a more noble purpose in life. . . .[2]

> I've had what I might term, and not facetiously, religious experiences when I've been dancing. You just get incredibly happy. You get filled with a real sense of joy. . . . The music is a religion. . . . If you've got a keyhole somewhere, that's the thing that puts the key in and turns the lock and opens you up.[3]

> For a lot of people, it was equal to a religious experience, but they didn't have to follow a religion. . . . On a ritualistic level, going into something and coming out feeling different, or feeling that you had become enlightened in some way. . . . You felt very connected to yourself and connected to other people. There was an incredible amount of energy, [a] feeling that you were energized when you left and this feeling of being very happy for a few weeks.[4]

It was what I always thought that religion was supposed to be, the community lightening of yourself, and to come out of a party and just be so filled with pure love and leaving the frustration of the week behind at the rave. It showed me true spirituality, from within flowing out of myself and joining it with other people. Undoubtedly the most spiritual feeling I've ever had.[5]

These are strong statements describing spiritual and religious experiences of a profound, life-changing nature. Such experiences are widespread among ravers, perhaps more so than even for people who participate in formal religious traditions. However, it is not simply that raves provide a powerful spiritual and religious experience, an encounter with the numinous that is at the core of all religions, although that in itself is remarkable enough. Raves also provide a form of ritual activity and communal ceremony that regularly and reliably produces such experiences through concrete practices. But it goes even further than that: Raves also provide a philosophy and worldview that makes sense of these experiences and translates them into a code for living, a map for integrating the transformative experience into the concrete details of day-to-day life. And, last but not least, raves provide a sense of community, a cultural identity, and an alternative social structure that exists in the "real world" outside of the rave. When one considers these powerful spiritual and religious dimensions of raves, combined with the fact that so many people regularly participate in them, it becomes clear that global rave culture constitutes a significant religious phenomenon, one worthy of closer investigation and serious study. Moreover, in examining raves as a significant religious phenomenon, what makes them even more interesting is the fact that they do not really resemble religion as we traditionally think of it, but rather are an innovative and unexpected development that has arisen in "secular" arenas of music, dance, entertainment, and popular culture. As such, raves also provide a template for new forms of spirituality and religion emerging in the rapidly changing social and cultural landscape of the twenty-first century. Therefore, a close study of raves will not only tell us a great deal about the spiritual and religious dimensions of this particular phenomenon, but will also provide general keys to understanding the dynamics of a wide variety of other innovative new spiritual and religious phenomena. What are some of these keys?

1. A combination of the sacred and the secular. While many raves have a general spiritual orientation, a sense of the sacred in the peak

dance-floor experience, and even explicitly religious components like altars or ceremonies, they also have many clearly secular aspects, such as paradigms of partying, "making the scene" (whether motivated by beauty, sex, status, or power), recreation, entertainment, artistic and aesthetic expression, and even good-old-fashioned commercial profit. The sacred and secular aspects are interwoven to such a degree that they often cannot be separated from each other, or they may even be the same aspect, but given a different conceptual gloss by different people. For example, one person's peak dance-floor experience might simply be construed as having a good time at a party, while another's might be a spiritual connection to the divine.

2. Expression within the arts. Raves combine several art forms—particularly music, dance, and the visual arts—in a unique manner to produce their characteristic experiences. Each of these art forms is a highly valued means of creative expression that in and of itself can lead to spiritual and religious experience and meaning. For example, the act of composing and producing a piece of electronic dance music can be a spiritual process. So can the act of DJ mixing, in which songs are strung together seamlessly in a creative fashion. Dancing to the mixed music on the dance floor is also a highly creative form of expression with spiritual implications. And the visual components—whether original art to decorate walls; flyers and websites to promote a rave; altars, lighting, or projected video/computer graphics—are taken seriously as forms of creative expression and spirituality and also contribute to people's dance-floor experiences of these art forms. Music is the most important, and in the rave context, music is more than just a means of creative expression. It is also a sophisticated and powerful tool for the induction of altered states of consciousness, particularly the trance state, and for opening access to the sacred.

3. Expression within popular culture. Raves are popular phenomena in several senses of the word. First, raves are not elite phenomena reserved only for the privileged few, such as a symphony orchestra concert or a religious ceremony closed to outsiders might be. Generally, anyone can come to a rave and, as I will show in greater detail later, the demographics often cut across traditional boundaries of race, class, gender, and ethnicity. Second, raves are popular in the sense that a significant number of people attend them, a number

totaling in the millions. One need look no further than the Love Parade to verify this point. Finally, raves are an expression firmly grounded in the forms and sensibilities of popular culture; they are youth oriented, mass-mediated, global, trendy, rapidly changing, disposable, have a high level of sensory stimulus, and so on.

4. Emphasis of experience over content. The incredibly powerful altered states of consciousness experienced by ravers on the dance floor are the single most important aspect of the spiritual and religious significance of raves. These states are brought on not only by the continuously mixed, highly amplified, electronically generated, beat-heavy music and uninterrupted high-energy dancing, but also by the innovative lighting and visuals, and the use of drugs such as MDMA and LSD. The content itself may be superficial, but that does not detract from the tremendous power and significance of the experience itself. Historian of religions Charles Long has touched on this shift in emphasis from content to experience in the "locus and meaning of religion," noting "Because of the *intensity of transmission*, the content of what is transmitted tends to be ephemeral; thus, the notion of religion as establishing powerful, pervasive, and long-lasting moods and motivations is shifted away from content and substance to *modes of experience*. Popular religion is thus no longer defined in terms of sustaining traditions, but in the *qualitative meaning of the nature of experience*."[6] Therefore, the powerful experiential states attained by ravers on the dance floor are the key to understanding raves as spiritual and religious phenomena.

5. The central importance of the body. As I will show in greater detail in chapter 3, these powerful experiential states on rave dance floors are bodily states, and the religious experience takes place in the body. Moreover, each person's distinctive style of dance, with its vocabularies of characteristic gestures and movements, correlates to specific experiential states that they produce, making raves not only an *embodied* religious experience, but also a *danced* religious experience. This central importance of the body is in stark contrast to Western culture's mind/body split, a split found in Christianity as well as in modern rationalism, which privileges the mind or the spirit and relegates the body to a status of subservience, repression, or even evil. From this perspective alone, the popularity of rave culture is a significant development in the religious history of Western culture.

6. Use of digital technology, multimedia, and global communication systems. Raves are high-tech affairs that take advantage of cutting-edge, state-of-the-art digital music production and amplification technology; lighting and computer graphic technology; and global networks for communication such as the Internet, cell phones, and satellite linkups. In contrast to earlier countercultures, rave culture does not see technology as negative and something to be avoided, but as a set of tremendous resources and tools that can be creatively utilized to enhance and intensify the dance-floor experience.

7. Postmodern, hybrid, cut-and-paste nature. Raves draw from a variety of different religious influences, from Hindu to Native American, Mayan to shamanic, neopagan to Christian, and combine them all together in a hodgepodge hybrid. From an historical perspective on religions, this is an extremely new development made possible by the advent of modern globalization that renders all cultures and religions accessible to everyone on an unprecedented scale. Today, not only can one choose to be a Jew, a Christian, a Buddhist, a Muslim, or a Hindu, but also a Wiccan, a Scientologist, a theosophist, or a UFO cult member and, more important, a combination of any or all of these. Raves clearly illustrate this hybrid, cut-and-paste nature of contemporary spirituality and religion. I use the word *postmodern* here in the sense that ravers have selectively appropriated elements from various traditions, placed them in an entirely different cultural context, and combined them in ways that suit their own purposes, which are not necessarily the originally intended purposes. In addition, many of these elements may not even come from spiritual or religious sources, but from arenas such as race, nationality, ethnicity, class, gender, and sexual orientation, as well as technology, communications, economics, and ecology.

The face of contemporary spirituality and religion is clearly changing, and global rave culture is an excellent example illustrating the nature of these changes. But what do these words, *spirituality* and *religion*, really mean? While there are no definitive or universally accepted answers, I think it is important to explain the approach I will take in this book. Here I will use a broader framework for the word *religion*, a framework that goes beyond the narrow reified institutions that the word is normally used to describe. This broader framework was developed decades ago by some of the pioneering scholars in the "history of religions" school of religious studies. In this approach, the emphasis is on the numinous as the central ordering structure for human beings. The human encounter with the numinous, the religious experience, forms the basis for subsequent developments that lead to the organized external forms that we call religion. Implicit in this perspective is the notion that religion, in a broader and more fundamental sense, is the underlying substratum for all cultural activity and serves as the foundation for culture in general. As Charles Long writes, "Religion is thus understood to be pervasive not only in religious institutions, but in all the dimensions of cultural life."[7]

For many people in today's society, however, our mainstream culture's traditional religious institutions are no longer a context in which they have a religious experience or an encounter with the numinous. So where do these people have such experiences? In other sectors of cultural activity. Historian of American religions Catherine Albanese has called this phenomenon "cultural religion."[8] Global rave culture is an outstanding example of how a significant number of people are having meaningful religious experiences in other cultural sectors outside of traditional religious institutions. Albanese has also provided an excellent approach to the word *spirituality* and, not surprisingly, this approach also emphasizes the primary importance of religious experience. In this approach, "spirituality [is] read and understood as the personal, experiential element in religion. . . . The task [is] to address aspects of experience that, for those involved, signal transcendence, sacrality, ultimacy, and/or a higher and purposive wisdom that empowers."[9] Here again raves are an outstanding example, clearly providing experiences of transcendence, sacrality, ultimacy, and a higher and purposive wisdom that is empowering for thousands—perhaps millions—of people.

In this book, I will examine all of these aspects of the spiritual and religious dimensions of global rave culture in detail. The first section provides an introduction to and overview of the rave scene. Chapter 1 traces the history of electronic dance music and its culture, from its roots in disco in the 1970s, to the emergence of house in Chicago and techno in Detroit in the 1980s, to the explosion of acid house and raves in the Summer of Love in England in 1988, to its growth as a global phenomenon in the 1990s and its current state in the twenty-first century. Chapter 2 surveys the many forms of electronic dance music events, including underground warehouse parties, large commercial "massives," mainstream clubs, outdoor raves, festivals, retreats, and unique phenomena like Burning Man and the Love Parade. These first two chapters provide the contextual backdrop for the second section, which is the real heart of the book, a close examination of the spiritual and religious dimensions of global rave culture. This section is based on research and fieldwork I conducted over a period of several years, primarily in the United States, but also in England and Germany, and includes my own firsthand observations and descriptions, extensive material from interviews with ravers, and scholarly analysis using a variety of methodological tools.[10] Chapter 3 examines the powerful experiential states attained at raves in detail and analyzes them as religious experiences, identifying key characteristics and themes. Particular attention is paid to the central importance of trance induction, feelings of ecstasy and love, connection and unity, transcending the ego, being in the body, the energetic field, spiritual worlds, and the presence of spirits. Chapter 4 examines the rave as a form of ritual and explores different ways of understanding its ceremonial dimensions, including ritualized time and space, opening and closing ceremonies, altars, ideas of "intention" and the "container," the role of the DJ as ceremonial leader, the incorporation of specific spiritual and religious traditions, and the use of themes and archetypes. Chapter 5 examines how ravers take the rave experience beyond the dance floor and integrate it into their daily lives and their spiritual paths. It also explores how they see themselves as part of a larger global rave culture and how this "alternative" culture articulates its vision for positive change in the world. Chapter 6 examines a number of West Coast rave communities and how they provide an important context in which this personal and planetary transformation can be concretely manifested. It also explores the emergence and growth of networks that connect these communities as a larger whole. Finally, in the conclusion, I place all of this material in a larger perspective by identifying key aspects of global rave culture as a spiritual and religious phenomenon, charting the current developmental stage of its growth, and exploring the broad implications for spirituality and religion in the twenty-first century.

Ravers themselves are very articulate on this subject and so I would like to end this introduction with the words of a raver, who notes,

> There's a little saying that "We are one in the dance," so if you get out on
> the dance floor, and you're all in that vibe, we suddenly become one
> regardless of cosmology. And that's what seems to be so transformative
> is that people aren't hung up on any particular dogma, like religion. It's
> more about sharing this spiritual nature that we all have with each other,
> and an understanding that we all do have it. . . . People are literally

listening to it [electronic dance music] in every corner of the planet and it's wonderful because it unites a planet in a language that is beyond language. It really isn't about lyric music, it's about a beat, and everybody can dance, so that's what's really great about it. I think that's what gives it hope to unify people in a way that maybe hasn't happened before.[11]

Shambhala, Salmo, B.C., 2004. Photograph courtesy of Quana Parker (Quana.net).

CHAPTER 1
A BRIEF HISTORY
OF THE RAVE SCENE

It was 1977, the height of the age of disco. The film *Saturday Night Fever* had swept across America, transforming the cultural and musical landscape into a series of fractal reflections of disco dance floors with mirror balls and blinking lights, John Travolta imitators in cheesy leisure suits, and the Bee Gees's enormous hit song *Stayin' Alive* endlessly repeating everywhere. I remember it well because, at the time, I was living in Chicago and working at a record store, and every few minutes a new customer would come in to buy the *Saturday Night Fever* soundtrack, which was in the midst of becoming the best-selling album in history to date. Unfortunately for me, I was no fan of disco. In fact, Chicago was home to one of the most virulent antidisco backlashes in the entire country, culminating with the public dynamiting of a huge pile of disco records on the baseball field in Comiskey Park, an event attended by a rabid crowd of thousands. Although I was not as extreme in my hatred, I definitely looked down at disco as an inferior form of music based on canned drum-machine beats, simplistic song structures, and mindless lyrics. So, like most people, when the disco fad faded and died, I did not mourn its passing, and moved on to other things. But, in point of fact, disco did not die; it merely retreated back to the underground gay, black, and Latino subculture from which it originally emerged. And there, far away from the harsh glare of the mainstream, it continued to live and thrive and evolve and mutate.

Fast forward twenty years to 1997. I am excited to be attending my first authentic underground warehouse rave in San Francisco. I have heard about the rave scene for the last six years and have only just now finally put myself in a position to have access to the real thing. I immediately love the space; the lighting and decorations; the people, fashions and the "vibe"; and I feel very much at home, but when I get out on the dance floor, all my old judgments about disco come rushing back to the surface. I can't seem to let go of my issues and enjoy the electronic dance music. These issues with the music would continue the rest of the night and on into several subsequent raves. However, a couple of events later, I finally have my epiphany on the dance floor and suddenly "get" the music, and go on to dance ecstatically for hours with a huge smile on my face. From that moment on, the music and rhythms somehow got deep into my body, and not only have I become a huge fan of electronic dance music, but I have developed an almost physiological need to dance to electronic beats regularly. My journey from 1977 to 1997 is tinged with enormous irony, as I have come full circle from being a fervent disco hater to a dedicated raver and electronic dance music enthusiast. My personal journey mirrors the trajectory of popular culture as well, and that journey is equally ironic, as house music (disco's direct descendent) exploded into the global phenomenon that is rave culture, a phenomenon that has made an enormous impact not only on the lives of the people directly involved, but also on many aspects of mainstream culture. It is an interesting journey, one with many such unexpected twists and turns, and one I will now briefly recount.

Disco

Disco is a shortened form of the word *discotheque*, referring to the dance clubs at which this music was first played. New York City was the primary center for disco, and the original audience was primarily gay African Americans and Latinos. As disco grew more popular, however, it became chic and trendy with the rich and famous at clubs like the infamous Studio 54 and then, spurred by the enormous popularity of *Saturday Night Fever*, spread throughout the United States into more mainstream demographic groups. As a musical genre, disco drew on the influences of African American soul and funk, but because it was first and foremost a dance music, its chief defining characteristic was its insistent, machine-like beat, which was foregrounded in the mix. The beat was in fact quite often produced by a machine; the first crude electronic drum machines were just being invented at this time, and disco record producers took advantage of the newly developing technology. Technology played a strong part in disco music in another respect, the prominence of the DJ (disc jockey) as the master of ceremonies at clubs. Unlike the rock concert, which featured live music played by musicians, discos featured recorded music, usually on special twelve-inch long-playing single records played by DJs over large, loud sound systems. The DJ was responsible for the selection of music, and used a mixer to segue seamlessly from song to song, thereby providing a continuous soundtrack for the dancers with no breaks in the energy. A kind of symbiotic relationship between the DJ and the dancers developed in which the DJ monitored the energy of the crowd and, depending on the context, either raised it to a fevered pitch, or brought it back down, creating several peaks in the course of an evening.

House

After disco retreated from the mainstream back into its core subculture, these musical and technological features continued to grow and evolve in the underground dance clubs of the 1980s. Catering to their core gay African American clientele, clubs like the Warehouse in Chicago and the Paradise Garage in New York pioneered the highly amplified, beat-driven music that came to be known as "house" (named after the Warehouse). One of the key figures in developing the distinctive sound of house music was the Warehouse's DJ from 1977 to 1983, Frankie Knuckles, who was so popular and influential that he became known as the "Godfather of House." Knuckles's approach was creative and experimental, and he invented new musical and technological techniques that other DJs were to follow, "such as playing a Roland 909 drum machine under old Philly records—thus emphasizing the beats. He would also blend in rhythm tracks that he'd created on reel-to-reel tape recorders to link and boost the music."[1] Over time, certain recognizable components of the music began to coalesce: "simple basslines, driving four-on-the-floor percussion, and textured keyboard lines."[2] As with disco, the importance of the beat was central to house music; as house music ethnomusicologist Kai Fikentscher explains, "House music is most easily recognized by the character and presence of its pulse, which is pronounced by an electronically realized kick drum. This concept is known as four-on-the-floor and is borrowed from disco music, house's precursor. That pulse, seemingly ever-present and ever-constant, actually fluctuates, often in minute increments within a range from 115–130 BPM [beats per minute]. It represents the stable order, the structure against which individual freedom can be asserted."[3] The driving beat of house music reflects its primary function as a dance music, providing a groove that serves as a rhythmic anchor for the dancers to lock into. The dancers then express their own rhythmic articulation of the groove through their individual body movements. There are strong continuities here with several principles of African music: the centrality of rhythm as an organizing principle, the groove generated from interlocking polyrhythms, the interconnection between music and dance, and the essentially participatory nature of the musical experience.

There are also strong continuities with some of the features of West African possession religion. Because of the high amplification and pounding insistence of house music beats, which are felt in the body as much as heard by the ears, the groove is often compelling to the point of trance induction for the dancers, carrying them beyond their normal consciousness into a powerful ecstatic state. When a large group of dancers enter this state together, it often results in what DJs and dancers refer to as "peaks"—palpable energy surges on the dance floor. Such peaks are one of the main goals of the house music dance club experience, and are sought after by DJs and dancers alike. There can be several peaks in the course of an evening of music and dance, each with its own distinct characteristic energy.[4] The religious overtones of these powerful group experiences are not lost on the participants. Fikentscher writes, "Awash in the sounds of house, the dance venue becomes a small version of . . . a social 'utopia' where music and dance become vehicles of individual and collective affirmation and celebration. The social model of the church . . . in African American culture is adapted to a secular setting, which for many participants is comparable in style and dynamics to actual worship."[5] DJ Frankie Knuckles, drawing from his many years of experience as a top house music DJ, has spoken explicitly of this analogy: "From my particular end of it, it's like church. Because, when you've got three thousand people in front of you, that's three thousand different personalities. And when those three thousand personalities become one personality, it's the most amazing thing."[6]

House music continued as a thriving subculture in Chicago throughout the 1980s, with superstar DJs like Knuckles, Ron Hardy, and Marshall Jefferson, clubs like the Warehouse and the Powerplant, and record labels like Trax and DJ International. At the same time, other local "scenes" also emerged, each with its own distinctive sound. In Detroit, for example, Juan Atkins, Derrick May, and Kevin Saunderson developed a style that came to be known as "techno," featuring strongly rhythmic drum machine programs and harder-edged synthesizer sounds influenced by European electronic music pioneers like Germany's Kraftwerk. New York became known for its "deep house" or "garage house" sound, the latter named for the legendary Paradise Garage club and its DJ Larry Levan. And in Chicago, classic house music gave birth to subgenres like "acid house," which was built around the characteristic squelchy sound of the Roland TBR303 machine that was used to compose the bass lines. Despite the growth and spread of these "dance music" genres, however, house and techno music remained primarily an underground phenomenon in the United States, with only rare breakthroughs to mainstream chart success.

Ecstasy

While house music was laying the foundation for the rave scene in the mid-1980s, at the same time, the emergence of Ecstasy as a popular recreational drug was also setting the stage for rave culture as well. Ecstasy, also known as MDMA, or 3-, 4-methylenedioxymethamphetamine, had been synthesized and patented back in 1912, but it was not until Berkeley biochemist Alexander Shulgin synthesized it in the late 1970s that it began to be more widely used. MDMA is classified by some as an empathogen, a drug that has the effect of increasing feelings of empathy, connectedness, and love. Because of these properties, psychologists and psychiatrists began to use MDMA as an effective tool in psychotherapy and other forms of counseling. Spiritual seekers also began to use it as a means of facilitating powerful ecstatic experiences that often had religious connotations, leading some to classify MDMA as an entheogen (from the Greek "bringing the God within"). During this early phase, use of MDMA was still primarily an elite phenomenon available only to a select few, remaining largely underground and hidden from public view. By the mid-1980s, however, all that changed as Dallas entrepreneur Michael Clegg, a former divinity student, gave MDMA the name Ecstasy and began to manufacture and distribute MDMA on an unprecedented scale through his Texas Group. From that point on, Ecstasy became an incredibly popular party drug that quickly penetrated into mainstream society, with Dallas as the epicenter. For our history of the rave scene, it is important to note that Ecstasy also began to be widely used in dance clubs as a means of enhancing the dance-floor experience, spreading beyond Dallas to house music capitals like Chicago and New York. The Starck Club in Dallas was the most popular of these clubs, catering to an eclectic mix of "rock and sports stars, musicians, stockbrokers, artists, and gay people," thus providing a preview of the inclusivity that was to become the hallmark of the rave scene.[7] Because it was still a legal substance, Ecstasy was sold at the door or at the bar, as well as at convenience stores and from toll-free phone lines taking credit cards. Of course, such widespread public drug use began to draw attention from conservative elements and, by 1985, the U.S. Drug Enforcement Administration had placed Ecstasy on Schedule 1 of the Controlled Substances Act, making it illegal and effectively ending the Ecstasy explosion of the mid-1980s. However, just as with disco, Ecstasy use did not die, but merely retreated back into its underground origins, remaining an illegal drug of choice for those drawn to its ecstatic properties.

Across the Great Water: Ibiza and the British Acid House Explosion

In 1987, both Ecstasy and variations of house music, particularly acid house and techno, made their way across the Atlantic Ocean and became established in underground scenes in Europe, setting the stage for a whole new series of developments. One of the first places where this potent combination of Ecstasy and house music took hold was the small Balearic island of Ibiza, off the Mediterranean coast of Spain. With its beautiful beaches and laid-back lifestyle, Ibiza has a long countercultural heritage dating back to the 1960s, featuring an eclectic mix of hippies, spiritual seekers, and wealthy jet-setters. It was also a popular vacation destination for Britons, particularly young clubbers seeking a relatively inexpensive place for a holiday getaway. In 1987, the heady mix of Ecstasy, house music, and countercultural freedom in the open-air clubs and underground parties on Ibiza made for some extraordinary life-changing experiences. As one clubgoer notes, "It was almost like a religious experience; a combination of taking Ecstasy and going to a warm, open-air club full of beautiful people—you're on holiday, you feel great, and you're suddenly exposed to entirely different music to what you were used to in London. This strange mixture was completely fresh and new to us, and very inspiring."[8] As another clubgoer put it, "We all had the same mentality, which was to have a really good time and try as hard as possible not to think about anything else. When we all came back to England, it really struck me that we'd got some kind of . . . it felt like a religion."[9]

Among the Britons on holiday whose lives were changed were Nicky Holloway, Paul Oakenfold, and Danny Rampling, and these three were instrumental in bringing this new religion back to England and establishing it there. They each organized influential club nights in London (the Trip, Spectrum, and Shoom, respectively) at which they attempted to replicate their Ibiza experiences, spinning acid house music to enthusiastic crowds on Ecstasy. Because the club plays a much more important role in the lives of young people in England than in the United States, when acid house and techno music hit England, young people flocked to the newly developing scene in unprecedented numbers and percentages that would not have been possible in the States. The acid house clubs quickly developed their own unique subcultural identity, which was strongly influenced by Ecstasy, a huge factor that contributed to the utopian "peace and love vibe" of the early acid house scene, a vibe that continues to be central in the rave experience today. Another effect that Ecstasy has, because of its amphetamine base, is to help keep people awake and energetic, an important feature that can make it possible for dancers to dance without a break for long hours on into the morning. For young people seeking freedom and novelty, adding this drug to the already potent combination of highly amplified beat-driven house music, trance dancing, and pyrotechnic light shows made for intense and wild experiences. Take, for example, one person's account of an acid house club experience in 1988:

> "I would suggest that Acieed [sic] House and the fundamental change in club culture it spawned was THE most significant cultural explosion to occur in this country (whose shockwaves have been felt worldwide) for over a decade. Talk about cultural revolution. It altered the course of my life and that of thousands of others. . . .
>
> Nothing could have prepared me for what lay beyond those portals. . . . The scene literally took my breath away. The club was rammed, the atmosphere was rich with whooping, enthusiastic, sweating party people. I'd never known anything like it. . . . But it was the music they were dancing to that really blew me away. . . . Unbelievable. It was like being

a blind virgin on his first visit to a brothel. Overpowering and completely overwhelming. . . . It was really Heaven on Earth. To the day I die I will never forget dancing on the main floor for the first time. . . . 2000 people dancing passionately, 2000 people's hands held aloft facing the DJ booth, their hands cutting through the green cascading laserbeams that bounce off their bodies as they chant . . . with an almost religious fervor."[10]

These wild all-night gatherings in London attracted thousands of enthusiastic adherents, who developed their own distinctive forms and fashions. In the hands of British musicians and DJs the music itself began to shift away from its American origins toward a more characteristic British sound, exemplified by electronic groups like 808 State, Orbital, and Future Sound of London and DJs like Oakenfold, Rampling, and Sasha. Advancing digital musical technology like samplers and sequencers enhanced this process. The same was true of visual technology, progressing from basic dry-ice fog and strobe lights to programmable lasers, fractal animation, and video effects units. Special spaces called "chill rooms," with soft cushions and relaxing music, were set up for people to temporarily escape the sensory overload of the main dance floor. Clubgoers began to dress in an identifiable acid house look: baggy, fluorescent, brightly colored clothing with psychedelic patterns, sometimes accompanied by visual paraphernalia and gadgetry. The so-called "smiley face" became the totemic symbol of this new psychedelic subculture, adorning tee shirts and posters alike. Numerous pirate radio stations sprung up, playing acid house and techno music and serving as information clearinghouses, along with a proliferation of acid house fanzines.

Acid house became so popular in 1988 that it crossed over to the mainstream, as songs like D-Mob's "We Call It Acid" hit the top of the record charts and tabloids like the *Sun* began to run sensationalist headlines and stories on the new subculture, emphasizing its drug use and bacchanalian nature. As acid house exploded into mainstream awareness, its psychedelic associations began to trigger a backlash from authority figures that some scholars have called "moral panic."[11] "We Call It Acid" was banned by the British Broadcasting Company, along with all other songs with any reference to the word *acid*. The police began raiding clubs, shutting them down and arresting people for possession of drugs. Such tactics forced the acid house subculture to develop more elaborate strategies in order to continue. One such strategy was to move out of the established legal clubs into abandoned warehouses or other large structures, where the acid house gatherings continued illegally, becoming known as "warehouse parties." This strategy worked for a time, until the police became aware of it, figured out the locations, and closed down the gatherings.

The Emergence of Raves and the Summer of Love

These cat-and-mouse games between underground organizers and the police gave birth to the next major development in the British dance music subculture, the rave. This appellation was originally given to the wild acid house gatherings described above, referring to the crazed activities and states of consciousness the participants engaged in, and used as both a verb and a noun. However, as the trajectory of these gatherings moved them out of legal dance venues into abandoned warehouses, aircraft hangars, municipal pools, and, ultimately, into open fields and other outdoor locations that could accommodate even more people, the term *rave* began to be applied more specifically to all-night events in these new contexts. The sheer logistics involved in organizing these raves gives an indication of the degree of fanatical dedication ravers had to their subculture and its ritual form. As Harvey Tyler notes,

> During the day, organisers would prepare the secret venue, setting up the required sound systems, lighting, lasers, refreshments, merchandise, etc. In the evening, via a mobile phone, they'd dial a computer that would record their spoken directions to a special meeting point. . . . Prior to this, tickets or flyers would have been sold for the event . . . with the special phone number printed on them. Party goers would ring this number to get directions to the meeting point and within minutes of the pre-recorded message being made available, thousands of people would be driving in their cars to the rendezvous. . . . A member of the rave organizers would be at the meeting point with instructions on how to get to another one. . . . After getting to the last meeting point you had the option of being herded onto buses to be taken to the venue . . . or just joining the convoy of cars, the atmosphere like that of a Carnival procession. The sheer amount of party goers descending on the site would prevent the police from stopping the rave.[12]

Unlike the clubs, the largest of which could accommodate two or three thousand people at most, these raves at secret illegal locations—particularly the outdoor events—could and did attract even larger numbers of people, often from five to ten thousand and sometimes as many as twenty-five thousand. There were two motivations for this on the part of the organizers. One was simply good old-fashioned profit. The money generated by ten thousand people at twenty pounds per person was enormous, making the logistics and legal risks well worth the effort. The second motivation was a strategy to thwart police intervention by sheer numbers. If thousands of people were already present at a rave, it was impossible for the police to shut it down. From the point of view of the participants, the cat-and-mouse tactics, the novelty of new locations, and the illegality of the raves made them even more attractive.

In the summer of 1988, the illegal outdoor rave became wildly popular, with dozens of events attracting tens of thousands of young people every weekend. Unencumbered by any external constraints, these raves took the wild energies of the acid house club gatherings even further, going all night into the daylight hours, creating intensely powerful group experiences along the way. For many of the participants, the raves were nothing short of revelatory, a life-transforming religious experience:

> For a lot of people, it was equal to a religious experience, but they didn't have to follow a religion. . . . For me, it was on the level of being in this situation of healing, very safe with a community of people. On a ritualistic level, going into something and coming out feeling different, or feeling that you had become enlightened in some way. . . . You felt very connected to yourself and connected to other people. There was an incredible amount of energy, feeling that you were energized when you left and this feeling of being very happy for a few weeks.[13]

The utopian feelings glimpsed in the heat of the peak rave experience were eventually articulated into the beginnings of a coherent ideology symbolized by the acronym PLUR, which stands for peace, love, unity, and respect. Such ideals, shared by the tens of thousands of young people who were attending the raves, are what led some to call that time period the Summer of Love. Like the Summer of Love of the psychedelic hippie counterculture twenty-one years earlier, it was probably the high-water mark of the rave subculture, attaining a critical mass in terms of sheer numbers and purity of shared experience.

The mainstream authority figures did not share this sense of love and community, however, and responded with more forceful tactics to try to shut down the rave phenomenon. As Tyler explains, "A special police unit was set up to deal with the parties. . . . A combined intelligence unit drawn from 12 police forces, the Home Office's most powerful computer system, sophisticated radio scanners, monitoring of underground magazines, light aircraft, road blocks and arbitrary arrests. . . . Phone companies were pressured into halting the use of their systems by organizers, and pirate radio stations promoting raves were shut down. . . . A new law was passed enabling a promoter to be jailed for six months with the confiscation of all profits."[14]

These tactics did eventually begin to have the desired effect of slowing down the momentum of the illegal raves. By 1990, faced with a virtual police state siege, most promoters chose to work legally and negotiated agreements with local authorities to hold licensed raves. Although the rave phenomenon continued to be huge in the 1990s, spreading to continental Europe and the United States and developing new articulations in these new locations, its character in England changed considerably. It became more commercial and more superficial, losing some of the sense of love and extended community that had characterized the Summer of Love. Within a few years, the British raves had degraded and, although still quite popular in sheer numbers, were no longer the same vibrant utopian centers of the culture.

Across the Planet: The Emergence of Global Rave Culture

It is interesting to note, however, that as the rave phenomenon spread to the United States for the first time, attracting a whole new audience, it seemed to carry some of its original authentic flavor with it. New York, San Francisco, and Los Angeles became particularly important centers for raves in the United States in the early 1990s. The "Stormraves" organized by DJ Frankie Bones were key in establishing the rave scene in New York. Likewise, Toontown, organized by Mark Heley, Dianna Jacobs, and Preston Lytton was seminal in San Francisco. In some cases, British ravers like Heley were instrumental in helping to reproduce the music and the feeling of the early British raves. This was also the situation in Los Angeles, where brothers Jon and Steve Levy organized a number of influential early events. Raves quickly spread and developed in most major cities across the country, with Ecstasy-fueled gatherings taking place in clubs and warehouses, and at outdoor locations. Young Americans were able to have the same type of revelatory experiences as their British counterparts, and they developed their own indigenous versions of the subculture, complete with clothing and accessory fashions, fanzines, pirate radio, Internet websites and bulletin boards, and so forth.

The rave subculture even followed a similar trajectory in the United States as in England, beginning as an underground phenomenon with a wild utopian sensibility and strong feeling of community and, as it gained in popularity and spread to the mainstream, gradually becoming more commercial and superficial, as evidenced by the proliferation of huge "massives" at arenas and stadiums attended by tens of thousands of people. The same kinds of developments were taking place in other locations as the rave scene spread throughout most Western countries. This process was fueled by the attempts of the major record companies in the mid-1990s to capitalize on the popularity of the burgeoning rave scene by marketing electronic dance music to the masses under the awkward appellation *electronica* with "bands" like the Chemical Brothers and the Prodigy. While the Prodigy did in fact become extremely popular and climbed to the top of the charts in England and the United States, this strategy eventually failed for a variety of reasons, but contributed nevertheless to spreading awareness of rave culture. This trend of commercialization in the mid-1990s also saw the rise of "superclubs" in England—huge, expensive, state-of-the-art venues booked with superstar DJs—pioneered by the Ministry of Sound and followed by the likes of Cream, Gatecrasher, God's Kitchen, and Renaissance.

In the midst of this commercialization, however, the underground rave scene was continuing apace, outside of the glare of mainstream attention. Dedicated crews sprung up in cities throughout Australia, Europe, Israel, Japan, North America, and beyond, each throwing small local events with their own distinctive style and flavor. For example, in Goa, India, a bastion of Western countercultural types since the 1960s, a unique kind of music called Goa trance, or psychedelic trance, developed in underground raves on its tropical beaches, strongly influenced by Hindu spirituality and LSD, and spread to establish strong local scenes in England, Germany, Israel, and the United States. In the San Francisco Bay Area, the Wicked crew began putting on its influential full moon raves in various outdoor locations outside the city. Following their lead in 1993, the Moontribe crew in southern California began to throw outdoor events on the night of every full moon in remote desert locations, building a close-knit community in the process. These raves continue today, and the Moontribe recently celebrated its twelve-year anniversary.

Yet the underground scene was not confined to small-scale events by any stretch of the imagination. Burning Man, which started as a small summer solstice ritual at Baker Beach in San Francisco in 1986 attended by several dozen people, moved to the Black Rock Desert in Nevada in 1990, where it began to take on its current flavor of a countercultural arts festival with a strong rave contingent, and grew throughout the 1990s from an attendance of several hundred to over thirty thousand while preserving a large measure of its underground character. A similar process was occurring with the Love Parade in Berlin, which began in 1988 as a celebration of the fall of the Berlin Wall and grew yearly from a small local street festival attended by hundreds to a huge international phenomenon attended by over a million, all the while maintaining its status as a free party open to everyone. For the last several years, the Movement Festival (originally called the Detroit Electronic Music Festival) has attracted a comparable number of ravers to Hart Plaza in downtown Detroit for three days of nonstop techno music and dancing. Interestingly, this kind of growth has not slowed even after the end of the economic boom of the late 1990s, a downturn that led to the scaling back of the commercial developments of the rave scene, best exemplified by the recent closure of superclubs like Cream and the Ministry of Sound. While this may be bad news for those people whose primary motivation is profit, it demonstrates the long-term viability of underground rave culture, and it is good news for those people who want to preserve the original "vibe" of the early rave scene.

I myself was first exposed to the rave scene in 1996 when I moved to the San Francisco Bay Area to do research for my Ph.D. dissertation. I was transformed by my experiences and I quickly became an enthusiastic participant. My involvement has continued and deepened in the years since and has led me to a variety of events in a variety of locations, many of which I will describe in the coming pages. It was not until 2003, however, in preparation for writing this book, that I returned to formal, focused research on the scene, based primarily on the West Coast and in the Bay Area. In the course of this research, one of the more interesting developments that struck me was the emergence of a new wave of underground rave crews with an "intentional" spiritual orientation who are working to create sustainable communities that integrate the rave experience into the fabric of their ongoing daily lives. I will discuss some of these crews that I was fortunate enough to come in contact with—the Rhythm Society in the Bay Area, Moontribe in Los Angeles, the Oracle in Seattle, and Tribal Harmonix in Vancouver—in greater detail over the course of this book; but for now let me simply note that I believe they represent the next step in the evolution of underground rave culture, a step that has been made possible by the fact that the culture has been around long enough to move from childhood to adolescence to the first signs of adulthood. It has now been more than seventeen years since raves exploded into the public consciousness in the Summer of Love in England and, despite the occasional pronouncements of its death, rave culture is still going strong. It has evolved into so many different styles of music and events that it is nearly impossible to make any generalizations about its overall trajectory except to say that it is still vibrant and vital and meaningful to thousands, perhaps millions, of people around the world. And for a significant number of these people, this vibrancy, vitality, and meaning has important spiritual and religious dimensions.

Burning Man, 2000. Photograph courtesy of James Romero.

CHAPTER 2
THE FULL SPECTRUM OF EVENTS: FROM WAREHOUSE PARTIES AND CLUBS TO BURNING MAN AND THE LOVE PARADE

There are so many different kinds of events the word *rave* might describe that it is almost misleading to discuss them as if they were all somehow the same thing. But the one key feature that they all have in common is the centrality of continuously mixed electronic dance music that people dance to for hours. This dancing can take place in warehouses or studios, in arenas or stadiums, in forests or open fields, on beaches, in city streets and plazas, at camps and retreat facilities, or in clubs and bars. It can be for free, for a small charge, or for a steep admission price. It usually takes place at night, but it can also happen in the day or for several days and nights continuously. It can be an intimate affair attended by several dozen people with only one room, or it can be a massive event attended by hundreds of thousands of people with many sound systems going simultaneously, or anywhere in between. It can be put on by an idealistic underground collective in its own space for the pure joy of it or by professional promoters primarily interested in making money. The music can be spun by local DJs or by internationally famous superstar DJs on records or

CDs, or it can be performed live over a PA. It can focus on one or several of an enormous variety of electronic genres: house, techno, trance, progressive, breaks, jungle, garage, downtempo, ambient, and an even larger variety of subgenres. In this chapter, I will survey the wide diversity of rave events, describing their basic structure and adding anecdotes drawn from firsthand experiences.

The Underground Warehouse Rave

I will start with the classic warehouse party, since that is perhaps the most archetypal form of a rave. While illegal abandoned warehouses were used quite commonly in the early days of the rave scene, typically these kinds of spaces are now legally rented, sometimes as a residence, sometimes as a business, and frequently under a combined live/work designation. In the San Francisco Bay Area, warehouse spaces are often residences for rave crews and/or collectives who wish to immerse themselves completely in rave culture and live "the rave lifestyle." Such residences make it easy not only to host a rave and its preparatory planning meetings, but other events as well. The Cloud Factory Collective and the Oakland warehouse space where they live, the Otherworld, are a good case in point. While a variety of underground raves regularly take place at the Otherworld—some put on by Cloud Factory and some by other crews—it also hosts a range of different kinds of events such as the Storm Sessions, a daylong gathering of networking, brainstorming, and workshops attended by different Bay Area and West Coast rave crews. I will describe a rave that I attended at the Otherworld in December 2003, an event called 2012, which was put on by the Koinonea crew. The year 2012 is widely known in rave and New Age circles as both the endpoint of the ancient Mayan calendar and the beginning point of planetary transformation in the late psychedelic philosopher Terence McKenna's time wave theory.[1]

Initial word of the event came out weeks in advance, through posting on the Internet; through 4 x 6 sized flyers distributed at other raves, at electronic dance music record stores, and from person to person; and by word of mouth. As is usually the case, these postings and flyers featured beautiful original digital art, made a brief statement of the theme, gave the names of the DJs, their style of music and/or affiliation (crew, record label, etc.), a date and time, and a contact phone number. As is also usually the case, they did not give the location, and the phone number was a temporary line set up for event information only. This is a protocol passed down from the early days of illegal raves in England, when this kind of precaution was necessary to guard against possible police action to shut it down. (In the current climate of antirave hysteria, this still remains a possibility today.) The location of the rave was then given out on the recorded message on the phone line on the evening of the event, mere hours before the doors opened. There are a tremendous number of logistical details involved in a successful rave—organizing DJs and musicians, sound, lighting, visuals, decorations, altars, furniture, security, insurance, the door, publicity, food and water, and the like—requiring a series of meetings to make sure the necessary arrangements are in place. The day of the event is spent setting up the space, which is a very labor-intensive process that takes many hours. For the 2012 event, this entailed setting up both the large main dance room and a smaller chill room. There was also a long entrance hallway with lighting and a series of quotations on the walls about the significance of each year leading up to 2012.

A typical warehouse rave usually does not open its doors to the public until 10:00 P.M. and the main dance floor usually does not really get going until at least 11:00 P.M. or often later, and 2012 was no exception. I arrived around 11:00, presented my ten-dollar ticket to the people at the door, and proceeded slowly down the entrance hallway, taking my time to read the quotations on the walls about the nature of transformation to expect in the years to come. This provided a nice transition from the outside world of gritty urban Oakland, so that by the time I entered the main dance room I was ready to take in and appreciate the colorful multisensory environment. A DJ was spinning progressive house music over a powerful sound system, and the dance floor was about one third filled with brightly dressed ravers, some dancing and some socializing. The lighting, decorations, and altars were beautiful, and thematically tied together by several distinctive archways that had a vaguely Tibetan feel to them. I spotted a couple of friends of mine, and we talked for awhile before going to check out the chill room, which was also very beautiful, but had no music playing as yet and very few people in it. We then went to the designated smoking area so my friends could smoke cigarettes and, about twenty minutes later, we made our way back to the main room—which was now tightly packed with a couple hundred dancers—for the opening ceremony.

The music stopped and a woman began speaking into a microphone, welcoming us and saying a little bit about the event. She then led us in a meditation/ceremony in which we closed our eyes, breathed together, did a guided visualization, and chanted the Hindu seed syllable mantra *OM* several times while she vocalized on top of the group chant. For myself, I had mixed feelings about this experience. On the one hand, I appreciated the creation of sacred space and the setting of a sincere spiritual intention. On the other hand, I felt the ceremony was a series of well-meaning but superficial clichés that were not particularly effective and seemed to actually dissipate the energy in the room rather than increase it. I would estimate that about half the people were participating fully and the other half were uncomfortable to one degree or another. However, once the ceremony ended and the electronic dance music came back on, the room exploded in a wave of high energy dancing and good feelings that continued for the rest of the night, so from that standpoint, the ceremony was a success. In the interest of providing an accurate overview of typical warehouse raves, I should note that while these kinds of opening ceremonies are quite common at warehouse raves I attend in the Bay Area, they probably only occur at a small percentage of the total number of warehouse raves.

After the ceremony, 2012 really entered the peak time of the night, which is often the case with most raves. The music was great, the floor was packed with enthusiastic dancers, the energy was high, and everyone seemed to be smiling. To use rave terminology, "it went off." There was a real "vibe" that could be easily felt and that many people were acknowledging. Although this shared ecstatic state is the goal of a rave, not every event succeeds in attaining it, so my approach is to enjoy this kind of fleeting experience when it happens. Accordingly, I stayed out on the floor trance dancing for a long time, carried along by the synergistic momentum of sound, rhythm, movement, light, energy, and a strong sense of connection with my fellow dancers and the larger field we were a part of. During this time, my friends had to leave in order to get home and get to bed in time to wake up for work the next day. We said goodbye, and I continued dancing. Finally, at a certain point, I decided to take a break in order to rest, give my body a chance to cool down, and rehydrate, so I went into the chill room and lay down on some soft cushions with my eyes closed, letting myself drift on the soothing sounds of the ambient music there. When I was rested, rehydrated, and cooled off, I returned to the main dance floor, which was still packed and now peaking, and resumed trance dancing for another long stretch of time. Some time after 3:00 A.M., happy and tired, I had had my fill and decided to leave and drive home. Of course, 2012 continued for many more hours into the morning light and ended with a closing ceremony.

There are plenty of folks like myself who do not stay all night. The dance floor often begins to thin out to some degree somewhere between 3:00 and 5:00 A.M., and the number of people left dancing at the end is usually less than half of the number at peak time. However, for those who remain, the rite of passage of staying all night forges strong bonds, creating a sense of closeness and connection that is very sweet. Many people stick around to help the crew break down the space and pack things up. Often there is an "after-party" for these people and the organizing crew at some smaller, more intimate location, which features food and chill-out music.[2] Finally, people go home and sleep until the afternoon.

The Larger Commercial Rave

Larger, more commercial raves are frequently held at concert halls, arenas, stadiums, and convention center facilities that can accommodate thousands of people. The really large events, called "massives," sometimes draw tens of thousands of people. Such events usually feature big-name DJs and have several large dance rooms with high-production sound and lighting systems, each showcasing a different style of music. These events are typically put on by more ambitious, profit-oriented promoters, sometimes with corporate sponsorship, rather than by idealistic underground collectives, although there are exceptions. These events also tend to be advertised in wide-circulation weekly listing newspapers like, for example, the *Bay Guardian* and the *Weekly* in the Bay Area, as well as with large glossy flyers and on the Internet, and unlike warehouse raves, the location is given out. Permits with the local authorities need to be approved and paid for, along with insurance and security. All of these factors are expensive, and this is reflected in a significantly higher ticket price, typically twenty-five dollars and often quite a bit more. Because these events are so big and public, they tend to lack the intimacy and underground feeling of smaller warehouse raves, focusing instead on providing a state-of-the-art multimedia spectacle that emphasizes the current "hot" superstar DJs and performers. The audience is typically on the youngish side—those in their teens and early twenties—and is more likely to be newcomers than veteran ravers. The best example of a successful massive in the Bay Area is the annual Cyberfest put on by Coolworld, which has been going since 1991. The 2003 event, held at the Cow Palace arena, featured five stages/rooms, a lineup of over sixty DJs and musicians, and was attended by twenty thousand people.

For those willing to pay the money and brave the crowds of a massive, a good time can be had dancing to high quality music with top-notch visuals, perhaps even to the point of having the kind of peak, religious, or life-changing experience that happens at smaller raves, and sometimes there can be a real vibe as well. One of the first electronic dance music events I ever went to was in 1997 at the Warfield in San Francisco, a small concert hall with a capacity of around two thousand people. It featured a DJ set by Fat Boy Slim and live performances by BT and the Crystal Method. I went with a friend, was amazed by the music, and had a fantastic time dancing, but it felt more like a concert than a rave. These kinds of commercial events usually do not emphasize a specifically spiritual orientation, and this is reflected in the absence of opening and closing ceremonies, altars, and chill spaces. Also, because the size of the crowd is so large, it is more difficult to make personal connections, especially with strangers, and one can sometimes experience a sense of aloneness and alienation. Finally, these events may not have the necessary permits to go all night long, which makes it more difficult to have a full-on transformational experience. Large commercial raves often serve as an introduction to the rave scene for the uninitiated and, if a beginner has a good time, she will go to more events and may develop connections that lead her to attend more intimate, underground raves.

Clubs and Bars

Clubs and bars are also an important context for electronic dance music even though club and bar events are not usually raves in the strict sense of the word. Although some clubs and bars do their own booking, they often do not put on the events themselves, but instead make arrangements with crews or promoters to use their space on a regular basis, usually weekly or monthly, and also for one-time events as well. The crew or promoter is primarily responsible for the lineup of DJs, the overall theme and flavor, and the target audience. However, depending on the arrangement, they can also be in charge of or collaborate on the creation and distribution of flyers and other advertising and, in some cases, the decor, lighting, and even the sound system. The profits are split, typically with the door proceeds going to the crew or promoters and proceeds from the sale of drinks going to the bar or club. If successful, these weeklies and monthlies can develop their own devoted crowd and a sense of community, as is the case in San Francisco, for example, with the Looq crew's weekly and monthly events, Qool Happy Hour and Qool Saturdays, which feature a top-notch lineup of DJs and maintain an authentic underground feeling.

However, while these kinds of events comprise a significant percentage of any given city's ongoing electronic dance music offerings and good experiences can be had on the dance floor, in general, most aficionados do not consider them to be raves per se for a variety of reasons. First among these is that they do not usually go all night due to city ordinances stipulating closing time, in many cases as early as 2:00 A.M. Second, the sale of alcohol and the prohibition of illegal drugs like MDMA and marijuana at a legal venue makes the vibe of a bar or club event considerably different than that of an underground rave—generally less ecstatic, utopian, and open, and more like a typical bar or club. This is not to say that people don't do illegal drugs at a club or bar, but recent antidrug pressures have made it much more difficult and have curtailed such use significantly. For example, in San Francisco, the leading electronic dance music club, 1015 Folsom, has been forced by the police to search people strictly at the door and to install video surveillance cameras throughout the venue, which has had the effect of not only cutting down on illegal drug use, but also on the number of people who choose to submit themselves to this kind of invasive scrutiny.

Yet, beyond these particularities, perhaps the most important factor distinguishing club and bar events from real raves is simply the fact that they are "above ground;" in other words, they are open to anyone who happens to come to the club with enough money to get in. So while the crews who put them on and many of the people who attend may be underground ravers (but they also very well may not be), there is no consensual framework that the purpose of the event is to generate the peak dance-floor experience and the sense of connection of a rave. For every raver who is there for that purpose, there may be someone else who is there simply to get a drink or looking to pick up a sexual partner or any of the many other reasons people go to a bar or club. A great example of this is 1015 Folsom. The club's Friday and Saturday night events, Sonic (produced by Spundae) and Release (produced by Martel and Nabiel), consistently book top DJs to play high quality music on their state-of-the-art sound system, and I have enjoyed many nights at 1015 dancing to amazing sets spun by the likes of Sandra Collins, Paul van Dyk, and Dave Seaman.[3] But the crowd is often mostly above-ground types and it has become increasingly rare for me to have a transcendent dance-floor experience with an underground vibe and a deep sense of connection at 1015. Nevertheless, because the logistics of putting on events at bars and clubs is considerably easier than at other locations, they will always be a major context for electronic dance music, and many people have a great time at them. In fact, the clubs and bars often serve as an introduction to the rave scene for the uninitiated, and once they've had a positive experience with electronic dance music in a club setting, many newcomers will then seek out more authentic underground raves. And sometimes underground crews will put on "one-off" raves at a club that will "go off" and have a real vibe. It is also worth remembering that the early acid house scene in London was essentially a club phenomenon, which demonstrates that despite their drawbacks, clubs were and continue to be an important context for authentic rave experience and culture, especially in England.

The Outdoor Rave

Raves that take place outdoors in natural settings have been part of the scene since the Summer of Love in England in 1988, where a significant percentage of events were held in open fields out in the countryside. Some of the seminal early raves in the United States were also held outdoors in natural settings. For example, the influential full-moon raves put on by the Wicked crew in the Bay Area in the early 1990s were held in natural locations such as Bonny Dune Beach, south of San Francisco. In the words of one attendee,

> The Wicked full moons were really special. It was clear that the whole thing of it being free and outdoor really brought out the depth of the experience, or the real potential of it to go deeper and to be more authentic and intimate and noncommercial and all that.[4]

The Moontribe crew in Los Angeles quickly followed suit and put on their own full moon gatherings at different remote locations on national forest land out in the Mojave Desert, an outdoor tradition that continues today. Here is a description of one of the first Moontribe full moon gatherings:

> It was on a flat lakebed. . . . The cars just kept coming. We just kept seeing headlights driving over the playa, the lakebed. And it was just like out of some movie, like Mad Max or something like that. And next thing you know we had, like, five, seven hundred people just dancing their butts off. For me, that was a very defining moment. . . . That was also the first time in the morning, you know, the sun came up and people just sort of spontaneously made a circle holding hands and started dancing around and then it was just lots of smiling happy people. . . . And one of the reasons I think it was so successful, as much as I'd like to think everyone came to see the DJs, I think it was much more about the location and what I would call now the spiritual aspect of that, which was . . . people living here in L.A., there's concrete, pretty stressful living here, and just to go out to the desert and release all that tension. It was all about the sun coming up. That was the focal point of the event. . . . People would find a little hill someplace and watch it come up and the sun cascade in the whole valley without any cars or smog or anything. Watching the sunrise in the desert with your friends after you've been dancing all night; that's a good thing.[5]

Outdoor campout raves are particularly popular in the Pacific Northwest, where the natural beauty of the land provides a spectacular backdrop. As one Portland raver says,

> It's why Oregon has such a unique scene is because of these outdoor parties that are just beyond anything I can even describe. They're usually free events and it's just this magic thing that happens.[6]

Another adds,

> It's not just an evening that you share with each other. You're out camping. . . . It's beautiful, very interactive.[7]

In Washington, for many years, the Starseed crew from Seattle put on full moon "events, mostly free outdoor stuff, up in the mountains, which became quite epic."[8] And the Tribal Harmonix crew from Vancouver has an annual summer campout rave out in the forests and mountains of British Columbia. Many Bay Area crews who regularly put on warehouse raves—such as Friends n Family, the Rhythm Society, or Sweet!—also make a point of having at least one outdoor campout rave each year in the summer at a beautiful natural setting. I should also add that outdoor events of varying sizes continue to happen in England and other parts of Europe as well. For example, in 2000, when I was in England to do research, I attended a small campout rave called Breathing Space put on by a psychedelic trance crew in a forest north of London.

There are a number of factors involved in an outdoor campout event that create conditions more conducive to having powerful experiences and making deeper connections. The first of these is simply the extra effort involved in attending, which necessitates making more of a commitment. It takes a lot longer to drive to outdoor events, often several hours. It is more than just one evening and sometimes as long as two or three days. One needs to pack all the necessary gear, including appropriate clothing, camping equipment, and, in some cases, food and cooking gear as well. Once at the location, it is difficult to just pick up and leave at any time. As one Moontribe veteran puts it,

> It requires a serious investment of time and energy and risk to get out to these things. It filters out a lot of people that don't have a certain kind of sensibility, and then people that have a similar sensibility naturally find themselves connecting and bonding easily. And often you're out there for a day or two and it's pretty powerful energy.[9]

Bonding is also enhanced because everyone is actually living together in a temporary community during the event, so interactions can go beyond the peak dance-floor experience to other activities that are more mundane, such as eating or camping. There are also more opportunities just to hang out and do nothing. These mundane activities are made more special by virtue of the fact that they take place in a liminal environment that is set apart from one's daily life.

The beauty and power of the natural setting, and one's connection to it, are also key factors in the outdoor rave experience. One raver notes,

> There's that connection I always feel going down into the earth. It's just a very core connection to warm, deep earth. And I feel an upward connection to the divine. It's just like right through my body, out with my dancers, into the mountains, out to the sunshine. It's all about nature for

me and I'm just in it. . . . For me, what it's about is being a true element of nature.[10]

Another mentions,

> I've noticed in my own movement that I'll consciously flicker in and out of drawing influence from the environment around me. . . . If I'm in nature, I've noticed that I like tuning into the shapes of form around me and allowing my movement to resemble the dance I see of plants and trees that are growing [there].[11]

And, of course, different types of natural environments have very distinctive feelings and energies. The dry, hot, desolate desert environment is very different from being in a lush green forest, which in turn is very different from being on a sandy beach next to the ocean with waves crashing.

Festivals

One important variant of the outdoor rave is the festival, which typically lasts two to three days (sometimes longer) and tends to be a larger, higher-production affair with numerous stages and/or tents. England has a particularly strong summer festival tradition and one of the best-known and longest running of these is the Glastonbury Performing Arts Festival, which began during the heyday of rock music and has been going strong for over thirty years. While Glastonbury is not exclusively devoted to electronic dance music, as are other festivals such as Creamfields or Homelands, there is nevertheless a very strong electronic dance music presence, with a huge dance tent that accommodates tens of thousands of people and features a first-rate lineup of DJs and performers, a second smaller dance music stage, and electronic dance music headliners like the Chemical Brothers or Moby on the main stage. I attended the Glastonbury Festival in 2000, along with 100,000 other people and, once I adjusted to the inconceivably vast, tightly packed ocean of humanity (which was no small feat), I ended up having a great time, dancing for hours to amazing DJs and performers day after day. And despite the enormity of the crowds, I was still able to make some nice person-to-person connections. Beyond the dance floor, some of these interactions took place in nonmusical contexts like the extensive vendors' rows and the "greenfields zone" that included alternative technology displays, a healing area, and a sacred space set aside for quiet reflection and meditation. In general, I was very favorably impressed by the level of friendliness displayed by most people and the overall good vibe of the festival.

England is certainly not the only place where rave festivals are held; they regularly take place throughout Europe, the United States, and many other locations around the world. One of the best and most popular festivals in the United States is the Movement Festival (formerly the Detroit Electronic Music Festival, or DEMF), which happens every Memorial Day weekend in Hart Plaza in the center of downtown Detroit. The Movement Festival began in 2000 as a celebration of Detroit's historic role as the birthplace of techno music and a showcase for the city's many local DJs and performers. From the very beginning, organizers were able to secure the support of the city government, including funding, sponsorship, and the use of Hart Plaza. This joining of forces between ravers and city government is extremely rare; in fact, government authorities are usually hostile to electronic dance music events and marshal their efforts and resources toward shutting them down. The festival offered free admission and by the second year had attracted a total of over a million people for the weekend. I attended the second DEMF in 2001 and found it to be a fantastic event. The setting in the heart of the city gave it an urban feeling very different from most outdoor festivals that take place in more natural environments, but at the same time, the normally bleak, barren urban landscape was transformed into a colorful throng of happy, dancing people. And these people were not just typical ravers, but Detroit area locals from all walks of life, including a high percentage of African Americans, who were united in obvious pride in their electronic dance music heritage. My experience was almost identical to that of a West Coast raver who attended the DEMF and described it as follows:

> I went to the Detroit Electronic Music Festival and I think it was Juan Atkins that was playing on the main stage. And I remember looking around and there was probably close to four thousand in this amphitheater. It was just unbelievable, just completely packed with people. And I looked around and there were old women with walkers and unhoused people and policemen and ravers—just this huge conglomeration of people, obviously a lot of them from Detroit. And I looked over and Juan Atkins is playing this hard, dark techno and everyone just starts screaming "Detroit, Detroit, Detroit!" over and over. I was just amazed at this place where you don't have anything to be proud of—this city, cars and

car factories, you know—then, all of the sudden you have people screaming and giving themselves a pride for the city that they're from. To me,
that is what the revitalization aspect is. Just the fact that it makes you
proud. And it seems like a way of transforming these cities into this really
ancient ritual that's performed in the most urban center of all.[12]

On the West Coast, one of the more popular outdoor festivals is the
Coachella Valley Music and Arts Festival, which takes place every year in
late April or early May at the Empire Polo Fields in Indio in the southern
California desert at the foot of the Santa Rosa Mountains. Coachella is a
classic commercial festival attended by tens of thousands of people that
features a lineup of top DJs and electronic dance music performers, along
with rock and hip hop acts as well.

Yet, of all the festivals, Burning Man stands alone as one of a kind, and
there are a variety of reasons for its unique and distinctive nature.[13] The
first of these is that it is not a rave festival per se. In fact, it is difficult to
say exactly what Burning Man really is. Some people describe it as an arts
festival and certainly the arts aspect is extremely important, as evidenced
by the plethora of unorthodox art installations, theme camps, and performances. Some might say the ceremonial and spiritual aspect is key, particularly with the central ritual of the "burning of the Man" and the wide
array of other ceremonial and spiritual practices that take place. On the
other hand, some might argue that it is really just a big party that cele-
brates hedonism and a variety of nontraditional approaches to sexuality.
Still others might wax rhapsodic about its articulation of alternative culture and community. And all of these approaches would be correct. However, there is no denying the strong connection between Burning Man and
rave culture, which was confirmed by ravers in many of my interviews. In
this regard, a second unique aspect is that the raves at Burning Man, like
most other activities, are put together by those participants who feel
moved to do so and, not insignificantly, at their own expense. Therefore,
there are many different sound systems and dance areas set up by many
different crews with many different tastes, and the DJ/performer pool is
primarily comprised of camp members and other fellow participants. It is
thus the ultimate playground of noncommercial underground rave culture,
a place where you can wander in any direction following the sound of the
beats and find another dance floor with its own distinctive flavor. Another
key aspect is that Burning Man now lasts for a full week, far longer than

most two- or three-day festivals, and this length of time makes it easier to go much deeper into the experience. As one raver put it,

> Burning Man was a seminal experience in my life. . . . At Burning Man, we got completely into that sacred space. As Burning Man can do, as the week goes on, everybody hits that space.[14]

When I asked another raver if Burning Man was connected to rave culture, he said,

> Absolutely. It's really confirmational. . . . And that experience has been really profound. . . . I went to Burning Man and got a way big jolt of hope and sense of belonging.[15]

Finally, no survey of rave festivals would be complete without mentioning the Love Parade. It is unique not only because of the number of people who attend (1.5 million in 2000; 1 million in 2001; and 750,000 in 2002 and 2003), and not only because of the distinctive format of the parade—the daytime procession of dozens of floats, each with its own sound system and DJs—but because for three days, the entire city of Berlin is transformed into a raver's playground with dozens of events to choose from, making it a pilgrimage destination for ravers from around the world and, for that weekend, the de facto capital of global rave culture. It is also one of the most powerful examples of how far rave culture has penetrated into the mainstream, and it demonstrates the complexities and contradictions of the dynamics of this interaction. For many years, the city government of Berlin was an active participant in helping put on the Love Parade, making the enormous central Tiergarten park available by giving the Love Parade the designation of a "demonstration" and providing massive resources for traffic and crowd control, portable toilets, garbage, and cleanup. In return, the influx of ravers pumped significant money into Berlin's economy and tourist industry. Over time, as attendance grew into the hundreds of thousands, organizers turned to corporate sponsorship to underwrite the spiraling costs of dealing with such a huge crowd, a decision that was the cause of some ambivalence among underground ravers. In addition, the massive crowds increasingly became a source of ambivalence for local Berliners, many of whom chose to leave the city during that weekend.

In 2001, the city government decided to revoke the "demonstration" designation, which significantly increased the organizers' expenses. Coupled with a marked decrease in attendance in 2002 and 2003 (although 750,000 is still a staggering number), the Love Parade began to suffer huge financial losses that became so crippling that both the 2004 and 2005 Love Parades were canceled. (At the time of this writing, it is unclear whether the Love Parade will continue and, if so, in what form.) However, even as these developments have thrown the original Love Parade in Berlin into question, a host of Love Parades have sprung up in other locations (Austria, Israel, Mexico, South Africa, Switzerland, and, most recently, San Francisco) over the last several years and have enjoyed considerable success. The annual Street Parade in Zurich, Switzerland, using the Love Parade as its model, has steadily grown from attendance of a few thousand at its inception in 1992 to 650,000 in 2002, 900,000 in 2003, and 1 million in 2004. Thus, it appears to have supplanted the Love Parade as the premier rave parade in the world, and its success demonstrates the continued popularity of the form, regardless of the fate of the original Love Parade in Berlin.

Retreats

On the opposite end of the spectrum from the Love Parade is a much smaller, more intimate rave phenomenon that has just started to emerge in the last few years—the retreat. Retreats are similar to campout raves, but they are held at retreat facilities with pleasant indoor sleeping accommodations, kitchen and dining facilities, a main room for music and dancing, and smaller rooms for workshops and other activities. Aside from these more comfortable physical amenities, the central distinctive feature of a rave retreat is the ongoing schedule of workshops, classes, spiritual practices and ceremonies, and a variety of other educational and interactive activities that take place throughout the days and evenings. Although retreats usually do include a rave-type electronic dance music event, the workshops comprise a major focus for participants, and there is also ample opportunity for people to spend time together informally as well. On New Year's of 2003–2004, I attended Intention, the annual retreat put on by the Tribal Harmonix crew up on the Sunshine Coast of British Columbia, which was held at a YMCA camp in a spectacular location right on the waterfront with views of the mountains. This five-day-long retreat was attended by several dozen people, featured workshops on everything from yoga to tarot to drug education to sustainable community to dance rituals, and culminated in an all-night rave on New Year's Eve. The rave featured both an opening ceremony and a ritual theater performance at midnight, and had two rooms for dancing as well as a chill space. I found Tribal Harmonix to be a close-knit alternative community that was very open and welcoming to outsiders like myself, and I made good connections and had several meaningful and transformative experiences.

A similar retreat is put on every spring by the Rhythm Society at a facility north of the Bay Area in a beautiful natural setting in Mendocino County. I attended the 2004 retreat, Inspire, along with several dozen others. I arrived on Friday evening just in time to participate in a Native American–influenced sweat-lodge ceremony. After dinner, there was an opening ceremony/circle for all the retreatants in the main room. On Saturday, I attended a workshop that drew on the work of choreographer and dancer Anna Halprin to create a movement ritual. Other workshop offerings included group drumming, a discussion on ecstatic dance, and a movement choir based on the work of Rudolf Laban. On Saturday evening there was another, more formal ceremony that featured smudging with sage (a purification ritual), chanting accompanied by Tibetan bowls, and a kind of circle dance. This was then followed by a rave-type DJ dance that lasted for several hours, but did not go all night long. On Easter Sunday, after brunch, there was a group discussion about where the Rhythm Society is headed in the future, and then a closing ceremony. For me, the highlight of the weekend was the opportunity to spend quality time with a number of people and get to know them better. I also had strong experiences with the sweat lodge, the workshops, and the ceremonies. Interestingly, the rave itself, although nice, was not particularly revelatory.

Several common threads stand out from both of these retreats. The first is the importance of the workshop format. As one participant in Intention puts it,

> The thing that makes those gatherings special is they're really not just parties. They're really more about workshops and sharing and learning and that goes on for many days and then there's a party at the end for New Year's. And it's almost like, "New Year's—whatever." It's all these workshops and all this learning that went on that was really memorable and powerful and empowering and awesome.[16]

A second thread is the importance of spiritual and ceremonial practice. The retreat format seems to lend itself to more focus on the explicitly spiritual aspects of rave culture, whether they are connected to the rave experience itself or not. Finally, the retreat format also seems very conducive to community building. The retreat provides an opportunity for those in the rave community to go deeper in their shared experiences and interconnections, to reflect on where they've been and to envision where they want to go. In this regard, it is important to mention the Gathering of the Tribes, a five-day retreat that began in 2000 for the purpose of linking up different rave communities. The June 2003 gathering, held in southern California, was organized around the theme *Evolution + Manifestation = Transformation* and included an opening ceremony, a DJ dance, and several days of workshops on assorted topics, some of which featured authors Barbara Marx Hubbard and John Perry Barlow. Although it is still in its formative stages, overall I think the emerging phenomenon of the rave retreat represents an evolutionary step forward for the rave scene because it provides more of a context for integrating the rave experience into one's daily life, especially in terms of spirituality and community.

PART II
THE SPIRITUAL AND RELIGIOUS DIMENSIONS OF GLOBAL RAVE CULTURE

In 1996, I moved to the San Francisco Bay Area to research and write my Ph.D. dissertation on the religious dimensions of popular music, focusing on four particular musical subcultures, one of which was the rave scene. It was during this two-year period that I was initiated into rave culture, attending numerous rave events, spending time with participants both in and outside of these events, and conducting formal interviews with a number of ravers. On an academic and scholarly level, this research was productive and resulted in the successful completion of my dissertation and my Ph.D. But my immersion in rave culture also had an unintended impact on a personal level as well: I quickly developed a strong affinity with the scene, became an enthusiastic participant, and my life was transformed through my involvement. In the years since that time, my involvement has continued and deepened, to the point where I consider myself to be an "insider." At the same time, my scholarly interest in the rave scene has also continued and deepened, as has my sense that rave culture is an important religious phenomenon that deserves in-depth study, a conviction that has been the driving force behind this book. In the summer of 2000, I used a research fellowship to travel to England and Germany to investigate the rave scene in Europe and was able to attend a variety of events and meet people involved in European rave culture. However, to be perfectly honest, of the dozens of rave events I've attended since my dissertation research, most of them were undertaken for personal and not scholarly reasons.

In the fast-evolving world of rave culture, seven years is an eternity, and I felt that in order to accurately depict the current state of the scene for this book, it would be necessary for me to undertake additional formal research. Accordingly, in late 2003 and early 2004, I traveled up and down the West Coast to check out rave events and meet members of various crews. During this time, I also conducted an additional dozen interviews. While much of this new material confirmed themes already identified in my earlier research, it also helped me to elaborate some of these themes in new and important ways and, more significantly, it turned up completely new themes and forms that demonstrate the evolution and maturation of rave culture. For example, the Street Parade in Zurich, the Rhythm Society in the Bay Area, the Oracle in Seattle, Tribal Harmonix in British Columbia, Earthdance, and the Gathering of the Tribes have all come into existence and had a strong impact during this time. Overall, I learned a great deal from this new research and I am excited to share this material.

In this volume I am addressing both a popular audience and a scholarly audience, each with its own sets of concerns, and I acknowledge that balancing these two audiences is a challenging task. On the one hand, ravers will want to verify my credibility as someone who has a sizable body of direct firsthand experience in rave culture, and I think my eight years of involvement and my own personal transformation meets this criterion. On the other hand, scholars will want to know I have not sacrificed my capability for objective research and analysis by being an insider, and to verify that I have a solid theoretical and methodological framework for this study. To address these concerns requires a bit more elaborate response, so if you are not interested in these issues, please skip ahead to chapter 3.

I conducted two kinds of formal research for this book, the first of which was fieldwork. Here my task was to immerse myself in rave culture and to attend a sizable body of events and activities. In conducting this fieldwork I have primarily used the participant observation approach so that, in addition to having direct personal experiences of the subject matter, I was also able to make detailed firsthand observations as well. For the second kind of research—formal interviews—I interviewed a number of ravers so that they could speak for themselves in their own voices on the subject, and I have included extensive direct quotes from these interviews in the chapters of this section. While I do not claim that these events and individuals constitute a representative sample, it is nevertheless clear to me that this research did allow me to significantly deepen my understanding of rave culture, its religious experiences, ritual forms, spiritual and philosophical meanings, and communities.

Once this research was completed, my next task was to analyze the material to bring out the dynamics, nuances, and complexities of rave culture as a religious phenomenon. As I have noted in the introduction, rave culture does not constitute religion as we traditionally think of it and, consequently, it does not fit neatly within the standard religious analysis. Therefore, it is necessary to develop theoretical and analytical tools to make sense of some of the key features of newly emerging religious phenomena like raves, features which I also noted in the introduction: a combination of the sacred and secular; expression within the arts; expression within popular culture; the emphasis of experience over content; the central importance of the body; use of digital technology, multimedia, and global communication systems; and a postmodern, hybrid, cut-and-paste nature. Historian of religions Charles Long has identified two important elements that I think are extremely helpful for understanding this new type of religious phenomenon, the first of which is "the mode of transmission."[1] Raves illustrate this point perfectly. Their mode of transmission is intimately bound up with beat-heavy music, electronic instrumentation and amplification, digital recording, record and CD manufacturing and distribution, DJ beat matching and cross-fade mixing skills, digital lighting and projections, a wide variety of crews and promoters, and a wide variety of physical environments (warehouses, clubs, arenas, outdoor locations, etc.), as well as each individual's unique way of receiving and processing the music, including dance, social interactions, and the ingestion of substances like the drug Ecstasy (MDMA, or 3-, 4-methylenedioxymethamphetamine). Each of these aspects has its own particular set of parameters and dynamics that, taken in sum, account for many of the complexities of rave as religion.

The second element is the "cognition afforded by the modes of transmission," which, because of the powerful technologies involved, has been greatly intensified. Long argues that "because of the intensity of transmission," "the qualitative meaning of the nature of experience" becomes the central defining feature.[2] In the case of raves, then, the key to unpacking their spiritual and religious significance lies in understanding the intense experiential states that they engender. Thus, the first and most important aspect of my analysis of the spiritual and religious dimensions of raves focuses squarely on the powerful experiential states ravers attain through music and dance, states that are clearly analogous to a variety of classic religious experiences. I see this focus on the primacy of religious experience continuing and updating a long-standing tradition of religious studies scholarship that emphasizes the encounter with the numinous as the central ordering structure for human beings. This primary religious experience then becomes the basis for subsequent developments that lead to the organized external forms that we call religion. In this section, I will look closely at three of these developments in particular: (1) the ritual and ceremonial forms that bring ravers together in religious communion; (2) the spiritualities, worldviews, philosophies, and codes for living that provide them an orientation to the world and a meaning system through which to construct their ongoing reality; and (3) the communities that provide ravers a context in which to integrate these religious experiences, rituals, and worldviews into their ongoing daily lives.

Religious experience is one of the most difficult subjects for scholars of religion to analyze because it is of a uniquely subjective personal nature that cannot be objectively observed or empirically measured. What one can do, however, is seriously examine the accounts of individuals who have had such experiences and to use techniques of comparative analysis to tease out consistent threads of similarity and difference. This is the approach that William James took in his classic study *The Varieties of Religious Experience*, an approach that could be characterized as a kind of radical empiricism.[3] While clearly useful for marshaling objective evidence of a subjective phenomenon and identifying structural patterns, such an approach, however, still leaves one on the outside looking in, separated by a glass wall from the interior texture of the experience. As a corrective, therefore, certain strategies have been developed within the discipline of religious studies that seek to overcome this separation. Joachim Wach's strategy is found in the hermeneutic enterprise, the attempt of the scholar to interpret the data using not only the intellect, but also the total person, which also includes emotion, will, and experience. He writes, "A love letter will appear meaningless and silly to anybody not in love. . . . By the same token a religious utterance will bewilder, frustrate, or repel anyone whose religious sensitivities have not been developed."[4] In a similar vein, Gerardus Van der Leeuw's phenomenological approach balanced objective techniques of epoché (bracketing and temporary suspension of presuppositions) and analytical categorization of phenomena with the scholar's empathetic interpolation of her own experiences; he called for "'a systematic introspection; not only the description of what is visible from the outside, but above all the experience born of what can only become reality after it has been admitted into the life of the observer himself.'"[5]

In terms of the life of this observer, I can say that music, and its spiritual and religious dimensions, has exerted a tremendous influence on me since my adolescence—an influence that has continued into my adulthood, with electronic dance music and rave culture as my primary focus for the last eight years. I regularly acquire and listen to vast amounts of recorded electronic dance music and regularly go to raves and dance clubs, all purely for my own personal edification, independent of academic concerns. Therefore, I have a natural empathy for the subject I am studying, as well as a set of powerful experiences I can draw from in making my interpretations.

In addition to this personal involvement, I think it is also important to address my scholarly work focusing on the spiritual and religious dimensions of music, as well as the work of other scholars in this area. The connection between music, spirituality, and religion is so widespread as to be nearly universal. Yet, strangely, there has been very little serious and systematic scholarly study on the subject, not only on the religious side of the equation by religious studies scholars, but also on the musical side of the equation by musicologists and ethnomusicologists. In my first book, *Traces of the Spirit: The Religious Dimensions of Popular Music*, a revised version of my dissertation, I developed a preliminary theoretical framework for understanding the tremendous spiritual and religious power of music, essentially arguing that because music integrates its multiple dimensions into a harmoniously functioning whole, it is the vehicle par excellence for conveying religious experience and meaning.[6]

> At the physiological level, it affects the body and its subsystems; at the psychological level, it affects the structure of the psyche and the state of consciousness; at the sociocultural level, it affects and reflects the social order and the cultural paradigms; at the semiological level, it provides symbolic structures which create affective meaning systems; at the virtual level, it creates compelling temporal and spatial worlds into which one is drawn; at the ritual level, it fits into a larger set of ritual activities,

with their own functions and purposes; and, finally, at the spiritual or religious level, it establishes a link to the spiritual world and the contours and dynamics of that world. Moreover, music affects people in all of these ways *simultaneously*, integrating all these levels into a harmonious whole that is greater than the sum of the parts. . . [and that] takes place in [a unique and powerful] *experiential* state.[7]

Drawing on some of the pioneering ideas developed by ethnomusicologist Steven M. Friedson in his excellent study of the vimbuza spirit possession complex among the Tumbuka of Malawi, *Dancing Prophets*, I took this framework further in proposing the concept of music as a unified field, a hyperdimensional continuum in which humans and spirits, as Friedson writes, "as equally viable presences, partake of the same experiential realm of sound and motion."[8] Thus, music allows human beings to enter a unified field where the spiritual dimension can be directly experienced in a powerful mode that is integrated with all the other dimensions.

In the years since I wrote my dissertation, an exciting new body of work has emerged that draws on new technologies in brain imaging that have led to new research in brain science confirming the unique capacity of music to transform consciousness and induce powerful religious experiences. In fact, I only discovered this work after I had already completed the manuscript of this book, and I was amazed to find that this new material uncannily paralleled many of the most important themes in the following section on the spiritual and religious dimensions of raves. So, while this new body of work did not influence my theoretical and methodological approach in this volume, it did validate the results and the larger themes of my research from a different perspective. I include a brief survey of this work here, not only because I feel it is important material on the connection between music, spirituality, and religion in its own right, but also because it sets up and illuminates the material on the spiritual and religious dimensions of raves that follows in the next section.

I begin with ethnomusicologist Judith Becker's *Deep Listeners: Music, Emotion, and Trancing*, a groundbreaking book that emphasizes the nearly universal importance of musically induced trance as an effective tool for accessing spiritual dimensions, a theme that is clearly central in this volume. She writes: "The interpenetration of music with trancing is ancient and universal. I suspect that most, if not all, societies have some form of institutionalized, religious trance ceremonies that also include music."[9]

"Music that accompanies religious trancing is . . . music whose primary function is to address, summon, or present an unseen world of gods, of deities, and of spirits."[10] Throughout her book, in characterizing the experiential states attained by musical trancers, Becker uses phrases that not only read like classic themes of religious and mystical experiences, but also that uncannily parallel themes that emerged in the course of my interviews with ravers: divine presence, transcendence, gnosis, out-of-body sensations, feelings of nearness to the sacred, loss of boundaries between self and other, experiences of wholeness and unity, joy, numinous luminosity, a sense of divinity, of the sacred realm, pure bodily experience, feelings of closeness to the holy, revitalization, a special blessing, a benediction, the ability to temporarily abide in an eternity, an enchanted world, and so on.[11] In addition, Becker identifies some of the key structural components of the musical trance induction complex and these also uncannily parallel key components of raves: musical immersion, music that is rhythmically vibrant and loud, dance or strenuous activity, and sensory overstimulation.[12]

Drawing on the new wave of brain science research, Becker gives her analysis of these structural components and spiritual/religious dimensions of musically induced trance greater depth and scientific validity by grounding it in biological and neurophysiological processes. Key among these is the arousal of the autonomic nervous system, or ANS. The ANS consists of physiological processes such as breathing, heartbeat, digestion, involuntary muscles, and so forth that operate independently of our conscious control, but are regulated by areas of the brain such as the encephalon and the brainstem.

> ANS arousal seems to be a central factor in precipitating trance. . . .
> Deep listeners experience strong autonomic nervous system arousal in listening to music that may result in chills or tears, changes in their heart rates, in their skin temperatures, and in the brain chemistry, resulting in a heightened sense of aliveness, an alertness, and, mostly, a joyfulness.
> . . . In trancing contexts, the ANS seems in overdrive, propelling the trancer to physical feats not normally possible, and to the feeling of numinous luminosity that encapsulates special knowledge not accessible during normal consciousness. [13]

Another important biological process is that of structural coupling, the synchronization of different bodies and nervous systems into a collectively shared brain state and consciousness, accomplished through the mechanism of musical rhythmic entrainment.

> Musical rhythmic entrainment can be seen as structural coupling, of a changed interior, personal consciousness in a musical domain of coordination. Bodies and brains synchronize gestures, muscle actions, breathing, and brain waves while enveloped in music. Many persons, bound together by common aims, may experience revitalization and general good feeling. The situation is communal and individual, music descends on all alike, while each person's joy is his or her own.[14]

Other scholars have developed similar ideas. For example, cognitive scientist William Benzon has also touched on the concept of structural coupling of brain states and consciousness through music in his outstanding book, *Beethoven's Anvil: Music in Mind and Culture*:

> For individuals sharing a common musical culture, there is a strong and systematic similarity between the tonal flow of music and its neurophysiological substrates that allows a tight coupling between the brains of those individuals. . . . This musical flow is not under the control of any particular brain system but rather reflects the joint interaction of all active neural systems, at all levels of interaction. . . . The music is a vehicle for a collective intentionality, one that slips beneath the barriers of individuality and the imperatives of autonomous selves. Music is a means of sharing what is otherwise an individual, private experience, that of trance. In music deeply shared, my rhythms and your rhythms are one and the same.[15]

In turn, both Benzon and Becker have drawn on the work of neuroscientist Walter Freeman, who considers musical entrainment such a powerful agent for social bonding that he believes it played an important role in the evolution of human society:

> I conclude that music and dance originated through biological evolution of brain chemistry, which interacted with the cultural evolution of behavior. This led to the development of chemical and behavioral technology for inducing altered states of consciousness. The role of trance states was particularly important for breaking down preexisting habits and beliefs. That meltdown appears to be necessary for personality changes leading to the formation of social groups by cooperative action leading to trust. Bonding is not simply release of a neurochemical in an altered state. It is the social action of dancing and singing together that induces new forms of behavior, owing to the malleability that can come through the altered state.[16]

This theme also uncannily parallels another theme that emerged from my research for this volume—how the trance states attained by ravers through music and dance lead to their personal transformation and the subsequent development of rave communities and rave culture.

The final theme relevant in this survey of new research and theory in brain science is that of ritual. In his influential book, *Why God Won't Go Away: Brain Science and the Biology of Belief,* brain scientist Andrew Newberg argues that ritual activity is another kind of rhythmic behavior that also shifts brain states and consciousness and produces religious experiences.

> The ability of human ritual to produce transcendent unitary states is the result of the effect of rhythmic ritualized behavior upon the hypothalamus and the autonomic nervous system and, eventually, on the rest of the brain. . . . The process of ritual begins as rhythmic behaviors subtly alter autonomic responses in the body's quiescent and arousal systems. If those rhythms are fast . . . the arousal system is driven to higher and higher levels of activation. . . . When the hippocampus senses that brain activity has reached excessively high levels, it exerts an inhibitory effect on neural flow— in effect, it puts the brakes on brain activity—until action in the brain settles down. As a result, certain brain structures are deprived of the normal supply of neural input. One such structure is the orientation association area—the part of the brain that helps us distinguish the self from the rest of the world and orients that self in space—which requires a constant stream of information to do its job well. When that stream is interrupted, it has to work with whatever information is available. In neurological parlance, the orientation area becomes deafferented—it is forced to operate on little or no neural input. The likely result of this deafferentation is a softer, less precise definition of the boundaries of the self. This softening of the self is responsible for the unitary experiences practitioners of ritual often describe.[17]

Once again, these themes are uncannily paralleled in ravers' accounts of their experiences of unity and transcendence.

And, as Benzon explains, again drawing on Freeman's work, these states of unity and transcendence are *collectively shared states*:

> Freeman suggests that such rituals involve a neuropeptide called oxytocin. He asserts that oxytocin "appears to act by dissolving pre-existing learning by loosening the synaptic connections in which prior knowledge

is held. This opens an opportunity for learning new knowledge. The meltdown does not instill knowledge. It clears the path for the acquisition of new understanding through behavioral actions that are shared with others." As the oxytocinated individuals move to the rhythms of well-established ritual, their synaptic connections are restructured in patterns guided and influenced by the events in the ritual. Obviously, the microdynamics of each individual will be unique, but they will be shaped by rhythmic patterns common to all. These rituals provide a space in which individuals can mold themselves to one another as the infant molds her actions to those of her mother.[18]

The material that follows, then, arises out of several disparate arenas of knowledge: my own lifetime of experience with music and spirituality; eight years of involvement with rave culture; formal research in the Bay Area, the West Coast, and Europe; methodological aspects of James's radical empiricism, Wach's hermeneutics, and Van der Leeuw's phenomenological techniques of epoché, analytical categorization, and empathetic interpolation; my own model of music as a hyperdimensional continuum and unified field; and an uncanny set of thematic parallels to Becker, Benzon, Freeman, and Newberg's research into the neurophysiology of musically induced trance, ANS arousal, structural coupling, rhythmic entrainment, ritual activity, and social bonding.

Groove Garden, Fairfax, CA, 2003. Photograph courtesy of Kenny Shachat (Beatstream.net).

CHAPTER 3
TRANCE FORMATION: THE RELIGIOUS EXPERIENCE OF RAVE

The Conversion Experience

Every raver has the first experience when he "gets it" on the dance floor, and this is a powerful moment that can change his life. Many ravers "get it" from the first moment they walk in the door at a rave and they are immediate converts; others attend several raves before this happens. Regardless of whether it happens the first time or the fiftieth time, the important point is that it happens. All ravers have a conversion experience when they "get it," and it seems appropriate to start this chapter with some of these classic accounts:

> That one night, it all came slamming together. I saw people celebrating, really celebrating for the first time in my whole life. I didn't know what joy was until that. In fact, I had the pretty distinct feeling that I had been living a black-and-white existence my whole entire life up until that day and it was suddenly like Technicolor kicked in. I had this amazing spiritual high for at least a good six weeks after that. I was unstoppably happy. . . . I had found this whole new world that I was completely psyched about. It was my first experience with ecstasy, not as a drug, but ecstasy as a state of being. I think I became an instant advocate of that

experience just by the fact that I felt it was an essential experience of life to have that experience.[1]

It really kicked in going to one of Martin's Gathering parties, which was a house break-in down on the docks. And that just was where it all kind of clicked. I said, *Okay, here we go. This is it.* And it was like, *Boom!* It was one of those situations where I just recognized instantly what it was. . . . It was kind of like finding the thing I had always been looking for.[2]

I flew to the Bay and went directly to a Toon Town. And this was '92, '93, so it was really popping. And I took my first drug ever and dropped Ecstasy one night and went to a Toon Town. And I'd never even smoked marijuana up until then. And this is the medicine that I really needed. I had my heart chakra blown completely wide open at this event. I'd never felt such unity. And I'd been in situations where it should have been there, like in a religious setting. But that just felt like there were so many issues that just kept that from happening. And here I was at Toon Town with maybe 3,500, 4,000 people on the dance floor and everyone was in this complete state of bliss. And Doc Martin was playing and the stage was set for this epic religious experience for me to happen. I should say *spiritual experience.* And indeed it did and I was a changed person from that day on.[3]

I moved here [Seattle] because I came to a dance culture event in '94 and was completely blown away and knew that I was looking for that, essentially. I moved here from Guam. . . . A friend of mine told me about rave culture events and I flew out to go to one. And I just knew that moment that that was what I was here to do. I just knew.[4]

I went and visited [San Francisco] and I was taken to my first real rave. I was there for four days and you cannot believe what I went to. When I think about it now, I just get the shivers. It was the NASA tour, and Jeno was playing, Moby, Richard James/Aphex Twin, and Orbital. I remember we did Ecstasy and it was just like, *Whoa!* like the heavens opened up. I can't explain it. It was amazing. It was like, *This is it! I have arrived. This is exactly what I've been looking for my entire life.* And I'm not trying to inflate it, but, *This is it! This is it!* And then I went to one of the very first Friends n Family events. . . . I just remember having these connections with people that were so incredible. And people just dancing, and the vibe just so good and so right and this felt so like, *This is home, this is what it's all about, this is what I've been looking for.* . . . And then I vowed to move to San Francisco.[5]

I hit this party and Doc Martin was playing. And he was the first DJ I'd ever heard and I just danced my ass off. I had never really danced that much, certainly not to a DJ where he's working the rhythms, sort of flowing from song to song, and I just ended up drenched in sweat and just going, *Wow, that is the most fun I've ever had.* And from that point on, every week, we'd just go dancing. . . . So yeah, I heard house music and it totally changed my life.[6]

I have included these lengthy testimonials from ravers because they vividly convey the euphoric intensity of the experience of "getting it" the first time at a rave, an experience so powerful that it immediately changed their lives in a complete and irrevocable way. These descriptions are uncannily similar to classic accounts of the religious conversion experience found in many religious and spiritual traditions, from the phenomenon of being "born again" in evangelical Christianity to miracle stories of seekers finding their guru or teacher, and they can be legitimately classified as such. But what exactly is *it* that ravers are experiencing, and to what are they being converted?

Electronic Dance Music

Any discussion of the experience of "getting it" on the dance floor at a rave must begin with the music itself. Electronic dance music is very different from most other kinds of music, not only in terms of its sounds, but also fundamentally in terms of its core organizational principles. As Jimi Fritz, author of *Rave Culture: An Insider's View*, notes, "With conventional music, we listen to the form and follow the lyrics, but with rave music there is no beginning or end. The music is cyclical and continuous and acts more as a catalyst for our own personal inner journey, more a transportation system than an end in itself. Rave music is specifically designed to make you move your body."[7]

A danceable groove is central in electronic dance music and beats are the foundation upon which the groove is built. The beats are constructed through drum-machine programming, or through manipulating recorded samples of drums, or other techniques. Then a series of sonic textures are layered on top of the beats in an interlocking polyrhythmic manner. One of the key compositional skills in electronic dance music is to weave these different layers in and out in different combinations so as to generate a sense of flow and dynamics. Also, producers are constantly creating new sounds and timbres using synthesizers, sound modules, and software, and these sounds are then enhanced by a variety of effects and processors; the freshness of these sounds is an important aspect of the music. Within the context of a rave, the music is played at an extremely high volume over a high-quality sound system, ideally with surround sound and a subwoofer that gives the bass register a physical presence, and the music becomes a totalizing sonic environment in which one is immersed. All of these aspects combine to make the music a powerful, unique experience, an altered state of consciousness in and of itself. Here are some testimonials from ravers to this effect, including Jimi Fritz and some of the people he interviewed for his book:

> People were dancing hard and smiling from ear to ear, as if amazed at the ability of the music to affect them so completely. The heavy tribal beats continued to grow, building in intensity. Just when any increase in power seemed impossible, a plateau of swirling sounds suggested an ultimate zenith. Then, suddenly, the music exploded into another rhythm even more penetrating and profound than before. This upward spiraling cycle of pulsating sound continued to build relentlessly hour after hour throughout the night. Like a musical river, it swept everyone along with an irresistible momentum. An incredible sense of optimism and enthusiasm pervaded the room as we surrendered to this new musical form.[8]

> Absolutely nothing . . . has taken me to the intense levels that this music does and hold it there. There is nothing like it in the world, it is like reaching an orgasm. . . .[9]

> The music made me feel both just free and inspired and more in touch with myself. . . . The music was so powerful to me that it just highlighted all the beautiful things. . . .[10]

> Electronic dance music is a new way of presenting sound. I think that part of the attraction is that some of the new sounds I'm hearing, I recognize from sounds I've generated in my own head before I ever went to a party or tried Ecstasy. It's like I'm listening to my own brain-wave patterns.[11]

> Electronic dance music is a brand new, cool musical genre, very progressive and modern. It is a new step of human musical progression and I think it is the music of the future.[12]

The repetition is primarily important—it is hypnotic and addictive. With a proper sound system the music is so loud you can feel it in every part of your body. The low bass notes connect you to the earth and remind us how physical and animal we all are. The melodies and higher frequencies extend us up out of ourselves into a higher state of consciousness. It is an embracing of both earth and sky. Its effect is the most liberating ecstasy possible.[13]

For many ravers, this state of ecstasy is one achieved through the music itself, without using the drug Ecstasy (MDMA, or 3-, 4-methylene-dioxymethamphetamine). However, the synergistic combination of electronic dance music and Ecstasy has historically been one of the key catalysts of the rave scene, and there is no denying that Ecstasy strongly enhances the already powerful effects of the music. Popular music critic and rave aficionado Simon Reynolds, in the seminal *Generation Ecstasy: Into the World of Techno and Rave Culture*, has written an excellent description of how Ecstasy (also called "E") enhances the experience of electronic dance music:

All music sounds better on E—crisper and more distinct, but also engulfing in its immediacy. House and techno sound especially fabulous. The music's emphasis on texture and timbre enhances the drug's mildly synaesthetic effects so that sounds seem to caress the listener's skin. You feel like you're dancing inside the music; sound becomes a fluid medium in which you're immersed. Ecstasy . . . melts bodily and psychological rigidities, enabling the dancer to move with greater fluency and 'lock' into the groove. Rave music's hypnotic beats and sequenced loops also make it perfectly suited to interact with another attribute of Ecstasy: . . . the drug stimulates the brain's 1b receptor, which encourages repetitive behavior. . . . Rave music instills a pleasurable tension, a rapt suspension that fits perfectly with the sustained pre-orgasmic plateau of the MDMA high. . . .

Over the years, rave music has gradually evolved into a self-conscious science of intensifying MDMA's sensations. House and techno producers have developed a drug-determined repertoire of effects, textures, and riffs that are expressly designed to trigger the tingly rushes that traverse the Ecstatic body. Processes like EQ-ing, phasing, panning, and filtering are used to tweak the frequencies, harmonics, and stereo imaging of different sounds, making them leap out of the mix with an eerie three-dimensionality or glisten with a hallucinatory vividness. Today's house track is a forever-fluctuating, fractal mosaic of glow-pulses and flicker-riffs, a teasing tapestry whose different strands take turns to move in and out of the sonic spotlight. Experienced under the influence of MDMA, the effect is synaesthetic—like tremulous fingertips tantalizing the back of your neck, or the simultaneously aural/tactile equivalent of a shimmer. In a sense, Ecstasy turns the entire body surface into an ear, an ultra-sensitized membrane that responds to certain frequencies.[14]

Trance and Peaks

A central aspect that is nearly universal in the dance-floor experience at raves is that of trance. The trance state is induced through the high-volume insistence of the continuous beat and the accompanying continuous dance. One veteran of the Chicago house music scene put it this way:

> You would definitely get rather hypnotized by the constant rhythm, the continual motion of the music. . . . You can get into a trance state without being high [on drugs]. . . . So much of it is repetitive dance, repetitive motion; you're getting into such a groove that you put yourself into a trance state.[15]

A San Francisco raver described it as

> a really powerful experience. It transports you. The volume, the sheer volume of the music, and just the repetitiveness of it is hypnotic. You're dancing, you're moving in time to the music and, after a while, you don't know what your body is doing. . . . You just kind of have this sense of your own motion and it goes with the music.[16]

These connections between music, rhythm, dance, and trance induction are consciously recognized by ravers, and induction of the trance state is a specific goal of the music:

> Rhythms have a real powerful influence on the mind. . . . The music definitely, definitely, definitely caters to this trance, trying to put your mind into it. When it starts getting these really regularly looping patterns, it goes into a state which is kind of hard to describe. . . . You start achieving some really unusual states of consciousness, which I think people really like. The music attempts to manipulate that sense of consciousness. It tries to take you to a place, tries to sculpt your experience in some way, by manipulating those mechanisms in your mind.[17]

It is also important to note that this is a *deep* trance state induced over a long period of time, one that "completely alters your state of consciousness."[18] As one veteran San Francisco raver put it,

> The periods of pure trance have been profound raving, simply because . . . raving's about eight, nine hours non-stop.[19]

The trance state, however, is not of a uniform texture. Another nearly universal aspect of the rave dance-floor experience, as was noted in chapter 1, is the notion of the energy building to a peak:

> A well-structured, a well-done DJ set really builds a flow and an ebb, builds it up and takes it back down again, and can bring you to the peak of something and then take you back down gently.[20]

Reaching these peaks is a conscious goal of both the DJ and the dancers, and DJs have developed specific strategies for how to get there:

> I will move the crowd up to a high level of energy by gradually increasing the beats per minute over time and then I will take it to a peak if I can, to some ecstatic peak where I'll just keep going as long as possible. And then, when the crowd seems to fade, or have enough of that, then I will gradually take it down again, rest them for a while, and then bring them up again. . . . As a DJ, I see myself as taking the crowd on a journey and through a number of different emotions and feeling states. And, at some point, letting all that break open into an ecstatic state. And, over the course of the night, doing this a number of times. And the feeling in the room grows.[21]

Another DJ put it more succinctly: "I like to definitely build up a crescendo and let it all explode."[22] It is important to note that the experience of peaks is often a *shared* experience in which many people on the dance floor acknowledge the collective entrance into this higher state. These are some of the best times of the night, when everyone can feel the palpable presence of the peak sweeping them up to an ecstatic, high-energy state:

> There's something about being in a room with more than a hundred people and everybody's experiencing this new thing for the first time. It's like being witness to two thousand births all at once, you know what I mean? You could almost just look at people and they'd look at you and

you'd just have this understanding about what was going on, but there
was no way to communicate it. It was just this physical electricity in the
air.[23]

Joy, Happiness, Ecstasy, and Love

One of the primary feelings associated with the peak experience on the
dance floor is that of joy or happiness:

> I've had what I might term, and not facetiously, religious experiences
> when I've been dancing. You just get incredibly happy. You get filled
> with a real sense of joy.[24]

And this sense of joy is not just a private, personal feeling, but one that is
shared by most everyone else present at the rave. One raver talked about
an ongoing event he helped organize that was

> positively notorious for this group joy that would happen. . . . They
> would walk into the space and they would just feel it. . . . They became
> truly joyful, truly ecstatic.[25]

For many, this sense of joy is the main goal of the rave. One stated that
"it's all about happiness,"[26] while another went so far as to call music "the
ultimate bliss."[27] This is not to say that there aren't other emotions and
feeling states experienced in the context of raves, but simply that the feeling of joy and happiness is central.

It is probably more than just simple coincidence that the drug most
often ingested at raves goes by the common name of Ecstasy, because the
feeling states induced by this drug certainly can be described as ecstatic. It
is clear that the use of Ecstasy in rave contexts is a major contributing factor to the feeling states described above. At the same time, however, many
ravers were emphatic in stating that these states were easily accessed *without* using MDMA, that the tremendous combined power of the music,
the rhythm, the dance, and the visuals was more than sufficient to produce
such states. One raver talked about experiencing profound altered states of
consciousness at raves long before ever taking Ecstasy, and that Ecstasy
"just confirmed the way I already felt about it, just enhanced it more."[28]
Another described the opposite sequence—after taking Ecstasy and having ecstatic experiences, that state became accessible without the drug,
solely through the music:

The connection I had with the music was real because I felt it when I wasn't high.[29]

In addition to its ability to induce ecstatic states, Ecstasy is also widely known for its ability to help people be in their heart and experience feelings of love, to feel a strong sense of connection and unity, and to enhance the internal somatic experience of the body. All three of these properties are important characteristics of the rave experience worthy of further examination.

With or without Ecstasy, for many people, the rave experience shifts them out of being primarily in their head and their thoughts into being primarily in their heart and feelings of love. As one Bay Area raver expressed it,

> For me, it's just the openness and the love, the heart vibration, that heart feeling . . . that feeling of opening and connection and love that just permeates. That's why I do it. That's why I go. . . . For me, this feeling of the sacred that I experience in the rave context, it's definitely a lot of heart, a lot of heart connection, a lot of heart opening. . . .The experience of [the sacred] is feeling all that heart energy in the group, feeling that love. I can feel it. You know, I walk through the door and there it is.[30]

Another raver put it more succinctly:

> I'm very aware that there's a heart opening when I'm dancing, especially when I'm in a place that feels safe and I can really let it go.[31]

And yet another raver referred to experiencing electronic dance music "in my heart, in my chest, feeling my heart cracking open and loosening and opening."[32] Interestingly, none of these three made any reference to having used Ecstasy during these experiences, clearly demonstrating that entrance into this state of being in the heart and feeling love at raves is not dependent on taking the drug. Nor is it limited to the dance floor or the rave itself; it often carries over into the rest of one's life. One aficionado talked about "coming out of a party and just being so filled with pure love,"[33] an experience quite common for many ravers. Another talked about connecting with people who "were much more loving and caring," and how "it definitely changed me and filtered into the rest of my life."[34]

Connection and Unity

This type of connection extends beyond simply connecting with other people into a sense of unity and being part of a larger whole.

> There's that unity that you experience, there's that feeling of connection, and a very loving sense of connection, sense of being connected to something larger.[35]

This experience of "something larger" can be very powerful and profound, and ravers' descriptions of it are strikingly similar to classic experiences of mystical union:

> I just remember the first time I caught the vibe; I'll never forget it. It was like—I'm getting kind of choked up thinking about it—it was this sense of this total union with everything in the universe, with everyone that was there, with everyone that was not there, with everything in the world. . . . I was stepping outside this world of limitations and stepping into this world that was just pure energy and this bigness, this space, I don't know, something. The use of the term *unity* so totally does not capture it at all; it so does not even come close to what it is. But this sense that all things were good, that everything was perfect, and that I was part of everything, and that there wasn't even this identification of the *I*. I don't know—there's no words to describe it. . . .There's this awareness of other beings, of other creatures, forms, something, but again, the sense that they don't exist as discrete forms. They are forms, but they don't exist as individuals. Again, there's that breaking down of separation. . . . I'm talking unity in the largest, most far-out, divine sense of the term.[36]

> I was subtracted from the individual and became part of the whole, blending into the field which binds all of the molecules of the universe . . . the energy that binds the entire world together. . . .There were definitely times where I felt like I was existing . . . as everything all at once . . . . I would blend into the cosmic mind. I felt like I was a part of that and not part of an individual consciousness, an individual experience with a sense of self.[37]

Though these experiences of mystical union are one-of-a-kind life-changing events of a profound spiritual nature, they are at the same time quite widespread and common for ravers, so much so that the ideas of *connection* and *unity* have become central in the discourse of rave culture:

Having that experience of connection—I mean, *connection*'s even the wrong word because *connection* implies separation, in that experience of unity. And I find that's something very prevalent in rave culture. I think that what rave culture is doing, that a lot of people feel it's doing, and they're articulate to one degree or another, is raising the level of our consciousness to a point where we're more aware of ourselves as a connected consciousness, as a connected being, and less as an individuated being.[38]

There appear to be two parts to this process; one must first transcend the individual ego in order to then become part of the "connected consciousness." As one raver expressed it,

You lose a sense of where you're at and it becomes so much more.[39]

Transcending the Ego

In the Western rationalist tradition of the Enlightenment, the Cartesian maxim "I think, therefore I am" forms the foundation for how our culture views and/or structures the psyche. The *I*, or the ego, or the self, is identified with rational thought, and most of our energy and attention is invested in that modality. Consequently, other human modalities such as feeling, the body, and spirituality are often relegated to the unconscious, where they continue to exist, but receive little conscious attention. However, what happens in the intensity of the dance-floor experience at raves is that the ego is temporarily relieved of its dominant position. As one raver describes it,

When you get so into the music that you're just dancing all night and you're grooving, you sort of lose your sense of self.[40]

And, in addition to losing a sense of self or ego, one also loses the petty, day-to-day concerns of the ego:

It was unlike anything I'd ever experienced in that I would, over time, not care how I was looking, not care about most of the things that I would carry around with me—you know, social concerns, even just root things like financial concerns, things like that would all be shed for those moments. . . . I no longer became this person with social hang-ups, this person with baggage and things like that. . . . I guess if I lost anything, it was more of an ego sense.[41]

In that moment, it's really hard to describe, definitely being set free from what people call ego—that identification of what am I doing, how do I look, how does this improve me, who will I be in the morning, any thought of that—and completely releasing.[42]

Most of the time, I'm consumed by the film of thought that's going through my mind. So the dance helps elevate me out of that into a more open undifferentiated place of unity. . . . Your self-conscious awareness of yourself is suddenly shifted away from concerning yourself about how you're seen by other people and you're in the pure experiential mode of feeling.[43]

Fundamentally, there's this sense of, I want to say *dissociation* of the self, but a loss of ego is what I had been referring to before. The sense of there's no separation between you and everything else. Like you are not you, like you are not this individual that has this stuff that is about this thing that happened three years ago, you know, all the things that come with individuation—your ego, your fears, your hopes, your dreams, all this stuff that is identified as *self*.[44]

Many ravers I interviewed had thought a great deal about this process of transcending the ego on the dance floor at raves and some had even developed their own model to explain the mechanisms of how this happens:

What people were doing was they were opening this gateway . . . they were just bypassing all their luggage to that place where they could feel, enjoy. . . . I look at ourselves as really complexly organized biocomputers. And when we come into this world, we're constantly programmed. We have all of these programs that are placed in us. And as these programs become more calcified as we grow, we start looking at life in a very rigid way. So I think in the experience of this transcendent dance, what happens is you can somehow bypass all these. Because that's what the Ecstasy was doing, too—you have all this luggage, you bypass the luggage. But it can happen the same way.[45]

Some ravers have developed an awareness of the transformative power of the dance-floor experience to such a degree that they consciously use dance as a practice to help solve problems and dissolve programming:

Part of what I love about how I use dancing is I use it to . . . address a problem. So, if I'm having issues at work, say, and I'm not communicating well with someone, I'll look at that and I'll use the dance to view it holographically, from all sides, instead of from my ego point of view. Because I do have some of a distanced perspective on that kind of stuff. And generally, it's informed by the heart. Who am I in this picture? How did I betray myself or someone else in this scenario? So I often use it to problem solve, to get to a solution. . . . It helps me analyze problems and have a new perspective on things.[46]

There's the aspect of a sort of freeing, using the dance to free yourself from condition—kind of routines, subroutines, behavior.[47]

Meditation

Some ravers have taken the idea of consciously using dance as a practice even further by comparing it to meditation:

I guess I kind of liken it to meditation, where when the waters are still, the light shines through. And I was definitely moving, so it's not a very good analogy, but I would get myself to a place where what really mattered was the fact that I was moving in a rhythmic motion to this music. And it's almost like, in meditation, you follow your breath, eventually you just become that breath. Well, that's the same with the dancing, it was like I became it. . . . And I was able to have these moments of incredible clarity and blissfulness.[48]

So, instead of focusing attention on the breath, as one might do in simple Buddhist meditation practices, and returning to the breath after distracting thoughts arise, ravers focus on the music and the dance in the same way.

To me, dance is my absolute meditation. And I started to discover . . . a lot of times when I would just be completely sober on this dance floor. And all of the sudden, I just began to, beyond just dancing, I would begin to really communicate with the music. And a lot of times I would just pull myself up in front of the speaker and just allow my body to journey through and with what was coming out of the speaker. I started to do this—I found that if I was thinking about something, if my mind was elsewhere, then I wouldn't be as into the music and I couldn't get into it quite as much. So that almost helped me to focus on, I guess, the traditional Buddhist style of meditation, which is to allow your thoughts to leave and just begin to observe your thoughts, as opposed to trying to push them out. So it just gave me a focus. And I found that hours would go by where I wasn't even aware of that happening. I was just so incredibly focused on the music that was coming out that moment that I wasn't even focusing on homework that I had or relationships that were going on, problems I was having with my parents. None of that was really apparent because I was just so in that moment.[49]

When you get so into the music that you're just dancing all night and you're grooving, you really, I think, to some degree, if it's a good night, you sort of lose your sense of self and you really become one with the music and everything else ceases to exist. It's called active meditation. You're not still but you're so in the music that you're not thinking, you're just being there, moving with the music.[50]

There is even a website dedicated to the idea of rave dancing as a meditation practice, called Enlightenment by Dancing, in which they draw on basic Buddhist concepts. Here is a brief summary of their perspective:

In a nutshell, dance is meditation! It is possible to gain direct access to our own enlightened qualities: peace, love, openness, understanding, energy and joy. The popular notion of meditation is to withdraw from the senses and suppress our thoughts. This is hard to do and doesn't last very long because it is an artificial state. It is also rather dull. Real meditation is being completely awake and open to what is happening right now. We recognize thoughts as just thoughts and return to openness again and again. This moment of recognition is effortless and natural and can become completely stable. Vivid dance experiences are the ideal time to practice real meditation. Real meditation is effortless and sparky. Effortless because we are simply opening up to what is already there, our natural awareness. Sparky because vividness is fun! Dance and meditation come together in the experience of absolute spontaneity! When we are completely in tune with the music, not a thought in our mind, and no idea where the next beat will take us, then we are in touch with our own spontaneous perfection. This is dance as a spiritual path to enlightenment.[51]

Being in the Body

Another key aspect of transcending the ego through dance in rave culture is a strong emphasis on being in the body and bodily experience. This emphasis is in sharp contrast to Western civilization's Cartesian maxim of "I think, therefore, I am," which has led to a primary focus on the mind as one's true identity and a culture-wide sense of disembodiment. One raver expressed this contrast very succinctly:

It's all about being in your body and out of your head.[52]

Another saw the dance floor as "a place to go deeper into your body."[53] For ravers, being in the body means bringing as much awareness as possible to one's internal somatic experience:

I totally feel it [the body], every bit of it.[54]

I notice that when I'm in dance the most, when I have that connection, I begin to feel every aspect of my body . . . really feeling it. And that's when I would feel the muscles in my arms actually moving and I would feel my legs do a turn or a backstep or something. So, yes, I feel more in my body.[55]

There's a tendency in this culture for our consciousness to be mostly directed outside of the physical body. And what I've found is that there's another direction, which is to go in the physical body and to really inhabit the physical body from another space, so that you're feeling your own consciousness participating with physical matter, so that consciousness starts to rest within physical matter. What I experience is that then I feel like, just as there's no separation between myself and a tree or another person, there's also no separation with my hands or my elbows, etcetera, so that I can rest in those areas and have a direct experience of moving from inside them.[56]

I've also experienced . . . an increased sense of body awareness, down to the very tips of my extremities, and that, to me, is the infusion of spirit into matter to the furthest degree. And that, to me, is where a lot of the magic lies.[57]

As I noted earlier, this increased sense of body awareness can be further enhanced or intensified by the use of Ecstasy:

When you hear something that is emotionally evocative when you're under the influence of MDMA, your whole body feels it. . . . It's like an almost physical reaction you have to the music. So it has a tendency to make music a very substantial experience. . . . That's definitely something that I always felt with MDMA—you get this sense of these waves

of abstract feelings washing through your entire body. . . . It really is sort
of like teetering on the edge of an orgasm for a very long time.[58]

What follows is a description of one raver's pivotal experience on the
dance floor under the influence of Ecstasy, and I have quoted it at length
because it vividly conveys the intense transformative power of the bodily
experience:

> I remember it completely transformed my relationship to my physical
> body. . . . I got on this pedestal and I danced for eight hours. It was the
> longest time and I just did not get off that pedestal. My experience of my
> body was just this pure column of energy. It was just this pure connec-
> tion from top to bottom of this pulsing. The beat just pulsed right
> through me and I could not stop. I was exhausted, but it didn't matter
> because I could not get enough of what that felt like. It was so cool and it
> completely rewrote my relationship to my body, like, in a night. . . . I just
> remember breathing in and feeling this rush from way above my head to
> way below my feet. It was just so cool. . . . It was really fun. It was great.
> That rocked my universe. . . . The music suddenly got into my body.
> And, to this day, I'll hear music, and I'll just be sitting there at work or
> somewhere, and some chord progression will hit, or some combination
> of timbres and beats, and I'll just be, like, *Whoa!* I'll feel it in my back.
> I can feel it right under my left shoulder blade a lot. . . . The music will
> just rush along a meridian. It's very integrated in my body right now. . . .
> Definitely [I experience it] in my body. My body opens and I am in it.[59]

Clearly this was an extraordinary personal experience. But it is also an
experience that many people have had on the dance floor to one degree or
another. What happens, then, when this kind of powerful bodily state is
shared by a group of people and experienced collectively, something that
often occurs at raves? As one raver noted,

> When you dance with people in this way over time, one of the things
> that becomes totally evident is the oneness, that we're all moving in this
> field, this vibrational field. . . . What I feel occurring is a sense of global
> consciousness, a sense of one moving world, one enormous dancing
> body that is felt in a physical sense.[60]

What is being described here, then, is a kind of *bodily* mysticism, in which
mystical union is experienced on physical, somatic, and kinesthetic levels.

Movement and Dance

At raves, dancing is the primary activity that opens the doorway to these powerful experiential states. Most ravers are dancers and they love to dance:

> I find everything inside of it. I can be anything. I can go anywhere. . . . The reason I find dancing is such a beautiful and deep experience is because it's completely letting go of, forgetting that you walk. I think it's a form of swimming or flying, it really is. It's a form of releasing in me. It's a form of entering a place that you can't just [by] walking around and observing the normal everyday. And it's a form of going inside the music. It's a relationship that you have with the music. And, once you come in harmony, you're in bliss, really.[61]

> There are moments when I'm dancing, but I'm dancing so effortlessly or so thoughtlessly that I'm not deciding how I'm going to dance. How my body feels is like, for a moment, my body's just moving to the music. And the music is just going through me. I'm more enjoying the music and enjoying the movement and that ecstatic state.[62]

Each dancer has her own set of unique characteristic dance movements that span a wide range of different forms and styles. Ravers typically do not perform these dance movements because they are aesthetically pleasing to watch from the *outside*, but because they produce powerful somatic states experienced from the *inside*. These states are not of a uniform nature. Different types of dance movements produce different types of experiential states. From this perspective, movement and dance can be considered a spiritual technology that ravers utilize to create and choreograph their own unique journey through a sequence of experiential states. Different ravers use different dance movements to pursue different experiential goals. One raver described using a set of movements to activate his energy:

> I remember I used to have a few things that would activate my dance if I felt sluggish; I would go through . . . a series of movements that would just activate me slightly more and bring me into a connection, so it's almost like a ritual I didn't know I was performing. Just having this set, a really quick thing that would take a four-count of music or a sixteen-count, that would just bring me back, activate my energy.[63]

Another raver uses the Taoist practice of chi kung in a similar way:

> I trained in chi kung for a few years. So, I actually do chi kung when I dance sometimes. And I'll do that just to get my energy moving around, so I can get in touch with it.[64]

Another approach is to dance with the polyrhythms of the music:

> It has layers and layers and layers, so I think it is the rhythm that really does it for me because I'll hear another rhythm come in, and another rhythm, and another rhythm, and so I begin to emulate those rhythms in my body. And it almost is a practice for meditation, and practice for dance, because I'll go deeper and deeper and deeper, with every new layer that comes in, I'll take myself a little bit deeper, and find myself juggling ten rhythms in my body at once.[65]

One raver uses this polyrhythmic approach to dancing as a way to work with different types of energy:

> I'll feel the bass and then I'll move up to the treble. I love skipping between the rhythms in a single dance move. What I love is interplaying the two or three different flavors of the rhythms at the same time. It's about energy manipulation for me. I manipulate my energy in a conscious way.

> Q: It sounds like what you're describing is a polyrhythmic approach to relating to the music.
> A: Totally.
> Q: So, you can pick out those different levels all simultaneously at the same time?
> A: I love it! That's how I connect to it. I hang different frequencies on different rhythms of the music at the same time. I love that! I love that so much! That's why I like complicated high-hats and good funky basses. When there's lots going on in the vertical spectrums of the songs, that's my favorite.
> Q: And you can relate to those different rhythms with different parts of your body?
> A: Yeah, it is different parts of my body. My arms will often do one thing where maybe my butt and my legs are doing something else.
> Q: Are there characteristic movements that help you modulate the energy?
> A: Hands. . . . One of the things that I started to realize recently is that low frequency music is down here and the center of weight is here.

The low frequency stuff is in the legs and the first chakra, down. There's sort of what I call warrior music or tribal music that's lower frequency and the moves I like to do with that are bent knees. The emphasis is getting my butt into that groove. And that's a root. And then above that is when it gets interesting. The arms pull that up and pull this down and there's a real interplay.[66]

This reference to the use of the hands and arms is echoed by many ravers, so much so that one could characterize it as a fairly universal movement form that some ravers have called "directing traffic":

One thing actually I think is pretty common is what we call *directing traffic*, where you have really dramatic rhythmic gestures with your arms. There must be some weird correlation with how you feel when you're on Ecstasy and doing that stuff because everybody does it. . . . The open arms, the extended arms, is you're kind of opening yourself, you're moving rhythmically to the music.[67]

The house music subgenre, on the other hand, produced a different characteristic movement known as "jacking the body":

In the early Chicago house music scene, all the parties were in really tight spaces. So, people were jacking their bodies, the whole concept of *jack your body*. . . . Jacking your body is all about . . . imitating sexual movements, you can take off your clothes, you're jacking yourself to the beat. And it's all in this really close environment where you are touching someone but you're not making love to them. And you're touching anybody around you. . . . And that was what a lot of the rhythm and motion was, in a really tight environment, where it was just like the sway of the ocean almost. That's how people danced. But now everyone has a lot more room in the raves, so they're like jumping around more, and it's a different type of trance.[68]

So, one factor in these different movement forms is how much room there is to dance. Another factor is the rhythm and the number of beats per minute (BPM):

When you have a very high BPM [135–50], that tends toward the techno genre, more ravey kind of stuff. And, as you move down the BPM, you start moving into the house genre. . . . House runs in the 110 to 120 BPM range. . . . House music has a tendency to get you into this kind of pelvic trance thing, whereas techno or rave music tend to get you more into an upper body trance thing.[69]

The "jungle" subgenre, also known as "drum and bass," has a different characteristic movement:

> There's definitely more footwork in dancing to jungle . . . more of a foot thing that goes on with jungle that you don't see in standard techno. . . . When you see people dance to jungle, there's definitely steps.[70]

Again, one of the factors in this different movement has to do with the rhythm, which has less of the pounding "four on the floor" kick drum and more complex, multilayered polyrhythms:

> If you listen to jungle, most of it, the bass line is half time from the drums, so it's usually 80 or 85 BPM for the actual perceived time of the music. . . . You hear these break beats that are totally sped up, you hear this crazy snare drum and cymbals and shakers going all over the place. . . .[71]

> What you do is dance half as fast you would normally dance to regular techno, even a quarter as fast, because you've only got a pulse in one place, you've got it one quarter of the time that you do in regular techno. And so actually you have to totally dance a different way.[72]

Overall, then, "rave music comes in a thousand different flavors. And, depending on the scene you're in, it dictates the kind of dance you're going to see."[73] Moreover, each different set of characteristic dance movements produces a different type of experiential state and a corresponding shift in the body. As one raver put it,

> The moment that we shift our movements, I think we're creating shifts in who we are, in our beings, in our body-mind.[74]

Thus,

> dancing permanently alters my perception and also alters my body and my body opens more and more. The alignment shifts and so the energies can flow through more clearly, more quickly, without resistance.[75]

Chakras

Another way of conceptualizing this interrelationship between the type of music, the type of movement, and the experiential bodily state that many ravers use centers on chakras; the term *chakra* is drawn from Indian yogic and tantric traditions, and chakras are also used in some types of healing work. Chakras are a series of seven energy centers located on the central axis of the human energetic body, an axis that roughly corresponds to the physical location of the spine. Each chakra is associated with a different type of energy. For example, the second chakra is associated with sexuality, the fourth with the heart and emotions, and the seventh with spiritual matters. Ravers describe their awareness of chakras:

> To me, it's all about chakras. . . . The higher the chakra, it starts to look trancy . . . so people look like they're in a trance, whereas people that are dancing more of a groovy, funky stuff with house or acid jazz, they look more sensuous, like they're in their lower chakras.[76]

> I definitely know about the lower chakra because that's a lot of where we carry this music when we dance. The center of our bodies are down here and this is where we use our hips. I have had the experience of music hitting me at different points, like in my heart or my head. IDM [intelligent dance music] is very head based electronic music. I've listened to IDM and I've written stories to the music. It's very heady, mathematical sounding. And then I've experienced other music, just very beautiful house music, in my heart, in my chest, feeling your heart cracking open and loosening and opening. And then there's other music, tribal, midtempo, you feel it in your lower chakra. It's sexy, it's sensual, and you feel it down in your genitals, that's where it resonates with you. And then there's drum and bass, you just get happy feet, you just move your feet around, jiggling.[77]

> Sometimes it's about communication [the fifth chakra], or some survival stuff. God, when I first started dancing, I had a lot of survival stuff. When I first moved here, *My God, where am I going to live?* I had a lot of survival, first-chakra stuff. And third, good Lord, I've got third chakra issues! So, yes, I use them all. Maybe I'm just a heart-centered person, but my heart informs a lot.[78]

According to this model, then, some musics affect the lower chakras and produce a more earthy, sensual experience. Some affect the heart chakra and produce more of an experience of love. Some affect the higher chakras and produce more of an out-of-body spiritual experience, which is also something that many ravers experience:

> I was outside myself looking down at myself. . . . I was above myself looking down, sort of in a helicopter if you will, looking down at all these people dancing.[79]

I talked with other people about this particular subject and that's a pretty common perception, to see yourself as if you're looking down on yourself.[80]

Yet perhaps the interesting thing about electronic dance music, according to some ravers, is that it seems to affect all of the chakras along the entire vertical axis at the same time.

I experience it actually affecting chakras above the head and all the way through to the earth. . . . Some of the techno is affecting the whole vertical dimension, so that the body will get a sense of both grounding and being very connected to the transpersonal. I'm getting that sense of both with techno.[81]

Therefore, electronic dance music appears to open up the whole range of experiential states, from the earthy to the cosmic, including some unusual and extraordinary combinations.

Energy

The system of chakras is one of many religious and spiritual systems that map the flow of subtle energy in and around the body. This energy goes by many names. In Indian Tantric traditions, it is referred to as *kundalini* or *prana*. In Chinese Taoist traditions, it is called *ch'i* or *qi*. Among the Huichol Indians of northern Mexico, it is called *kupuri*. Ravers don't have a specific name for it, but they do know from their firsthand experience that very powerful energies are generated on the dance floor, and they frequently used the word *energy* to talk about these experiences:

I was stepping outside this world of limitations and stepping into this world that was just pure energy. . . . Energy, high energy, lots of energy, but very big and light.[82]

For me, there's a tremendous amount of energy, a tremendous amount of—it's almost electric at times, a great deal of joy, and chi in movement. . . .[83]

My experience of my body was just this pure column of energy, it was just this pure connection from top to bottom of this pulsing. . . . I just remember breathing in and feeling this rush from way above my head to way below my feet. . . .[84]

There is simply a flow of energy that has no beginning or end, that starts with no one and ends with no one, there's no one person or thing that's causing it.[85]

The energy of the earth can come through the body in a very unimpeded way, the energy of anything, another person's energy. . . . I experience it as a universal force that is present in every one of my cells and that moves through me.[86]

In many cases, not only do ravers recognize that energy is being generated, but they also seem to be able to consciously work with the energy by moving it and channeling it in specific ways.

I like to dance on the dance floor and move the energy around, around me and through me.[87]

It's about energy manipulation for me. I manipulate my energy in a conscious way. . . .You're weaving energy around. You're moving energy in. I feel like that's what I'm doing. . . .When I'm dancing and I'm cleaning out all this garbage, inviting new energy in, and working with it . . . that kind of realignment of my energy is absolutely grounding, it's refreshing, it gives me hope, it helps me analyze problems and have a new perspective on things, and that's all energetic.[88]

It's about channeling energy, for me. I think that would be a primary, the channeling energy is a big part of it, especially when I get into a spinning thing, that really takes it there. But channeling energy and creating sort of like, there's a feeling of a vortex or an elevator or a portal of some kind that's defined by the sound and the perimeter of the dance floor. . . . It has more to do with frequencies of energy that normal society does not allow you to go there into those spaces, into these certain kinds of energy states.[89]

As this last quote indicates, the energy is not confined to the body, but can be found throughout the dance floor. This can include specific identifiable formations:

I have distinct memories of, like, balls of energy sweeping a room, hitting everybody in a row, just like *shwoo, shwoo, shwoo,* spiraling. And you could watch it go. And it was just like hitting people and people are doing their thing.[90]

You can get sometimes just a vortex of energy coming. . . out of heaven into the DJ, out of the turntable and into the speakers and into the people. And you can just see this energy, you know, almost a physical wave downloading into everyone.[91]

The Unified Energetic Field

The experience of energy can also go beyond specific formations to include the entirety of the dance floor as a unified energetic *field*, a term used by several ravers:

> There's an interesting phenomenon that occurs with speakers. You can take two subwoofers and let's just say that they're running at 110 DV and they have a certain amount of voltage through it. If the speakers are in phase, when you put them next to each other, they actually increase the output even though no more energy has been put into it. And I think what happens is, when you have a group of people in sympathetic resonance, not just individually but in this group, you start producing a field that is generating more energy than any one person could accomplish on their own. And this energy is in some way helping to dissolve the programming. And what happens is, you lead an experience like that, you feel like something transcendent has happened.[92]

> If the setting's good, and the general vibe of people is good, and people came with positive intention, and they're not too sketched out, and the music's good, you have this kind of feedback looping effects that start to happen, and everything builds on itself. For one thing, people get tuned to each other by the process of seeing each other, hugging, connecting, and then moving together on the dance floor, and all of these different components start to feed into one another and it just creates a spiraling energy field.[93]

> When you dance with people in this way over time, one of the things that becomes totally evident is the oneness, that we're all moving in this field, this vibrational field.[94]

The Connection to Spiritual Worlds

This experience of a unified energetic field is remarkable in and of itself. What is even more remarkable, however, is that this field also seems to include access to spiritual realms as well. This was clearly articulated when

I asked one of my interviewees about his use of the words *vortex* and *portal* and pressed him to say more:

> There's a feeling of a vortex that you get from the dance floor, where the vortex is going—it's like it is connecting different levels somehow, which is similar to what the shamans probably visualize with their whole thing of going up a world tree, although I don't generally have that kind of imagery myself, for the most part. But there's a feeling of making a connection between different realms somehow and allowing a flow to happen between those worlds.[95]

Another image or metaphor that traditionally expresses the idea of access to spirits and spiritual worlds is that of a vertical connection that begins in the earth and touches the divine realm as it reaches upward. This is an image that goes all the way back to shamanism and the axis mundi, or the world tree that stands at the center of the universe. In fact, one raver specifically used the image of a tree in trying to express this connection:

> It's like having the experience of seeing the illusory nature of reality, or seeing it through a different lens where my body is not just my body, my little window to the world walking around. Suddenly, it's like this entity and I step out for a moment and experience it from a different angle. And experience, let's say, myself as a leaf; the leaf is just one little element on this tree but it's part of a little branch, which is part of a big branch, which is part of the trunk, which is connected in the root system, and everything is branching off from everything else at all different levels. I see that unfolding in my moves as I'm flowing with the music.[96]

In a more general sense, the idea of verticality as a connection between different worlds was mentioned by several ravers:

> There's that connection I always feel going down into the earth. It's just a very core connection to warm, deep earth. And I feel an upward connection to the divine.[97]

> I have a transcendent quality to my experiences. I have a lot of vertical connection.[98]

> My experience of my body was just this pure column of energy, it was just this pure connection from top to bottom of this pulsing, the beat just pulsed right through me and I could not stop. . . . I just remember

breathing in and feeling this rush from way above my head to way below my feet.[99]

Some of the techno is affecting the whole vertical dimension, so that the body will get a sense of both grounding and being very connected to the transpersonal. I'm getting that sense of both with techno.[100]

What is interesting about this vertical connection to the divine or the spiritual realms is that there is also a connection to the earth, the body, and physical reality that is happening at the same time. In fact, just as with the image of a field, the physical and spiritual are integrated into a unified whole.

The Presence of Spirit(s)

These images of a unified field or a vertical connection provide a framework for understanding how it is possible for someone to experience the presence of spirits on the dance floor at raves. And, while there are many ravers and electronic dance-music aficionados who are uncomfortable with framing their experiences in spiritual terms, on the other side of the spectrum, many of the ravers I interviewed had no trepidation whatsoever in speaking about spirits in a clear and unmistakable manner:

There's all sorts of different forces and spirits in the world and some can come and visit, have things to say to you or through you.[101]

I sense various spirits that help me in the other world, you know, spirits that I talk to.[102]

I operate in a belief that this world is filled with energies and entities and forces that we have just, in our Western way of perceiving things, very limited concern for.[103]

There's this awareness of other beings, of other creatures, forms, something.[104]

What is more, it is not simply that spirits are present in the dance-floor experience at raves, but that ravers can develop a conscious and mutually beneficial relationship with them:

While we're dancing at the event physically, we also have a lot of help on the other side dancing with us, moving energy on the other side for us, and they want us to live beautiful lives as much as we want to live beautiful lives and they're willing to help us if we have a way of connecting with them and inviting them to participate with us. . . . The light beings, the ones you really want to be dealing with, are polite. And they'll wait for an invitation. And the guys you don't want to deal with are impolite and you have to keep them out—you know, the darker ones. Spirits are just like people. People are spirits. And there's people you want to invite in your home and there's people you don't want to invite in your home. It's just common sense. And the same with spirits. There are spirits that you want to invite into your ceremonies and there are spirits you don't want to invite, that you want to keep out. And that's part of what the ceremonial container is about.[105]

When we're in a tribal dance culture sort of situation, we are even further vulnerable to whatever energies are present or being released, for that matter, into the atmosphere. And I've heard from healers or friends of mine that this is cause for one to make sure you clear your energy field after you've been at a gathering of that nature, because you may have accumulated excess energies or dark energies that were released unconsciously that have looked for a vehicle and they find you. So that said, I think I've had experiences where I consciously will say, *I dedicate this dance to my relationship with the planet, with the environment where I'm finding myself dancing, with the ancestors of that land, with the elemental forces*, using dance as a way to actually actively engage communication, and feel myself in harmony.[106]

I'm shamanically inviting those spirits in and asking them to flow through those that are open, as DJ.[107]

In these quotes, people are discussing spirits in the plural, implying a multiplicity. However, other ravers use the word *spirit* in the singular form:

At those times I'm really glimpsing how spirit is, there's a true is-ness of spirit in this endless creation, this vibrational play, that I get to see. It carries through to my own life. In other words, I get to see more and more that spirit is this endlessly moving creating playful energy that the dance has made very apparent to me.[108]

Checking in with spirit is how I've always thought about it. For me, spirit is not something out there but something that manifests.[109]

I became a little less human and a little bit more spirit.[110]

Still other ravers have formulated things in a kind of spiritual hierarchy that includes both the plural and the singular:

> There's spirits of all kinds and then there's the Great Spirit.[111]

> From a shamanic viewpoint, also, if you want to go up the ladder, you can also talk about angelic beings who want to participate and you can talk about God-consciousness that wants to participate. I mean, as we reach up to God, God is reaching down to us. We meet in the middle.[112]

Possession

In my previous book, *Traces of the Spirit*,[113] I examined the influence of Yoruba and Fon possession religion on American popular music, following the route of this musicoreligious complex as it came to the Americas in the slave trade and went through a series of transformations in order to survive and adapt to the radically different circumstances of the New World. In their original West African context, possession dances were ceremonial gatherings where drum ensembles and singers supplied beat-driven polyrhythmic music and initiates danced themselves into ecstatic trance states in which the gods would take possession of their bodies and be physically present among the community for the purposes of counseling, healing, and divination. The primary metaphor for possession is that of the rider and the horse, in which the possessing spirit is the controlling rider and the dancer is the horse. When the Yoruba and Fon were brought to the United States as slaves, these religions were outlawed, but many of their musical practices and experiential states were preserved in the cultural arena of African American 'secular' entertainment musics like jazz and blues, albeit in a highly transformed fashion.[114] These musics then formed the basis for what was to become rock and roll when it crossed over to a mainstream white audience, carrying within it this hidden religious sensibility. As rock and roll evolved into a major cultural force and spawned a variety of different musical youth subcultures, including the rave scene, several generations of Americans of all classes and ethnicities came of age under the influence of this hidden religious sensibility, which became part and parcel of the fabric of our common cultural heritage.

I mention all of this in exploring the idea of the presence of spirits on the dance floor at raves because many ravers' descriptions of their experiences sound uncannily like the possession experience of the rider and the horse:

I feel like, for me, another force takes over and I let go and my body just starts doing this dance, which is more intricate and patterned and fractalized than anything I could possibly come up with if I was actually trying to do it with my head. So my mind lets go and I'm watching myself, possibly even from a space slightly outside of myself. And just executing this geometric spiraling pattern.[115]

There is a point that, when you achieve it, it's truly wonderful and it's kind of a mystical thing where the music literally—I mean, this all sounds so trite—where the music really sort of sinks its teeth into you . . . my boyfriend always says, "It's got you," or, "It's got me." And it's that kind of thing where the music just completely—it's in you, it's around you, and your body is moving despite yourself.[116]

For me it's also a feeling of something bigger than me looking through me and participating in what I'm doing . . . being aware of itself through me and through other people. And for me, the experience is of recognizing myself looking at myself through other people, and feeling that.[117]

Moreover, it is not only the dancers who are having this kind of experience, but the DJs as well:

When I'm doing my best DJing, it's the exact same thing, something hops in and takes over. I see my hands do things on the mixer they've never done in practice that sound amazing on the sound system. And everybody is getting off, just going nuts, when I get in that space as a DJ.[118]

I was completely in a trance state. . . . It seemed like I could just do no wrong. . . . And, in those times, I feel like, seriously, the spirit's taking over. . . . I definitely feel like there is some spirit force that comes over my body. . . . Someone, something is assisting me. . . . And I don't really know who that spirit is that's inside me. I've talked about it with a couple of friends. They agree that something just sort of takes them over. . . . And I don't know what is guiding me that way. I can just assume that it's a great mixture of my talent and a spirit that's taking over the set.[119]

I feel like something is traveling through me, that I am a servant of something. This sense of being so deeply in service to something, like I'm a conduit for something, and all I'm doing is anything that's happening through me—it's like, it's happening, I'm making it happen in a sense, but also not at all, there's something that's traveling through me, there's something that's coming through me that I'm expressing or I'm helping to deliver. . . . I'm in service to something higher that's going on, something bigger than me. I am part of some sort of beautiful transcendent thing that exists but we don't have access to it all the time. I'm a servant of the vibe. I am a priestess of the church.[120]

I do have a sense of opening to something larger than myself when I play. . . . I do have a sense of being divinely guided in the choices of the music and, when I'm truly in a flowing place, the sense of what to play is just coming. That's the place where, as a DJ, I like to get to, where each piece of music is just flowing from one to the next. And I believe that I can most help people enter that state of flow when the music is happening that way, when it's just coming through me.[121]

Interestingly, in all of these quotes, no one specified what spirit was coming through them in these situations, which seems to indicate that this awareness of spirits in the dance-floor experience at raves is in an early developmental stage, especially compared with West African and Afro-Diasporic traditions that can skillfully identify the particular spirit and its domain of expertise. In all of the interviews, there were only two instances where anyone came close to identifying a particular spirit. The first was as follows:

One of the energies of the heart that we worked with was what this teacher called a *Christ force*. And I love that one. It's this massive warmth. It's this huge benevolent, compassionate—it is grace. I do a lot of body work and oftentimes I will invoke the Christ force and that sends this chain reaction of all this warmth and this energetic flow, even when I'm not dancing. It's a label for something that I also often experience on the dance floor, often will invoke, although not intentionally . . . one just kind of happens with the other.[122]

The second was when, in framing my question on this subject, I used the example of Kali, the fierce Hindu goddess of destruction, as contrasted with the serenity and enlightened quality of the Buddha, to illustrate the vast difference in types of spiritual energies that exist, and a DJ was able to see that contrast in her own experiences:

The experience that I had the very first time I went out and DJed, and had that experience of humility, it was very churchlike, sacred, benevolent thing that was happening. But then, there are other times when I've DJed, like at Burning Man, this huge dust storm was happening and all of the sudden there were all these people in the dome and I was playing this serious tribal set. And the energy, the force was the same, but the manifestation of it was different. So, when you said Kali, as opposed to Buddha, I immediately identified with that. There's something up here that's the highest, and then there's this manifestation of it; the energy of it's a little bit different, though the purpose of it is the same. And that is this thought of being in service and serving this higher good and helping create higher good and helping enable higher good and helping enable beauty and truth and freedom—but the manifestation of it could be a Kali manifestation that's kind of aggressive, and "urrr!" And then there's the Buddha manifestation that is this beautiful mid-tempo groovy, sensual thing. But the overarching thing or force that it's coming from is the same.[123]

The identification in both these cases is still pretty nonspecific. Nevertheless, the language of all of these descriptions does seem to confirm that something akin to possession is happening, and this is remarkable in and of itself.

As far as a more specific identification of particular spirits, I should also mention the events put on by the Oracle crew in Seattle, which has designed its own Tarot deck consisting of twenty-three images, each representing a spiritual archetype. Every rave they produce is based on one of these images, and they are very clear that the whole point of the event is to manifest that particular archetype:

What we have been finding, through this process, which has been really amazing, is the archetypes absolutely play themselves out in our lives. . . . So they really are our teachers and the Oracle literally is its own entity. And it just tells us how it works day by day. And we're ultimately in service to what it's asking us to do as a community.[124]

While it is common for many rave crews to name their events based on spiritual themes or figures, the Oracle is unique in that they are consciously trying to manifest these archetypes, not only on the dance floor at these events, but in the larger life of their community. It is a subject worth investigating more thoroughly and, accordingly, I will examine the Oracle in much greater detail in the next chapter on the ritual and ceremonial dimensions of raves.

Sacred, Spiritual, Spirituality

Of course, not every raver or rave crew articulates the religious nature of their rave experience in terms of spirits, archetypes, manifestations, or possession. There are a couple of general terms that are more widely used; *sacred* is one of them:

> You're definitely touching something sacred, for sure. . . . People have an experience of the sacred, of something they recognize as sacred, as transcendent.[125]

> It's a sacred space.[126]

> I definitely consider that to be sacred. I began to hold those moments as my most sacred time.[127]

And for many ravers who may feel a lack of the sacred in other areas of their lives, having an experience of the sacred at a rave satisfies this powerful human need:

> *Q:* I take it you have a sense of the sacred when this is going on?
> *A:* It makes my hair stand up just talking about it. I definitely do. . . .
> *Q:* Do you experience the sacred at a rave, on the dance floor?
> *A:* Absolutely. Absolutely. I see people transformed when they pass through. . . . People come into it just longing for that feeling of the sacred and feeling of the divine but not really knowing how to get it, coming from a spiritually damaged background, which I partially come from, so I can recognize that. Or coming from a spiritually powerful background but not having it anymore, not having that spiritual background of their upbringing to support them anymore, and coming . . . and finding it again, or finding it for the first time.[128]

Another more general term that is widely used by ravers also appears in this quote—*spiritual*—and it is often used interchangeably with the word *spirituality*. It seems appropriate to conclude this chapter with some quotes from ravers on this subject.

> It's definitely a spiritual experience. And I never had any spirituality before, so this was my first time that I had ever experienced that.[129]

I consider it to be a very spiritual experience. In fact, I can say that prior to doing that, my sense of spirituality was pretty weak, pretty undeveloped, pretty dormant in me. . . . I definitely felt a very strong sense of spirituality.[130]

It showed me true spirituality, from within flowing out of myself and joining it with other people. Undoubtedly the most spiritual feeling I've ever had.[131]

The Oracle, Seattle, WA, 2003. Photograph courtesy of Shawn "Skoi" Lass (Archivist@oracle.com).

CHAPTER 4
TECHNO TRIBAL CHURCH: THE RITUAL AND CEREMONIAL FORMS OF RAVE

In the last chapter, ravers spoke at length about the sacred nature of their powerful experiences on the dance floor at raves and beyond. These experiences are extraordinary in and of themselves, particularly in a secularized world where genuine, transformative, religious experience is extremely rare. What is even more extraordinary, however, is that these experiences are not accidental or even unusual, but are instead the products of events that are deliberately designed and consciously constructed to facilitate just such experiences. Raves do this by combining certain identifiable structural components (e.g., DJ-mixed electronic dance music, lights and visuals, decorations and altars, opening and closing ceremonies, and so forth) in a consistent manner that has proven effective and reliable at producing these powerful experiential states. Used in this way, these structural components of raves function as a ritual technology and the rave itself can be understood as a religious ceremony, a view confirmed by ravers:

> There are some basic elements to ceremony that engender primary
> religious experience. . . . For me, all of the effort that I do for ceremony,
> and I see the purpose of ceremony, is engendering that. From what

97

I understand of how it works, and how it works for me, is the ceremony is part of creating the container for that experience.[1]

There are two important and complementary aspects to the ritual dimensions of raves, and I will examine both in detail in this chapter. The first is what ritual studies scholars have called *ritualization*, a term used to describe the repetition of certain activities or practices in a consistent and identifiable manner.[2] In terms of raves, this would include activities or practices such as planning, publicity, set-up, transportation, DJing, dancing, chilling out, opening and closing ceremonies, breaking down the rave at the end, and the "after-party." It also includes the temporal sequencing of such activities, the spatial arrangement, and the roles people play. The second aspect is the implicit understanding that the goal of these ritualized activities is to facilitate powerful experiential states and a connection to the sacred. Here I draw on the ritual studies work of historian of religions Jonathan Z. Smith, who argues that ritual serves as a kind of focusing lens through which the ordinary "becomes sacred by having our attention directed to it in a special way."[3] This aspect is seen not only in the explicitly spiritual orientation of a number of structural components such as themes and archetypes, decorations and visuals, opening and closing ceremonies, altars, and the incorporation of material from specific religious traditions, but also in the overall intention of both the organizers and the participants. As the creators of the Oracle events in Seattle eloquently articulate it, the goal is to "call upon new ritual experiences based on the wisdom of our own culture, creating sacred space, transformational experiences, and art with intention."[4]

The Weekly Rhythm and Comparisons to Church

As I have shown in the last chapter, newcomers typically begin their involvement in rave culture with a conversion experience. Following this experience, ravers often immerse themselves completely in the scene by going to raves once a week or even more frequently.

It [the rave experience] blew me away and suddenly I found myself going to parties every weekend.[5]

It definitely, for a good number of years, was all I did and all of my friends were doing the same. . . . Everything we did revolved around going out to parties and going out to clubs and stuff like that. . . . There was a time where it was several nights in a week, you know, five, six nights in a week, we'd be going out somewhere and just dancing and carrying on.[6]

Considering that raves are typically all-night affairs that require enormous outputs of physical energy (and, for many, the ingestion of consciousness-altering drugs), this kind of temporal frequency and regularity of practice is strong evidence of the central importance of the rave as an ongoing ritual in their lives.

For many ravers, this weekly rhythm led to comparisons with church:

Raving was Saturday but, suddenly, raving was Sunday morning, too. We used to talk about [how] we should just find an old church and throw a rave every Saturday night on into Sunday. It was my first hit of religion as far as something organized.[7]

We were all sitting around at the end of one [Saturday night] Sunday morning tweaking our brains out. And we were going, "Yeah, we really should start a Sunday morning thing and keep the vibe going." And my friend Frank said, "Yeah, and we should call it Church because that's what it is. I mean, I go to a club on Sunday morning for my church." And so we did. . . . We actually started another one-off kind of thing that went on intermittently and we called it Church. And it started out at six on Sunday morning and it ran all Sunday. And Carefree [the main club] kind of bled into Church.[8]

Although, at first glance, this comparison to church may seem superficial, on closer examination, it is actually very accurate. Just as churchgoers attend church consistently, so ravers attend raves regularly, often on a weekly basis, and they regard them as a central activity in their lives. Just as with churchgoing, there is a consistent ritual structure that ravers can rely on. Just as with church, they experience a sense of communal solidarity and bonding with their fellow participants. And, finally, just as with church, they experience a connection to the sacred that recharges them and carries over into their day-to-day lives, providing them with meaning, direction, and purpose. In fact, as I will show in detail later in this chapter, raves and churches have had an interesting history of interconnection, beginning with the Reverend Chris Brain's "Rave Masses" in Sheffield, England, in 1993, and continuing to today with Episcopal priest Matthew Fox's "Techno Cosmic Masses" in Oakland, California.

Ritualized Time

In addition to this regular weekly sequencing, there is also a strongly ritualized temporal sequencing of activities that occurs within the raves themselves. First of all, there may be a period of time spent just tracking down the location of a rave through phone calls and driving to a series of informational check points. Raves usually begin no earlier than 9:00 or 10:00 P.M., and often the dance floor(s) will not really get full until 11:00, 12:00, or even later. Many raves have opening ceremonies, and these usually either precede the first DJ set or follow it. (I will examine these ceremonies in more detail a bit later in this chapter.) DJs will typically spin two- to three-hour sets, starting slowly and then building to peaks. A good set will include several peaks, which take the dancers up and bring them back down repeatedly, leading them on a musical journey. Because of the strenuous nature of the dancing, it is necessary sometimes for the dancers to take a break to recuperate, both physically and psychologically. For this, there are chill rooms where one can relax with friends in a relatively quiet, safe, comfortable environment. In the course of the evening, there is a rhythmic temporal oscillation between the intensity of the dance floor and the relaxing break of the chill room.

Generally speaking, the overall peak of the rave, in terms of density of crowds and intensity of dancing, will typically happen between 12:00 midnight and 3:00 A.M. This is the most highly coveted DJ time slot, and the headline DJs are usually scheduled during this time. The dancers have been dancing long enough to be well warmed up and inducted into deep trance states, and those who are taking drugs are by now well feeling the effects. During this time DJs tend to keep the musical peaks going for longer periods, and therefore the dancers tend to have their most powerful experiences of the night. Each DJ has his own idea of where he wants to take the dancers, and his own strategies and techniques for doing so, and I will discuss these in greater detail a bit later in this chapter. Sometimes, this peak time on the dance floor can go on for many hours, keeping the intensity level high until dawn.

In many raves, however, there is an energetic scaling back in the predawn hours, when the crowd thins out somewhat and the music becomes more downtempo and ambient. This time can be very sweet and intimate, in which the energy and connections that have been established over the course of the night can be more personally expressed and savored. Finally, for those who stay all night, the onset of dawn and the light of the new day provide another kind of peak, one that culminates the whole experience with a sense of uplift and completion. There is a feeling of having gone on a collective journey together and arriving at the end transformed, renewed, and unified, and, as noted earlier in this volume, many raves formalize this sense of completion by concluding with a closing ceremony. Organizers then begin the tedious process of breaking down the space, which can take several hours, often assisted by participants who have stayed all night. After this, many crews have an "after-party," at another smaller location that has the feel of a chill-out room and features downtempo or ambient music. The after-party is an opportunity to decompress from the rave and continue to hang out with fellow ravers in a more intimate setting. Inevitably, however, one must return home and sleep in order to recover from the high level of intensity and exertion. The nocturnal nature of the rave, followed by daytime recuperation, leads to a lifestyle in which the daily rhythms of ravers are nearly the opposite of the mainstream world—up all night and sleeping during the day.

Rave as Rite of Passage: Turner's Concepts of Liminality, Communitas, and Anti-Structure

This nocturnal lifestyle is a powerful example of the liminal aspect of raves. Liminality is a term coined by anthropologist Victor Turner to describe the "betwixt-and-between" state of initiates in traditional rites of passage. In his classic book *The Ritual Process*, Turner developed a number of important concepts that laid the foundation for the field of ritual studies, and several of these concepts are useful in bringing out the ritual dimensions of raves.[9] In traditional cultures, rites of passage mark the transition from one phase of life to the next, and one of the most important of these transitions is from adolescence to adulthood.[10] The hormone-driven rebellious quest for intense experience characteristic of those in this age group is often channeled into various types of initiatic trials, such as body mutilation, fasting, dancing until exhaustion, use of psychotropic plants, and going on vision quests. While there are many mixed-age raves that include people in their thirties and older, the vast majority of ravers are in their late teens and early twenties, and raves clearly serve the function of just such a rite of passage, an initiation experience for many of them.

Traditional rites of passage emphasize the liminal quality of this transition from adolescence to adulthood by separating the initiates from the rest of society, stripping them of their normal social identity, placing them in their own temporary form of alternative community—which Turner called *communitas*—and initiating them through a powerful encounter with the sacred. Raves do all of these things in almost exactly the same sequence. Furthermore, Turner identified the trajectory of these rites of passage in a threefold arc of movement from structure to antistructure and back to structure, in which the middle stage of antistructure contains the heart of the initiation. Again, the same arc can be found in the rave, with the dance floor as the perfect example of antistructure where initiation takes place. The enormous difference between the rite of passage of traditional cultures and those of raves, however, is that traditional cultures provide a framework within which young people can complete their initiation and be reintegrated back into society in their new social status as adults, and raves do not. One might argue that this leaves many ravers in a state of permanent liminality and adolescence, where they function at the margins of mainstream society, seemingly unwilling to grow up and become adults. While there is some truth to this critique, in my experience there are just as many ravers who are fully functioning, responsible adults with real jobs and careers, children, and families who are making important contributions to society.

Ritualized Space

In addition to having a temporal aspect, ritual also has a spatial aspect; in other words, ritualized activities unfold in space as well as in time. Ritual takes place in a controlled environment where everything is in its proper place and all activity unfolds in the correct sequence. In this regard, Smith has emphasized the importance of place, arguing that "a sacred place is a place of clarification (a focusing lens) where men and gods are held to be transparent to each other." Furthermore, he notes, "if we take seriously the notion of a temple, a sacred place, as a focusing lens, the ordinary . . . becomes significant, becomes sacred. . . ."[11] Raves are a perfect illustration of this point—particularly the warehouse rave. What could be more ordinary and secular than a warehouse, whose drab, faceless environment is the embodiment of utilitarian functionality? Yet raves consistently transform decrepit warehouses into magical places of wonder. Here is an account of just such a transformation from the early days of the Los Angeles rave scene:

> People would break into warehouses, huge monstrous warehouses downtown, and just spend days decorating and putting the sound systems in and black lights and Day-Glo paint. It was madness, always madness. Now, this was back in the day of map points, secrecy, you know, it wasn't just *there's a location*. You find the flyer, you call the number the night of the party, it would tell you to go to this location, and you go to that location and they tell you to go to *this* location, [and then] you go to that location. Then you pay your money there and they actually finally tell you where the party's at. So, everyone was like a secret agent, the whole outlaw thing. That sort of mystery just added to the excitement of what you were getting involved with. When you finally did arrive, you'd see like five hundred to a thousand people just going crazy, dressed up in costumes.[12]

The mystery and excitement involved with the step-by-step process of simply getting to the location is another example of the liminal aspect of raves. It can also be seen as a kind of pilgrimage, which is another form of religious ritual that has a strong spatial dimension. The account continues:

> How the warehouse was set up—it was three massive rooms but they were separated by brick walls. So, these guys came in through the main entrance and broke holes through each wall and put slides in one side and steps in the other so you entered up stairs to go into the next room and, to get out, you'd go through a slide to get down. Huge rope swings hanging from the ceiling. They even put, in one room . . . a small school bus totally painted in Day-Glo paint and it had black lights. So, after going to around three map points and then arriving in a scene like that, actually, it's a bit overwhelming, it's like an assault on your senses, but in a good way. It's very much like being a kid going to Disneyland.[13]

And, to finish the metaphor, as we all know, for a kid, going to Disneyland is definitely a numinous experience.

The warehouse spaces are often very large and dark, with an almost cavelike atmosphere and an urban, postindustrial ambience. Bright multicolored decorations, elaborate lights, and projected visuals are an important part of enhancing the visual field so that it has a strong psychedelic and cybernetic feel. Just as DJs invest time, energy, and money to hone their musical craft, decorative artists and light technicians do the same for their visual craft. For many ravers, this visual element is just as critical in their experience as the music:

> The lights and visuals are really important to me. It definitely alters my consciousness. It's crucial to have visuals and lights for me.[14]

> The lights and the setting and the decorations and all that—they bring you out of your ordinary self. . . . It prepares you to go into a transcendent state. The lighting and the decorations and all that wonderful beauty just brings out a state of awe when you walk into it.[15]

In many cases, there are also altars set up throughout the space that contain fabric, figurines, paintings, candles, incense, and various assorted sacred objects. (This is a subject I will examine in more detail shortly.) The altars, decorations, lights, and other visuals are often organized around particular spiritual themes. For example, for the subgenre of electronic dance music called Goa trance (or psychedelic trance), which originated in Goa, India, and subsequently spread to England, Germany, and the United States, rave visuals are likely to include images of such various Hindu deities as Ganesha, Kali, Krishna, and Vishnu, among others.

The visual and decorative aesthetic of the rave also extends to the ravers themselves. Brightly colored psychedelic-patterned clothes are de rigeur and the designs often have a high-tech, cybernetic edge to them. Hairstyles also reflect this aesthetic, with brightly colored dyes, dreadlocks, and unusual shaved patterns being quite commonplace. Many ravers have small high tech accessories such as glow-in-the-dark wands (called glowsticks) or flashing lights. Modification of the body itself occurs in the form of tattoos and multiple body piercings. The pain involved in such procedures closely parallels the ordeal aspect of traditional initiation rites. In this regard, the phrase *future primitive* is a pretty accurate summation of a lot of the rave fashion aesthetic. In some rave circles, this aesthetic is important:

> Once you adopt the look of a raver, it definitely can open doors later. If you look like a raver, people are going to not be suspicious of you. They're going to tell you all kinds of crazy things.[16]

On the other hand, there has always been a strong element of the rave scene that has consciously devalued the importance of any particular fashion aesthetic and the judging of people based on external appearance. As one veteran of the original raves in England said,

In Britain, it's so much to do about what you're wearing and how you're talking and who you know, etcetera, etcetera. It just wasn't like that at the raves. You could go in designer clothes or you could go in a tee shirt and nobody cared. It was very nonjudgmental.[17]

This element has carried through to the present day rave scene:

I could dress the way I wanted, which was very casual, jeans and tee shirt.[18]

Thus, in addition to the future primitive fashion aesthetic, there are also plenty of ravers dressed in nondescript clothing, as well as in a wide variety of eclectic styles.

Many raves have multiple rooms with dance floors, each decorated in a different style, with DJs spinning different types of music. At such raves, one can move from room to room, depending on which atmosphere one is most drawn to at the time. Another option in this regard at most raves is the chill room, a quiet space where one can escape from the sonic assault of the dance floor music. The chill room is usually filled with couches, beds, soft cushions, or carpeting, where ravers can recline and relax. The lighting is low and, often, there is soothing downtempo or ambient music being played. People can have conversations here because it is possible to actually hear what is being said. It is a space where more intimate personal interactions can take place or people can just lie down and catnap. Most raves also have some sort of a bar area where water is available, as well as, often, chai tea, other beverages, or even fruit or other solid foods.

The dance floor at a rave is configured in a very different spatial arrangement from that of a performance or concert in that there is usually no stage with a performer as the main focal point of the crowd's attention. There is also no bank of speakers facing unidirectionally, but instead speakers that are distributed equally throughout the space. Therefore, for the most part, the dancers' attentions are focused primarily on the dance floor as active participants and cocreators:

When you're on the dance floor, who you're looking at, if you're looking at anybody, is each other, and that's really a big difference. You're not watching the stage; you're looking at each other.[19]

Sometimes, one focuses on friends and other dancers who are in close proximity, and certain kinds of movement interactions can develop; but to

a large degree, most of the dancers are deep within their own interior
trance state, not directing their attention outward at all. If there is any
reliable external focal point, it is often the DJ, who has a special space for
her equipment and records, which is off to the side or slightly raised or
even in a small, self-contained booth. Sometimes a significant percentage
of the dancers are paying attention to the DJ, with their bodies facing in
her direction. In fact, there is a high degree of interaction between the
dancers and the DJ, a topic I will examine in greater detail shortly.

Conscious Recognition of the Importance of Ritual and Ceremony

The role of the DJ, altars, opening and closing ceremonies—all of these
are important examples of the ritual and ceremonial dimensions of raves,
and each is worthy of close and thorough examination. Yet, before under-
taking such an examination I feel it is important to establish that, for
many ravers, these components are intentionally used as a ritual technology
to facilitate spiritual and religious experiences. In other words, there is a
conscious recognition of the importance of ritual and ceremony in the
context of the rave and, conversely, of the importance of the rave as a ritual
and ceremonial context. Some ravers are highly articulate on this subject:

> I find it very important to do it in a ceremonial context. . . . I think
> people really have an innate craving for a spiritual context in our lives . . .
> so I think people will create ceremony in their lives, given the opportu-
> nity. Because there is such a spiritual potential and content in raves, peo-
> ple are . . . creating ceremonies in them.[20]

> I am a big fan of ritual. . . . I've had some incredible experiences at rituals
> in the RS and Sweet! has some really fantastic rituals. But, yes, I think
> overall, absolutely, whether it's done in the community or alone or with
> a few friends before, however it's executed, it's a big deal. . . . I like the
> intention of opening the space. I like what they do. . . . And they would
> be a very different event if they didn't happen, without a doubt.[21]

This conscious recognition of the importance of ritual and ceremony can
be seen in a number of different ways, beginning with raver terminology.

Intention

A word that is often used by ravers in discussing the importance of ritual
and ceremony at raves is *intention*:

I'm looking at ways that we can create ritual at personal and collective levels where . . . we are engaging our intention. We're setting intention and we're trying to connect with what the fruit of that intention is.[22]

Setting intention, what your intention is as you enter into the space and enter into the ceremony, is key towards the kind of experience that you have.[23]

It's just such a catalyst for really cool things to happen because of that intention. I'm trying to think of a better way to put it, but it really is because that's what everyone wants. That's what we're doing there. It's not a party. And that makes such a difference.[24]

That is the thing that sets Moontribe apart from pretty much anything else [in the Los Angeles rave scene]—there's a real element of intention to it.[25]

This aspect is so important to the Tribal Harmonix crew in British Columbia that their annual New Year's retreat is named Intention. The basic intention of most raves is to have a smooth-running, safe event that has a good "vibe" and that "goes off." As far as raves with ritual and ceremony, the general intention is to create "sacred" space in which people can have a meaningful and transformative experience. There are also more specific intentions tied to the themes of particular raves, which I will examine in more detail a bit later in this chapter.

The Container

In discussing the use of ritual and ceremony to create sacred space, ravers often use the word *container*. The Rhythm Society, for example, writes the following on the information sheet each participant must read: "A foundational element of our divine celebrations is the creation of a ritual safe 'container' in time and space." In my interviews with them, ravers elaborated on this idea of the container:

The ceremony is part of creating that container for that [religious] experience. You've got the lighting, the music, the space, the security so you don't have to worry about ruffians showing up off the street, and also, ceremony is just another aspect of it, but one which in our culture isn't really very well understood. There are some basic elements to ceremony that engender primary religious experience. Among them are an energetic container, so that the experience can be a sweeter one and less problematic. Having really good energetic grounding works a lot better because the more you ground, the higher up you can reach, the more transcendent you can get, if you're well-grounded. Having a good perimeter is good. . . . What else? What kind of help and spirits are invited to participate from the other side, in a shamanic term or way to look at it? There are spirits that you want to invite into your ceremonies and there are spirits you don't want to invite, that you want to keep out. And that's part of what the ceremonial container is about.[26]

I'm stunned by how important the container is. . . . It's shocking to me how important it is to have. I'm really spoiled, between the Rhythm Society and various groups like it who really know how to create a vibe. They really know how to make that container beautiful. And I'm convinced it has to do with the whole clarity of the group, about why they're doing it. . . . Everybody's bought off on that; that's the point. And so everything informs that goal, everything informs that idea. . . . Connecting with spirit, connecting with each other through spirit, connecting with oneself. Recognizing one's own needs in a container that's safe.[27]

A lot of what I put my efforts towards, within the context of the things that I go to, is creating a container for that feeling [of love] to occur. So that's why I say for me the ceremony is very important because that creates that container to hold that energy, to make it more palpable.[28]

It was in San Francisco that a big shift had occurred for me. I had a visit in which I experienced a different style of party that really awakened me to the possibility of what could occur as the experience creating a container for potential transformation for people.[29]

There is a spatial metaphor in the image of the container as a physical object—such as a bowl or a box—that holds all the contents of the rave and sets boundaries for what is inside and what is outside. Everything inside the container is safe; everything inside the container is grounded; everything inside the container is in its proper place; everything inside the container is sanctified. And, most important, everything inside the container is there in the service of the stated intention of the rave, and everything inside the container is held in place in this way for the duration of the rave.

Opening and Closing Ceremonies

As I noted earlier in this volume, many raves begin with an opening ceremony and end with a closing ceremony. The mere presence of these ceremonies clearly demonstrates the explicitly spiritual and religious nature of raves. However, these ceremonies are more than simply window dressing; they are consciously used as a way to create sacred space and to facilitate religious experience and, therefore, they serve exactly the same function as a ceremony in a traditional religious context. Typically, the opening ceremony occurs either at the very beginning of the rave, before the DJs have begun playing music, or after the first DJ's set, around 11:00 P.M. or 12:00 midnight. In either case, the music is brought down to a low volume or there is no music at all, so that it is easier to hear the ceremonial leaders, who often have a microphone to help in this regard as well. Most ceremonies start with a call for quiet and for everyone to come into some kind of designated formation; a circle is the most popular, but it can be difficult to achieve if the space is tightly packed. Announcements and perhaps a brief explanation of the theme of the rave and the structure of the ceremony then usually follow. The ceremonies themselves are eclectic and diverse, and can draw elements from a variety of different spiritual and religious traditions and cultures. For example, one element that is widely used is for everybody to breathe together, followed by the chanting of the Hindu seed syllable *om*. Other ceremonies might "smudge" people with smoke from the burning of sage as a ritual purification, followed by calling in the four directions, both of which are derived from Native American ceremonial practices. Still others might lead everyone on a guided meditation or visualization. The pool of potential elements is vast, as is the number of permutations for combining them. Nevertheless, there are some particular influences and traditions that seem to be especially popular at raves, and I will explore these in greater detail shortly.

In general, closing ceremonies tend to be simpler and shorter than opening ceremonies, perhaps because there are significantly fewer people still at the rave and, since they have been up all night dancing, those who remain tend to have less energy and patience. However, there is also more of an intimate bond among those who have stayed up all night together. Often the closing ceremony will simply involve gathering everyone into a circle, holding hands, and offering a prayer of thanks. In other cases, it is more elaborate. For example, when the Rhythm Society's events took place in the Episcopal Church of St. John the Evangelist in San Francisco, as they did for seven years, the closing ceremony would end with someone playing Bach organ fugues live on the church organ and ravers could watch the light of the new day as it illuminated the beautiful stained glass windows of the church.

Each crew has its own particular approach to ritual and ceremony, creating its own distinctive style and feeling, and participants come to expect this. The Moontribe is a great example:

> One of the things that really set the Moontribe apart on that spiritual level that was totally spontaneous but deep at the same time was the hand-holding circles. You'd have that somewhere in '94 or '95, the hand-holding circles that Moontribe started to kick in. And that became a defining feature of Moontribe. . . . Almost every single Moontribe, at least once and sometimes at multiple points, you'd have big hand-holding circles start to spontaneously form. And then freeform chanting will go on—*om*, whatever, we'll jump up and down, different things kind of come out of it. And there's usually a point where it breaks and everybody rushes into the center and there's this giant mush pile, basically.[30]

Another key Moontribe ritual is watching the sunrise in the desert:

> That was also the first time in the morning, you know, the sun came up and people just sort of spontaneously made a circle holding hands and started dancing around. . . . It was all about the sun coming up. That was the focal point of the event, was the sunrise. . . . People would just find a little hill someplace and watch it come up and the sun cascade in the whole valley without any cars or smog or anything. It was definitely—watching the sunrise in the desert with your friends after you've been dancing all night—that's a good thing.[31]

While the Moontribe ritual began as a spontaneous occurrence involving hand-holding, chanting *om*, and watching the sunrise, the midnight ritual for the Oracle Gatherings in Seattle is a tightly choreographed theatrical performance planned months ahead of time to express the theme of the event, with elaborate costumes, sets, and props. The ritual for the gathering I attended in November 2003, called Ocean Deep, took place on a set decorated with aquatic motifs, began with a procession of masked costumed dancers and stilt walkers accompanied by original electronic music, and culminated with an aerial dance duet on a piece of fabric hung from the ceiling. In my opinion, the Oracle has taken the ritual aspect of raves to its most sophisticated level of articulation thus far and, accordingly, I will explore the Oracle in more detail a bit later.

Those people who plan and lead the ceremonies take their responsibility very seriously and put a lot of time and effort into making sure it runs smoothly and effectively. In this regard, some even go so far as to do preparatory ceremonies before the rave ceremony:

> I do ceremony usually starting a month or more before our events to invite in the [spirits] we want and keep out the [spirits] we don't want and start creating a container for events. And there are often people who participate with me. . . . In the last several years, I've been doing pipe ceremonies, prayer ceremonies, with the teams as the teams come together at their meetings. And then, usually before an event, I'll go into the space and do a ceremony there. I do a banishing and a warding and a blessing of the space. Those are all steps that take place before the event.[32]

All of these preparatory ceremonies clearly entail a lot of extra work. Why would someone choose to go to all this trouble? First and foremost, they want the ceremony to be successful at a spiritual level. One ceremonial planner/leader expressed this idea with an interesting metaphor:

> The ceremony and the spirits and that kind of ritual, it's more like plumbing or electricity, there are ways to wire a house that work, and I do them that way.[33]

Another reason is to protect oneself from any negative energy that might occur, to continue the metaphor, as a result of incorrect "wiring":

> What happens is when you plug into the energy of an entire event with five hundred people like that and you lead a ceremony, if you haven't built a container around it, you don't have the directions, you don't have the elements in place, you don't have all the spirits in place, you don't have your helpers in place, then you're very connected to the energy of the dance and if you haven't cleaned it out and smoothed it out and saged the place and smudged it off and balanced everything out and gotten everything contained, then whatever kind of murk or mud passes through that event as a result of not having done the janitorial work beforehand can effect you really strongly. The first few times I tried it, I made myself physically ill for a few days afterwards, so I really took on trying to figure out how to do it with the proper kind of preparation.[34]

This level of dedication to preparation for a ceremony is impressive, and compares favorably with that undertaken by ceremonial leaders in any religious tradition.

Obviously, not every rave ceremony is going to have that level of forethought and preparation. And not every rave ceremony is going to be successful or effective. In fact, not every rave even has a ceremony at all. However, my overall sense is that the inclusion of ceremonies at raves is becoming more widespread, and this was confirmed in my interviews, as exemlified by the observations of this raver:

> I'm definitely seeing a lot more ceremony. I think it's growing. . . . I'm noticing over the last five or more years, having the ceremony becoming more prominent in events, starting to see opening ceremonies and closing ceremonies, and sometimes ceremonial aspects that go through. I'm seeing altars, things of that sort, which were less common, even when I started five years ago. . . . So now it's common to have ceremonies and it's common to have an altar and speak on spiritual themes and things of that sort.[35]

The DJ as Ceremonial Leader

In addition to the person or persons who lead opening and closing ceremonies, there is another important figure who can also be considered a ceremonial leader—the DJ. Opening and closing ceremonies comprise only a tiny portion of the total activities of a rave, where probably over 95 percent of the time is spent dancing to or listening to electronic music spun by DJs. While the DJ's primary concern is to make sure people are dancing and having a good time, on a deeper level, the DJ is responsible for leading dancers into the powerful experiential states that connect them to the sacred. In this regard, the DJ is the de facto ceremonial leader of the rave, the one who guides the participants through their spiritual experience. Both ravers and DJs are very clear on this point and they often use the words *shaman* and *journey* in describing this function:

> You do have a navigator, and I think a lot of people feel that with the DJ—the tribal connection to the shaman guiding you through and bringing you where you to need to go to experience what you need to experience.[36]

> I realized I was playing the role of the shaman, having a tribe, and bringing a tribe on this ceremonial ritual. . . . I facilitate realizations and transformations and healings, and all these things are completely shamanic.[37]

As a DJ, I see myself as taking the crowd on a journey and through a number of different emotions and feeling states. And, at some point, letting all that break open into an ecstatic state. And, over the course of the night, doing this a number of times. And the feeling in the room grows.[38]

And just like a shaman or any other skilled ceremonial leader, the DJ has a set of tools and strategies he employs to most effectively facilitate the peak dance floor experience. As one veteran raver put it:

A well-structured, a well-done DJ set really builds a flow and an ebb, builds it up and takes it back down again, and can bring you to the peak of something and then take you back down gently.[39]

One of the musical techniques used by DJs to produce these peaks is to gradually increase the beats per minute in a sequence of songs over a period of time:

I will move the crowd up to a high level of energy by gradually increasing the beats per minute over time, and then I will take it to a peak if I can, to some ecstatic peak where I'll just keep going as long as possible. And then, when the crowd seems to fade, or have enough of that, then I will gradually take it down again, rest them for a while, and then bring them up again.[40]

The speed of the music is one thing that the DJ uses to control the peak of the set. You start out playing slower music and it gradually speeds up with each song. . . . If you start out slow and then build it up, then definitely people are kind of forced to go along with it, you're forced to higher levels of exertion to keep up with it.[41]

This increase in tempo, called *accelerando* in musical terms, has been identified by ethnomusicologist Gilbert Rouget as an extremely effective and nearly universal cross-cultural musical technique for the induction of trance and possession states, particularly in combination with *crescendo*, an increase in volume and instrumental density.[42] Not surprisingly, DJs also employ the use of crescendo in their bag of tricks as well:

I like to definitely build up a crescendo and let it all explode.[43]

In his groundbreaking book *Music and Trance: A Theory of the Relations between Music and Possession*, Rouget also identified another nearly universal musical technique to induce trance and possession: the musical motto, a short musical phrase that serves as a kind of triggering device.[44] Electronic dance music certainly has a multitude of such musical mottoes, and DJs intentionally employ them in their arsenal of techniques. The most popular of these is well described in the following quote:

> There's definite motifs in electronic dance music you can use for a desired effect. If you want to build a peak, you bring in a sixteenth note snare roll and you change the pitch of the snare roll up as it quickens and that just all of the sudden gets everyone's attention and everyone's waiting for the payoff. Then you drop out the pounding kick drum and just have one long bass note, and it's like, *Boom!* And everyone—all of the sudden—it's like they hit a bump in a car and they're floating in the air and they're about to hit the ground. . . . It's like the whole room has just opened up. It's like the floor fell out from under you and you're just floating in space all of the sudden. And when it comes in again, it's like a big kick in the ass. It just sends you flying down this tunnel.[45]

In addition to this build-up/drop-out/payoff motto, which is nearly universal in all genres of electronic dance music, there are also musical mottoes that are more specific to the particular style of electronic dance music, and these vary widely from genre to genre. For example, in jungle, or drum and bass, it is often the thick, distorted, rumbling, sinister bass line that serves as the motto. In trance, the motto can often be the build-up of melodic, arpeggiated, layered synthesizer parts. In diva house, it is usually the soulful female vocal (which is why it is named for the singing diva).

One of the skills of the DJ is knowing when to employ these kinds of mottoes and other techniques, and this depends to a large degree on paying close attention to the dancers. A good DJ watches the dancers to see how they are responding to the musical flow she is creating and where she can take them with that flow:

> I'm basically interacting with the crowd and trying to feel where their energy is that night, where the room can go as a whole, how I can have the most bodies dancing at once, and experiencing the most ecstasy at any one time.[46]

Likewise, the dancers are paying attention to the DJ, especially to let him know when he is in a good flow or creating a peak, often through vocal exclamations or bodily gesticulations. Thus, there is a high level of interactivity between the dancers and the DJ that flows both ways:

I think it's a two-way thing. Not only is the DJ . . . part of this reality that's created somehow slightly outside of the normal day-to-day experience where I'm not really doing it per se, I'm letting go into it and everybody else is letting go into it and collectively we're all getting into this state of ecstasy.[47]

When I'm playing music, I'm actively attempting to connect to as many people in the room as possible, which has become my spiritual thing. When you're in a room and music's playing and people are dancing, the mood is elevated into sometimes, most of the time, in my case, a spiritual realm. People are opened up, people are happy, they're just more open, their hearts are open. So I love that environment. And to be playing music is a complete and total honor to me. So I feel incredibly of service when I'm playing and, ideally, I'm really connected to the people that are there.[48]

These observations identify another important aspect of the DJ as ceremonial leader, the idea that DJing is a spiritual practice through which the DJ accesses the spiritual realm and takes everyone else along with him; as other DJs noted,

I want to facilitate a moving spiritual experience for people, bring out the funk and the soul and the love and the joy, and just let that channel through people. I guess you could say I'm shamanically inviting those spirits in and asking them to flow through those that are open, as DJ.[49]

That was a very defining moment, for me DJing, in that it all clicked for me. So that became a very spiritual thing for me, too. For the first time DJing, I got so into the music that I really lost myself in the music, to where DJing became very—I wasn't even really aware of what I was doing with my hands so much, I was just so into the music and the beats and everything. . . . DJing is more than playing records, people don't realize. I definitely got to the point where I wasn't really thinking about what I was doing. I was in the same place that those people were dancing, where I was DJing and I was just into the beats. . . . When I get to that place, that's when you rock the dance floor. You're in there and everyone's on your ride and you're just taking people for a nice funky dance ride. . . . And for me, performing becomes a very spiritual thing.[50]

In the previous chapter I compared some of the powerful states attained on the dance floor to the classic possession experience, and this comparison included not only the dancers, but the DJs as well. Many of the DJs

I interviewed were very cognizant that some larger spiritual force was moving through them:

> It's the exact same as being on the dance floor. When I'm doing my best DJing, it's the exact same thing, something hops in and takes over. I see my hands do things on the mixer they've never done in practice that sound amazing on the sound system. And everybody is getting off, just going nuts, when I get in that space as a DJ.[51]

> Usually my greatest sets are the ones [in which] I just get myself out of the way and I just understand. . . . Usually I will say a prayer to the universe, saying I just ask to be a vessel, you know, and get out of the way, and just to give as much as I can to those people that are here. . . . There'll be situations where I've pulled the wrong record, but it turned out to be the right one. And I realize, *Oh, it's not me*; you know what I mean? It's like I'm doing this, I'm just a vessel, and it's doing itself.[52]

The prayer that this DJ recites before his sets is very similar in function to the prayers in the opening ceremonies at raves. And just as some ceremonial leaders do preparatory work and ceremonies well in advance of the rave, so too do some DJs:

> It's a huge responsibility, you know, because really it's . . . not about just externally changing the lights or this or that—the work has to be done internally. And if the work isn't done internally, then something, it's going to in the music, it's going to be in the party, it's going to be in these things. And so it's a process where one has to cultivate their own life in order for these things to start. It's kind of like putting into the forge and tempering the metal until you do it so much, the blade cuts through anything.[53]

This idea of cultivating one's own life in the service of the rave indicates a sophisticated spiritual awareness and demonstrates that some ravers are beginning to take the spiritual dimensions of the scene beyond a rudimentary level to the next developmental stage.

Several DJs spoke of their role in terms of being of service and feeling honored, and I'd like to include one such quote that uses this language:

> The gift that a DJ gives is a really huge one and I never really understood that until I started to do it. I really got it the first time I went out and played in front of a bunch of people. . . .

It's like creating that vibe, it's being part of that vibe in the sense there is no self, there is simply a flow of energy that has no beginning or end, that starts with no one and ends with no one, there's no one person or thing that's causing it. It's not me because I'm putting a record on, I'm putting the record on because I'm feeling this thing. . . . And then, when that comes out and you see people really getting off and you see people getting the vibe and you see people finding that sweet spot that happens for them, and you experience the energy just kind of moving and flowing, I get this sense of incredible humility, like I am just this tiny thing, not in a bad way, but I am just this thing, and I am so honored to serve. I am so honored to be part of this experience. Whatever's traveling through me, I'm honored that I get to be the conduit for it traveling through me. I am honored to get to be the person that people on the dance floor are focusing their energies on. . . .

Q: So you feel like, as a DJ, you're skilled enough to call in these different types of energies?
A: Yeah, appropriate to whatever is called for.[54]

If the DJ can be considered a ceremonial leader, then ravers can likewise be considered ceremonial participants, and listening and dancing to music are their primary ceremonial practices. Ravers love their electronic dance music and see it as a vehicle through which they connect to the sacred:

Music is the enabler to have a primary religious experience, destruction of the ego, sense of oneness with everything or nothingness, or how it is each person describes having that primary religious experience. . . . Music is a spiritual thing; if you choose to go there, it's available. . . . Some tracks will take me there immediately, and everything, all the chakras will align and the energy will start shooting out of the top of my head and my whole [experience] will just be electric and I'll be brought to tears because this piece of music is so there, it's so hit it.[55]

Ravers intentionally use the music spun by the DJ as a vehicle to shift their consciousness into powerful experiential states that open access to spiritual realms. And, as we saw in the last chapter, dance and movement are important tools in this process. Moreover, this is not just an individual experience, but a collective one that is often shared by everyone on the dance floor. As one raver put it,

The music synchronizes everybody's motion, synchronizes everybody's breathing, synchronizes everybody's energy, you can just open up into a resonance of energy.[56]

Altars

The DJ's musical selection provides ravers with an important focusing lens through which sacred energies are generated and configured. Altars do the same thing in physical space and, for this reason, they are far more than just aesthetically pleasing decorations. As one raver put it,

> It creates a good vibe for people. Setting is an important aspect of it—the altar becomes a focal point, like an anchor for people's trips and it creates sort of a sacred space.[57]

Altars go back to the early days of the rave scene but, in the beginning, they were created spontaneously. For example, the following description is from a Gathering rave in San Francisco in 1990:

> I had a friend who was into Temple of Psychic Youth and he started laying out a psychic cross with trash on the dance floor, like making a mini–ritual altar kind of effect, and I tried doing it by collecting water bottles and making a magical circle around his psychic cross. And that was without having much theory about anything.[58]

Spontaneous altars of a different nature began to appear at Moontribe raves held out in the Mojave Desert:

> Sometimes people would make big pieces of earth art. Like, one time, I don't even know who did it, but right before the party started, somebody did a giant swastika in the sand, like dug out, like a trench thirty or forty feet long going both ways. You'd see things like that just pop up. People would do earth art, stacks of rocks, and it was different people doing things at different times without any particular coordination.[59]

Over time, however, spontaneous altars began to give way to more formal, planned creations. For example, one veteran West Coast raver remembers

> the first altar; this woman, Mona Bryant, in San Francisco, I think she started the first altars at the Full Moon parties in San Francisco back in '92 or so.[60]

These formal altars typically are set on a table covered in fabric, lit by candles and strings of Christmas-type lights, and tend to feature images and icons drawn from a wide variety of religious and spiritual traditions, as well as beautiful objects such as rocks, feathers, crystals, and so forth. Here is a description of a typical altar from a rave in Portland:

The Temple of Sound became one of the first places where I started to really see altars at a rave event. And there were these giant altars up against the front of the decks. Just a lot of different images on them. They had different styles, depending on who created the altar. But a lot of times you'd have Christmas lights underneath fabric, and candles. Really eclectic, they were always extremely eclectic. I guess anyone who saw it would categorize it as New Age, just having Ganesh, Siddhartha Buddha, Mother Mary, you know, every kind of religious iconography, all sort of belched up into one specific altar. And it was called The Altar, and people left various trinkets at the altar. It wasn't uncommon to see candy bracelets or lollipops, feathers.[61]

While this kind of eclectic syncretism is pretty standard, rave altars can also be designed with a unifying motif, such as one particular religious or spiritual tradition (e.g., Buddhist, Mayan, Wiccan, etc.), an element (e.g., water, fire, earth, air), a season, or a wide variety of other themes, including everything from space aliens to teddy bears. In the San Francisco Bay Area, the Rhythm Society's events usually have two main altars. The first is called the High Altar, which is designed according to the theme of the event. Participants can place their own sacred objects on this altar, both to contribute their energy to the altar and for their objects to receive energy from the event. The second is called the Sharing Altar. Here, participants place objects as an offering to be given away and also can take objects they feel drawn to. It is not uncommon, in the course of the event, to see people spending time in front of these altars, focusing, praying, and meditating. In fact, many raves have a special meditation or shrine room for just this purpose, and these rooms almost always have an altar designed to help facilitate this. Although not every rave has altars, they are extremely widespread, to the point where one San Francisco raver estimates that "75 to 80 percent have altars or try to at least have a few candles, tapestry around the DJ or in front or on the bar or on the table or wherever, somewhere to keep the element."[62]

Specific Religious and Spiritual Traditions

Altars illustrate a number of important features of the ceremonial dimensions of raves, the first of which is that they draw from specific religious and spiritual traditions. Many ravers take an eclectic, syncretic approach, acknowledging that all religious and spiritual traditions have something to offer; therefore, there are a wide variety of forms to choose from. One of the cocreators of the Oracle articulated this approach:

> I've been influenced by all kinds of religions. And seeing people seeking a deeper connection with God. And, obviously, all religions, all mystical sides of religions are saying the exact same thing. So that kind of intention came into the tarot deck of "well, we can explore all these religious archetypes or paths and actually learn from them in the process. . . ."[63]

This view is shared by many other crews and ravers; one noted,

> I'm trying to learn how to do it [ceremony] in our context in a good way and use all those things that I learned along the way in other paths, other traditions, to do that.[64]

This kind of approach is clearly seen in rave altars, where images and icons from a wide variety of different traditions are placed alongside each other. It is also seen in the ceremonies themselves, which include practices from a wide variety of traditions combined together in different ways.

What are some of the more popular traditions? Perhaps the most popular influence is from Indian/Hindu traditions. I have already mentioned the Goa/psychedelic trance scene, which began in India and is strongly influenced by its religious ethos, featuring Hindu images of deities like Ganesha, Kali, Krishna, Shiva, and others. Beyond the Goa scene, I have also noted the widespread practice of chanting the Hindu seed syllable *om* in all sorts of rave ceremonies. Many raves now also offer yoga stretching practice before the start of the dance music. Other Eastern traditions are popular as well. Buddhist images are very common at raves, and simple Buddhist breathing meditation practices are often used in rave ceremonies. Although less common, Taoist influences are also found in the form of yin/yang symbols and practices like chi kung or tai chi. In addition to Eastern traditions, another popular influence is that of indigenous cultures. This includes Native American–influenced practices like smudging with burning sage for purification, calling in the four directions, and even pipe ceremonies. The use of Mayan iconography and cosmology is particularly strong among certain rave crews—especially the Mayan calendar, its end date of 2012, and the glyphs associated with it. Shamanism is also very popular, but in a more general way as a metaphor for the rhythmic trance induction of the rave experience and the role of the DJ as a guide for the journey rather than for specific practices, although images from traditional shamanic art often appear at raves. Wicca is popular as well, as evidenced in images of goddesses, raves held on solstices, equinoxes, and their midpoints, and the use of ritual practices like the spiral dance. The influence of Western magical (magickal) traditions is seen among certain crews and, in this regard, the Temple of Psychic Youth has been particularly influential. It is not unusual to see images such as pentagrams or ritual implements like cauldrons or wands. The Oracle is based on the tarot and also has a strong connection to mystery school traditions. Other religious and spiritual traditions referenced in raves include African religion, Australian aboriginal religion, Celtic/Druid religion, ancient Egyptian religion, the Kabbalah, Sufism, and many others. In fact, it would be difficult to find a religious or spiritual tradition that has not been incorporated into a rave.

This also includes Christianity, which has been conspicuously absent from this discussion thus far, probably because most ravers are alienated from their Christian upbringing and more interested in alternative (and exotic) forms of religion and spirituality. Nevertheless, some of the earliest experiments in combining raves with specific religious traditions were, in fact, Christian. For example, in Sheffield, England, in 1993, there were a number of experimental ritual gatherings organized by Reverend Chris Brain, which combined aspects of rave music and dance with a weekly Anglican church service, known as the Nine O'Clock Service, and also as the Rave Mass or Planetary Mass. As one raver remembered them in an online article, "The services, produced by and largely for a young working-class group, incorporated elements of rave-ambient house music, large video screens playing computer generated images and video clips with ecological and social themes, nightclub-style lighting and the freedom to dance."[65] Although these gatherings were to end in allegations of sexual misconduct that forced Brain to resign, thus bringing the rave masses to an end, the innovative combination of raves and Christian liturgy inspired other such experiments in England, including one version called "Rave in the Nave."[66]

These experiments continue today in the United States with maverick Episcopal priest Matthew Fox's Techno Cosmic Masses, held regularly in Oakland, California. These events are not really raves per se, in that their primary activity is not dancing to electronic music and they typically last for two hours at most, rather than all night. They are actually more of a "hip" liturgy with a rave-influenced aesthetic, and their participants are liberal Christians rather than hard-core ravers. Nevertheless, the Techno Cosmic Mass is still an important development in combining raves with ritual components from a specific tradition, Christianity, and one that culminates in a very familiar ritual, the taking of communion.

Themes and Archetypes

Another approach ravers take in order to unify diverse religious traditions and components is to organize the rave around a particular spiritual theme. The Rhythm Society's events are a good example of this approach. Each event has a theme that is given a name, spelled out in an explanatory paragraph, and expressed in the decorations, the altars, and the ceremonies. Some of the names/themes have included Alchemie, Anima Mundi, Beloved, Creation, Chrysalis, Essence, Gift, Intimacy, Nirvana, Resonance, Rites of Spring, Shine, Terra Firma, and Wheel of Fortune. Obviously, some themes loan themselves to certain kinds of spiritual/religious traditions, ceremonial components, and decorative motifs. Anima Mundi, for example, focused on animal and plant spirits, and a connection to the earth. Beloved featured Sufi influences in the form of Rumi poetry and the motif of divine love through mystical union with the Beloved. Nirvana, of course, had more of a Buddhist influence. The theme for Rites of Spring was fertility and new growth and, appropriately, in the opening ceremony, participants were given a seed of corn that they then planted in small pots of soil. As one member reflected on the importance of themes,

> I love the themes. I love that we think about that kind of thing and that the themes are somewhat archetypal and transcend all religious structures or schools of thought.[67]

In my own personal experience, I have found that the theme of a particular rave, especially as articulated in the opening ceremony, is often very timely and meaningful, providing a context in which I can make sense of events in my life and in the world, resolve important issues, and move forward with a fresh outlook and renewed energy. In this way, the theme transforms the entire rave into a rite of passage.

The Oracle crew in Seattle has taken this approach to an even higher level of articulation by developing their own tarot deck of twenty-three specially designed cards, each of which embodies a different spiritual archetype. Every rave event they produce is based on one of these cards, and the card for the next event is picked in a ritualized manner at the closing ceremony of the current event. The total sequence of the twenty-three events is a series that forms a larger whole, a kind of meta-tarot casting. At the time of writing, the events that have been held took place in the following order: Father Sun, The Myth, The Elements, Alchemy, The Senses, Harmony, The Gypsy, In the Garden, Mystery School, Behold the Buddha, Atlantis, Imagination, Ocean Deep, Faery Magick, Mother Earth, Space Traveller, and Journey of the Shaman. Aside from the obvious associations for each name, the card images also reference particular spiritual or religious traditions. For example, The Myth featured the sword-in-the-stone image from Arthurian legend; The Senses featured a Hindu-style sadhu in a meditation pose; Harmony featured a Sufi Mevlevi whirling dervish; In the Garden featured Adam and Eve standing before a Kabbalistic Tree of Life; and Mystery School included Egyptian religious iconography like the Eye of Horus. The creators of the Oracle are very clear about the archetypal nature of each of the cards and the events, and how each archetype is a step in a larger spiritual path:

> The Oracle is based off of a twenty-three-card tarot deck of archetypes. We started thinking about any spiritual path one could go on, such as Buddhism, or alchemy, or mystery school, going back to the Garden of Eden. For this one, Ocean Deep, the mysteries of the ocean, kind of moving into the abyss, and we created twenty-three archetypes. . . . Each of the cards have a symbol, dance movement, and kind of an affirmation poem that describes the archetype. . . . The function of the midnight ritual is to essentially express what the archetype means to us, to the community, or inspire our vision of the archetype to the community so they can take that seed and let it tap into what they feel it is. And the whole event is centered around the archetype. We choose musicians based off the archetype. We get submissions from musicians for that archetype. We obviously decorate according to the archetype. We have ceremonies centered around the archetype. And the whole community dives into that world for a little while because it's one element of the many paths one can take but it's discovering what that aspect of that path has to teach you. So you're kind of learning from all these different worlds and bringing them together for your wholeness. That's the intention. We definitely feel they are intense initiations.[68]

In the course of my interviews with the Oracle crew and the stories they shared about their events, I was struck by the degree to which each particular theme or archetype manifested its distinctive energy in very specific ways. Here is the first of two examples that demonstrate this point very clearly:

> Gypsy's a clear example. We found this amazing space in Everett. We spent a week decorating the space. Gorgeous, totally ready. We were two days ahead of the event. We were stoked. The fire marshal came in and said everything here had to be fire retardant. So we had to take everything down and spend twenty-four hours fire retarding everything and put everything up, be done by 8 A.M. the day of the party. Then the police came and said, "You guys can't have a party here." There's this new law that no one nineteen and younger could be in the same room dancing with anyone twenty-one and over. So, basically, at 9 A.M. we were told we couldn't do our event there. So we had to take everything down and packed everything up like a little gypsy tribe and came back to Seattle. Got turned down for another space, found another space, and didn't get a finalized *yes* till about 7 P.M. The doors opened at 8. So we started decorating at 4 or 5, without agreements. So we ended up being like a gypsy tribe, essentially.[69]

The second example has to do with the Mystery School card and event. At the time of the interview, the Oracle folks had become involved with an actual mystery school, so I was a bit confused as to which came first, and I asked them to clarify:

> What's interesting is how we found the mystery school was somebody from the Rocky Mountain Mystery School heard about the Mystery School Oracle [event], went to it, and started talking to some of the people from the Oracle, saying "Hey, I'm a part of this mystery school that I want to share with you guys." So it took a couple Oracles before we connected with the mystery school. But now, we're actually working with the mystery school. . . . So it did literally come from the event. But the interesting thing was, which is really the way it has to be for this process to work, was that the card came first and we had to, from an outside perspective, not really having a direct experience through a mystery school, create the mystery school archetype. That's what allowed it to be a new ritual experience.[70]

I will explore the Oracle's involvement with the Rocky Mountain Mystery School in more detail in the next chapter. For now, however, the key point is that the theme and archetype gives each Oracle event its distinctive energy and ties all of its elements together as a unified ritual:

We've found that every event and archetype is absolutely an initiation for all of us into a deeper part of our learning process and ultimately breaks our stuff down so we can be more open channels for what the Oracle has to share with us. Not just us, but the community, everybody. . . . We're finding that there's a process through each—before, during, and after the event—a longstanding ritual that the Oracle is expressing to us how it needs to play out, you know, to get more of the intention in there, the magic.[71]

While not every rave has the same high level of thematic articulation and spiritual orientation that is found in the Oracle or the Rhythm Society's events, nevertheless, most raves do have some kind of unifying theme that is often spiritual or religious in nature. This is especially true on the West Coast, and particularly in the Bay Area, which has a strong history of alternative spirituality. As one Bay Area raver put it,

That kind of offbeat spiritual interest in the Bay Area just naturally took hold within the rave community. So, there's a big part of the rave community that's taking the New Age movement and moving it into the next century with a whole new technology built around dance. . . . They do want to have a transformative experience. And so there's a lot of people who have been in the rave culture for ten years now. They're not kids anymore, and they're throwing these pretty sophisticated parties that have . . . ritual with intention.[72]

An Experimental Approach

The experimental nature of these rituals is a crucial aspect of rave culture's distinctive approach to ceremony. Ravers are very clear that they are not trying to mimic or reproduce traditional religious ceremonies, but instead to create something new through experimentation:

We live in such a time that this kind of experimentalism with spirituality is actually very much of benefit because we need to experience—not ritual in the sense of what I think a lot of people are afraid of, you know, this mindless adherence to customs that we have no base of true connection with, we're just parroting and miming through things that have some supposed meaning. I'm looking at ways that we can create ritual at personal and collective levels where we're in the purity of experience.[73]

I think because people have an experience of the sacred, of something they recognize as sacred, as transcendent, as relating to the deepest and most important aspects of our humanity, when they touch that, then that entrains a whole series of other imagery and associations that just kind of naturally go with it, so people start experimenting with what seems to work.[74]

Part of the fun of this whole group is that everyone's got their own idea of what a ritual looks like. And that's cool. And I love that we're always experimenting with different ones.[75]

In this experimental approach, ravers can draw from traditional religions and their ceremonial forms, but they do so in order to create something new that gives expression to a newly emerging religious and spiritual sensibility. One of the creators of the Oracle beautifully expressed this idea:

We're tapping into magic from the past to support magic for the present to guide us into magic for the future.[76]

However, combining elements from different cultures and traditions in this experimental way runs the risk of also becoming a scattershot, hodgepodge approach, and ravers are very clear on this point as well:

I think it's a hodgepodge. I mean, I think there's stuff that people have absorbed from the broader culture, just their general exposure to all kinds of things we have in modern cosmopolitan society where you can pick up all kinds of tidbits from all over—cultures, history, all over the world, things that sort of make sense in the moment can be picked up on and tried out.[77]

One of the consequences of this hodgepodge approach is that many rave rituals do not work very well, an experience I myself have had on numerous occasions, and one shared by other ravers:

Once in a while, I've had incredibly powerful experiences at a [rave] ritual but, more often than not, I don't. . . . I like what they do. I just don't always like how they're done.[78]

Not everybody really has the same idea of what a ceremony is. For me, some people do what looks like performance. And I don't feel the energy of it all. And that's just how it goes.[79]

In the larger scheme of things, however, this kind of hit-or-miss success rate is not surprising. Traditional religions have had hundreds or even thousands of years to develop effective ceremonial forms, and even these ceremonies don't always hit the mark. In contrast, rave ceremonies are, at most, seventeen years old, and clearly in a very early developmental stage. Ravers seem to understand this larger perspective and, for this reason, are not so quick to judge what they see:

> The ceremony that I'm seeing in rave culture, in my opinion, is actually very immature. And I don't mean that in a derogatory way, I just mean it hasn't matured, it's very young.[80]

> We, in what we call tribal dance culture, are mimicking—kind of like almost babies mimic—our ancestors, as far as how far we've gotten. And there's no call for us to profess any level of mastery. At the same time, though, we're in an experiential frame of mind that will allow us to take what we can out of the experience. And that is very much worthwhile.[81]

Recognizing that rave ceremonies are very young and erratic in their effectiveness, some ravers have taken their experimentation with ritual outside of the rave itself in order to try to focus more specifically on finding what works and cultivating it:

> I'm working on a very specific vision. . . . Something that I would like to be involved in would be a collective of people that would start working together and create sort of a laboratory for much more intimate events with a very definite ritual structure to try to really explore what the ideal nature of that container would be, that ritual container, and how to bring, get people into a resonant state without the use of psychedelics. And then be able to go on a trance journey together, sharing and generating the same kind of energies, and also bringing them down, grounding them, a whole process basically that would be more formal and more structured. . . . I think there's a wing of [the rave scene] that is and will continue to move in the direction of more ritual, more intention, more deliberateness. It's a small wing, in terms of size, it's maybe five percent of the broad techno dance music thing, but it's the source where the real dynamism, the real energy of the scene comes from mostly. [82]

Such ritual "laboratories" are, in fact, happening in the Bay Area and elsewhere and, although they are in an even earlier stage than the ceremonies themselves, they would appear to represent the next evolutionary step in the development of rave ceremonies.

Shambhala, Salmo, B.C., 2003. Photograph courtesy of Quana Parker (Quana.net).

CHAPTER 5
TRANSFORMATION: RAVE WORLDVIEW, RAVE SPIRITUALITY, AND GLOBAL RAVE CULTURE

In the last two chapters, we have been focusing on "trance formation"—the ritual of trance dancing to electronic music at raves that generates deep experiential states and opens access to the sacred. For many ravers, this experience can be incredibly powerful and revelatory. However, while trance formation is clearly at the core of the rave phenomenon, this experience does not remain limited to the dance floor, but spills over into the lives of ravers in a variety of important ways, irrevocably and profoundly transforming them. The rave experience has been articulated into a spirituality, philosophy, and worldview that makes sense of it, contextualizes it in a larger perspective, and translates it into a code for living, a way to actualize its potential in the concrete details of daily life. Moreover, this transformation is not simply an individual experience, but one that has spawned a multitude of rave communities around the world and, indeed, a global rave culture that in turn has had an impact on mainstream culture. From trance formation to transformation—this trajectory exactly follows the model of religious development proposed by the 'history of religions' school of religious studies that I mentioned in the introduction.

In this approach, the human encounter with the numinous, the religious experience, forms the basis for subsequent developments that lead to the organized external forms that we call religion. Religious experience is the underlying substratum for all cultural activity and serves as the foundation for culture in general. As Charles H. Long notes, "Religion is thus understood to be pervasive not only in religious institutions, but in all the dimensions of cultural life."[1] In terms of the rave scene, then, the religious experience of trance formation on the dance floor at raves forms the basis for the subsequent transformation of ravers in the rest of their lives and leads to the organized external forms of rave spirituality, rave philosophy and worldview, rave lifestyle, and rave culture. In this chapter, we will examine each of these in detail.

A Shift in Perspective

As I noted earlier, many ravers begin their involvement in the scene with a powerful conversion experience and they usually then follow this experience by attending as many raves as they can and immersing themselves in rave culture. In the process, they are transformed on virtually every level of their lives. To begin with, there is often a profound shift in perspective, encompassing one's own life and how it fits into the larger world:

> I found myself getting reconnected with myself, just picturing what I needed to do and what I wanted to do and how I wanted to enjoy myself, all in the course of an evening, just from the music, you know, losing myself on the dance floor. . . . It definitely gave me a larger sense of the world and how I fit into it and what I needed to do for myself.[2]

> To me, music is something that is so much bigger than this reality. Sometimes I feel like, you know, I live downtown and when I go to my job or go to school, do homework, hang out with my friends, I get these blinders on, I think the world is everything that I can see. And I think that the whole world is just my world. Then, once I listen to music, it just brings me out of that and it just makes me realize that there's something so much bigger out there. Specifically this music, it doesn't have a lead singer who's putting the words, putting the thoughts in. You're actually hearing that and maybe you're translating that into your own life, maybe you're translating your own life into it. I don't even know if those two can be separated. To me, it's something that has always put perspective on things, always just made me realize that life is good, not

to get caught up in these little tiny details of life—*Oh my God, I didn't get this raise! I got a B-minus on this paper!* It really puts things in perspective that life is amazing and that there's really nothing beyond that.[3]

When I'm dancing and I'm cleaning out all this garbage, inviting new energy in, and working with it, and wiggling it into my elbow, feeling it in my heel, there's a kind of experience that it's all going to be okay, it all is okay, it's exactly what it's supposed to be. . . . So that kind of realignment of my energy is absolutely grounding, it's refreshing, it gives me hope, it helps me analyze problems and have a new perspective on things.[4]

I realized what it was I wanted to do with my life. . . . Things really transformed in me. I really started feeling like I had a more noble purpose in life. . . . There was something unique about a rave and that unifying experience that helped you on that path to just feeling like you were part of the big whole. . . . I knew I had gotten involved with something that was much, much bigger than I'd ever imagined I would be involved with. . . . I started realizing what was going on and my whole life transformed.[5]

I got the big picture. I got a picture of the universe as a whole and my involvement in it. . . . I finally put it all together and I began to realize . . . . exactly where I'm supposed to be.[6]

There was one particular experience I had at a party that was almost like a revelation as far as, not specifically what I wanted to do with my life, but like the general direction of it. . . . It really was a momentous occasion. I remember very clearly it was a dramatic change in the way I perceived what I should be doing with myself. . . . It had pretty profound effects in my life. . . . The basis, the foundation of it all, just kind of shifted.[7]

Unity in Diversity: Kinder, Gentler; More Open, Loving, and Compassionate

Another key feature of the rave phenomenon that also facilitates a shift in perspective is the ecstatic feeling of love, unity, openness, and inclusivity people experience together on the dance floor. One important aspect of this experience that goes all the way back to the early rave scene in England is the ability to transcend normal social barriers of race, class, ethnicity, education, and even religion. One veteran of the original British scene put it this way:

In Britain, I think it is so much about who you are in terms of what class you come from and how you talk and what clothes you wear. I think this was the first time in our contemporary history that this was broken away and it really gave this opportunity for people from all different classes and races just to be together.[8]

This same experience of unity in diversity has continued as a hallmark of the rave scene in the United States as well:

It was a composition of a lot of disparate groups of people—gay, straight, men, women, black, white, Hispanic. It was a polyglot of a lot of cultures and races and mind-sets and orientations coming together in a very positive way. . . . Everybody was getting off on it.[9]

You're able to incorporate a lot of diversity. Maybe some people don't even have a high school education. Other people have three Ph.D.s. And they're all dancing together and dance is a great leveler in that we're all simply moving our bodies in a vibrational field.[10]

The concept that I love about it the most is the concept of the beat as something that unifies dance floors and that unifies people. That has always been my goal in music because, on the dance floor, you can break down color barriers, sexual barriers. . . . It becomes universal and it brings a lot of people together.[11]

A second important aspect of this experience of unity is the ability to be unguarded and open and loving with other people, including strangers:

I was really impressed with the vulnerability that everybody showed to each other. . . . That really shook me at the time because it didn't occur to me that it was possible to be so unguarded with complete strangers.[12]

Here was a place for me to go and dance with other people, to share love with people who are openly giving love. I never ever found that anywhere else, at least not that amount of love and nurturing.[13]

This open and loving attitude toward other people is something that ravers then seek to carry over into the rest of their lives. One raver said that raves "actually, I think, make people kinder and gentler and more compassionate."[14] Another talked about his realization that "there was no reason why this openness can't carry over to the rest of my life."[15] Still another sought the answer to these questions:

> How can I live a better life? How can I be a better person? How can I know more about myself so that I can be in the world in a conscious, compassionate, and loving and connected way?[16]

Concrete Life Changes

This shift in perspective then quite naturally leads to making concrete changes in one's life, beyond simply being more open and compassionate and loving:

> I had to make decisions about how my life was going to be. . . . And the only person who could make them quite right was me and I had to do that all for myself. . . . I think this is part of all the things that coalesced during this one time where I was just dancing. . . . And so I started realizing I've got to make my choices, I've got to do this, I've got to do that, and this is how I will live.[17]

The decision to change one's life can entail a wide range of choices. Many ravers make the biggest change possible—moving to a new location in order to be involved in the scene:

> I moved here [San Francisco] because of the dance music scene.[18]

> Honestly, I moved to San Francisco for the rave scene and the rave scene only.[19]

> I moved here [Seattle] because I came to a dance culture event in '94 and was completely blown away and knew that I was looking for that, essentially. I moved here from Guam.[20]

Other ravers made equally momentous life changes, such as changing jobs or dropping out of school:

> I changed my direction. I left school, actually. I said, 'Because I've found my new school. Why am I in the freaking school of classical music composition? That's not what I'm doing. I want to work with these people.' So I dropped out, started doing this. Spent every dime I had on records and CDs and music equipment instead of tuition.[21]

I was doing [high-tech marketing] for a living at that time. So I was really headed in a direction that was much more a part of the corporate-America lifestyle. . . . It's funny, I went from wearing a suit and tie and having a real conservative haircut, going to a job where people expected me to be very corporate America—I went from that kind of a lifestyle to becoming more of a hacker, an on-staff hacker.[22]

These kinds of life changes are often based on an unwillingness to compromise one's ideals, and choosing instead to live life according to one's most deeply held values and highest vision. In this regard, there can also be a strong sense of altruism in deciding to do certain things, a desire to be of service and help bring about positive change, a subject I will return to shortly.

Many ravers also begin to shift their circle of friends to reflect the new importance of raves in their lives:

It definitely changed me and filtered into the rest of my life. I stopped hanging out with all my friends so much. I couldn't deal with what they liked. . . . The people I started meeting were a whole different group of people from what I had ever known before. People were more open-minded and spiritual and much more holistic. They were much more loving and caring.[23]

It [the rave experience] blew me away and suddenly I found myself going to parties every weekend and meeting new people that blow my mind—artists and dancers and visionaries and people that were creative and doing all kinds of things with their energy to promote this great vibe. . . . I started meeting all kinds of people that were very spiritually inclined and doing all kinds of spiritual work in all different levels.[24]

Some ravers choose to become involved with particular rave crews and help put on events:

I just dove into the Rhythm Society, basically spent the next three years just really intensely involved in the RS.[25]

Some ravers may even decide to live in raver households or warehouse collectives so that they are completely immersed in the scene on a continuous basis.

Integrating the Rave Experience into Daily Life

While not every raver makes these kinds of momentous changes, never-theless, there is an overall sense of wanting to integrate the peak rave experience into the rest of one's life:

> You have an experience like that, you feel like something transcendent has happened, and then you go back into the other world of the program and you start going, *Oh*. And then you have to reconcile the two worlds: what did I experience and what is going on now? And that's where the change starts slowly happening. You start thinking, *Oh, I need to read a book*, or, *I need to investigate*. And that's what I saw happening in my own life. And now, as I go farther on that journey, it's looking for more things that don't use a specific external tool, cultivating more internal technology that's available to all of us.[26]

> A big part of the challenge of rave culture is that it opens up a lot of pos-sibilities and moments of real human connection and communication and sharing, but . . . not having a structure and a system of knowledge for how to implement those kind of states, how do you translate those spaces of opening and possibility to the rest of the situations in life?[27]

> Something that I'm really enjoying watching and being part of is the sense of taking it beyond the realm of music and the occasional all-night party or celebration . . . and taking it into the realm of, Okay, how are we going to apply the experiences we have here to our daily lives, what is the daily practice of unity and loss of ego that we get to experience when we're out there on the dance floor? How can I live a better life? How can I be a better person? How can I know more about myself so that I can be in the world in a conscious, compassionate, and loving and connected way?[28]

One of the key answers to the question of how to apply the rave experi-ence to one's daily life is to create more lasting, ongoing structures in the form of rave communities, and I will examine several of these communi-ties in more depth in the next chapter.

Yet there are many other ways to integrate the rave experience. Many ravers go more deeply into the music, either through learning to DJ, learning to produce their own original electronic music compositions, or simply by acquiring music on record, CD, or MP3 and listening to it in their daily lives. Other ravers express themselves creatively through other art forms like dance, painting, sculpture, computer visuals, fashion design, poetry, writing, or theater, and some even share their finished products in showings or performances. Still others undertake spiritual practices such as meditation, yoga, or chanting, or work with various ceremonial traditions, and some may go so far as to facilitate these activities in a public setting. Some ravers may choose to organize or lead educational events, and a number of them have even formed nonprofit organizations to help facilitate their efforts. Many ravers become politically active in a variety of causes, including the environment, the peace movement, gay and lesbian issues, human rights, and indigenous cultures, to mention just a few. In this regard, one issue particularly relevant to ravers is fighting the current reactionary wave of repressive antirave legislation,[29] and the Electronic Music Defense and Education Fund and the San Francisco Late Night Coalition are two great examples of ravers (and nonravers) banding together to become an effective political force.[30]

Integrating the Rave Experience into One's Spiritual Path

Since this is a study on the religious and spiritual dimensions of rave culture, I'd like to focus more specifically on how the rave experience is integrated into ravers' spiritual paths. Here are a few examples:

> I had an even more profound illumination. I was looking at my friends and thinking of how interconnected we were and how everything in our lives had brought us together in just this way. I was just thinking on how grand the scale of perfection of synchronous occurrences and all this was. I think I just fell into this realization of God. I realized that I was praying in a moment and realized that this consciousness was in fact behind everything and not just nothing. It seems so obvious once you get there but a little curtain got pulled aside that night and I realized that it was not just all random. And it wasn't even a realization. It was just like it was a gift, something that was given, an illumination, just from that experience of that connection, of realizing that everything was God and everything is God and that's what's making everything what it is. That is everything, in fact. Since everything is God, that forced me to start this process. I had to completely break down everything I had ever thought about, asking questions, getting answers. It was just all right there. And once you get in there, there's no going back. I think that was the real beginning of what I would call my life and my path, just who I feel I am and what I feel I am, which is to say, just like God, part of all that is. . . . It started me on the path.[31]

I started to see something deeper and just really started to open up to various practices that would make me feel better. So I stopped taking so many drugs and started to look at other ways of getting high, just dancing all night, etcetera. I had these conversations with people. It would start getting in focus, and it would make me have different realizations. Also, The Temple of Sound had a gigantic library of just any book you can imagine on religion or spirituality. I spent a lot of my time there.[32]

I came to a place where I realized that actually changing the external environment of a party actually doesn't really move it to that place that I was looking for, that really you can't change the external environment, truly move it into a different vibration without making changes internally within yourself. So during that time, I . . . started to try to cultivate some tools. I started doing Vipassana. . . . I definitely saw things in the meditations that made me question why I was doing what I was doing. . . . I have grown tremendously in the experience. And in that growth, I'm still coming to places like, What am I trying to do with this? Where am I trying to go with this? Where am I growing as a person? I think it's a lifelong journey in facing yourself and really being honest and going deeper.[33]

I put together my own construct for my own spirituality, which I'd say is . . . that basic idea that, stripped of dogma and creed and specific practices, we can say that there are certain commonalities between all spiritual faiths. So I've made it a niche for myself to combine that with my experience of music dance culture. Because, in there, I was finding something that nourishes my soul and something that connects me with something larger than myself, including community, the world, and some larger rhythms than just my own day-to-day rhythm.[34]

In each of these cases, the rave experience not only brought about a shift in spiritual perspective, but also was an impetus for ravers to take their spiritual paths deeper and to integrate the spirituality they found in raves into the larger framework of their overall spiritual paths.

Rave Culture: Philosophy, Worldview, and Code for Living

These transformations in ravers' lives are not simply accidental, isolated individual occurrences, but take place within the context of a larger rave culture that sees itself as the leading edge of a planetwide cultural transformation. This culture goes all the way back to the very beginning of the rave scene in the Summer of Love in England in 1988, and even earlier to its antecedents like the acid house scene in London, the Balearic party scene in Ibiza, the original house music scene in Chicago, and the Dallas Ecstasy scene. Each of these scenes was more than just a pretext for people to have a good time or a peak experience; participants developed a sense of community and cultural identity that also had a strong social utopian component. Many ravers have used the word *home* to describe this feeling:

> I had come home.[35]

> We felt like, yeah, this is our thing. We finally feel at home.[36]

> This is home, this is what it's all about, this is what I've been looking for.[37]

One raver talked about how "it helps you feel part of something, like you're part of a bigger network of people than just yourself."[38] Another raver said that it

> creates a template and a way to be that can influence other people and can influence the way people relate with each other. I think there's a lot of people all through the whole rave culture that, to one degree or another, see that happening and are part of that and are facilitating it.[39]

Still another raver spoke of "the idea of rave culture as a sort of petri dish for the evolution of a new culture, one of the most vital fertile areas where a new planetary culture is being elaborated."[40] In this context, the word *culture* means more than just the external forms of fashion, music, art, language, and so forth, but more crucially, the deeper underlying way of looking at the world that gives meaning and order to life. For most ordinary people, this underlying perspective is preverbal and preconceptual, typically remaining below the threshold of consciousness. However, in rave culture, the deeper meaning of the rave phenomenon and its implications has been the focus of intense exploration and discussion, and many ravers have articulated this meaning into a philosophy, worldview, and code for living. I will now examine several of the more important of these articulations.

PLUR

The first, and most influential, of these articulations came in the form of the acronym PLUR—peace, love, unity, and respect—back in 1993.[41]

It seemed to capture succinctly the main principles of the burgeoning rave scene and quickly spread to become almost universally used as a central credo. The peace and love part is an obvious throwback to the idealistic 1960s psychedelic hippie counterculture (as is the phrase Summer of Love), with which rave culture clearly has significant continuities. However, there are also significant differences as well, and I will explore these in some detail a bit later. *Peace* here includes both inner peace (i.e., tranquility) and outer peace (i.e., living in harmony without conflict and war). Similarly, *love* is not only self-love and love of other ravers, but also a higher, spiritual, unconditional love that is understood to be the true nature of all things. In the same way, *unity* refers not only to the experience of unity on the dance floor at raves in which social boundaries are transcended, but the application of that same unity to the whole world, thus transcending nationality, ethnicity, race, religion, class, gender, sexual orientation, age, and the like. Finally, *respect* is both self-respect and respect of others, even if they are different, including nonravers, and extending that even to the policemen who might come to shut down a rave. PLUR is obviously both very idealistic (perhaps to the point of naïveté, some would argue) and very difficult to put into practice. It has also been the subject of a great deal of ridicule and cynicism by ravers and nonravers alike over the years. Yet, no one can argue its central place in the philosophy of rave culture, and it exerts a huge defining influence even today. As one contemporary raver put it,

> I'm looking at things in terms of the old school word PLUR. It's so basic and it's just so true. So for me, just the principles of peace, love, unity, and respect go deeper. . . .[42]

Thousands of ravers were initiated into the rave scene with this simple credo, and thousands are striving to live their lives according to its principles, even if they might not admit it.

An Alternative Culture

Rave culture is an alternative culture in two important ways: First, there is an implicit critique of mainstream culture and the problems it has created, both on a personal and a planetary level; second, rave culture sees itself as an alternative model that solves these problems, a working template for a healthy, harmonious, sustainable, and spiritually conscious culture. Ravers are extremely articulate on this point:

> How things are going is not working, so let's be exploring the different ways that we can be creating goodness in the world and beauty and love and compassion and tolerance and unity.[43]

> I think what the world really needs now is to learn to live from the heart in a world of connection. What we really lack as a culture is connectivity with each other. . . . I think what humanity has been going through is, it started out just about survival, about living to the next day. And then the human collective consciousness moved into the second realm, which was about reproduction and growing, and the third one, which is about power and control and building. I think we're still there as a race. But I think it's time for us to start thinking about living in the heart, living in connection, and in love. I think that a group like the Rhythm Society, what it does, it patterns that.[44]

> There's this huge force of aggression and an eye for an eye kind of warrior energy out there right now, and here's this counterforce, if you will, that doesn't have an aggressive bone in its body. How does it make a dent in this other part? I mean, it's wonderful, we all have these wonderful experiences, and we all make more choiceful decisions as a result, and we all eat better, don't finance evil companies, we're aware of that and starting to think that way, we all have more of a global perspective, and maybe that's enough, maybe that will eventually help. . . . George W. Bush is running the show and . . . there's this scary external world. But that having been said, there's this energy that I have to believe has some larger force for positive evolutionary heart-centered ends, or development, that direction, I really do. I mean, if there's anything that's going to help usher in the next era of light, it's this, in my opinion.[45]

> The Bushes, you know, I think of . . . the petty tyrant and I think that's what these characters are. They're showing such the archetypal imbalances of the world that now the other side is rising up. And I think it's causing a huge acceleration. And I think what we're really involved with has been known in the beginning of time. It's the fulfillment of a stage. This isn't really like a surprise, this is what was supposed to happen. We were told to forget ourselves, become mired in compartmentalizing and dissecting everything, and at some point in time, it would get to a place where it's just completely breaking down. And that that community has to find itself in that breakdown. I think that's what drew so many people

to the rave scene. . . . I actually think we live in really auspicious times. And that the emergence of this culture and its transformation isn't just arbitrary. It's happening as other things are happening in the world. Things are bubbling up in the world. The world wants change. The earth wants transformation. The people want healing. And I think as we do the work and we get more out of our way, that there's something seeping up through the creation.[46]

Rave culture is certainly not the first alternative culture with this perspective, and ravers definitely see it as continuing and updating a lineage of a succession of alternative cultures, particularly the 1960s psychedelic hippie counterculture and 1950s beat culture:

Rave culture is kind of that wave that you can trace back to the fifties beat culture, it went through the hippies, went through punk, and I think rave culture's kind of like hippies with jobs.[47]

I'd done my own take and study on the culture, as it were, everything from the Beat generation up to the hippies, the psychedelic movement, and into the rave movement, and just seeing this movement of consciousness waving through time, through young people.[48]

It's a different movement, but I think the movement of the '60s was a similar revolution. It's happening much more quietly here.[49]

As the last quote suggests, there are also differences between rave culture and the 1960s counterculture, and these differences are not insignificant:

Hippie was tune in and drop out, you know, leave culture. Try to live in right livelihood, try to live in a good way, but they thought you couldn't do that and be a part of society. But I see rave people trying to do that and be part of society, be part of culture. I think that's really the major difference there.

Q: So you see it as carrying on that countercultural tradition, but in a slightly different mode.
A: Yeah, and in a more engaged way. People in the rave community, there's lawyers and doctors, people of all sorts, who do professional web design, all kind of stuff.[50]

It's not just a bunch of hippies running around getting psychedelic in the desert. There's people who have very respectable careers, a lot of people involved in music and art and multimedia. Definitely very into technology . . . . Everyone's got jobs, kids.[51]

In this respect, ravers see rave culture as the next evolutionary step in the lineage of alternative culture.

TAZ

In the mid-1980s, postmodern anarchist philosopher Peter Lamborn Wilson, a.k.a. Hakim Bey, developed a new strategy for countercultural resistance, an innovative model he called the TAZ, or Temporary Autonomous Zone:

> The TAZ is like an uprising which does not engage directly with the State, a guerilla operation which liberates an area (of land, of time, of imagination) and then dissolves itself to re-form elsewhere/elsewhen, *before* the State can crush it. . . . The TAZ can "occupy" these areas clandestinely and carry on its festal purposes for quite a while in relative peace. . . . As soon as the TAZ is named (represented, mediated), it must vanish, it *will* vanish, leaving behind it an empty husk, only to spring up again somewhere else, once again invisible because undefinable in terms of the Spectacle. The TAZ is thus a perfect tactic for an era in which the State is omnipresent and all-powerful and yet simultaneously riddled with cracks and vacancies. And because the TAZ is a microcosm of that "anarchist dream" of a free culture, I can think of no better tactic by which to work toward that goal while at the same time experiencing some of its benefits in the here and now.[52]

The idea of the TAZ struck a chord of resonance throughout many sectors of alternative culture and became a well-known and widely used concept. When the rave scene emerged in the late 1980s and early 1990s, many ravers saw the rave as the perfect manifestation of a TAZ—they are clearly temporary; they occupy areas clandestinely, especially cracks and vacancies like abandoned warehouses; they are festal in nature; and they are certainly a microcosm of a free culture whose participants experience its benefits in the here and now. One raver put it this way:

> Raves are sacred spaces or Temporary Autonomous Zones. . . . These TAZs are to free ourselves and others of the ideas and mindsets forced upon us by the fucked up corporate entity which passes for

culture. The TAZ is a direct response to and escape from the crap—the mass media brainwashing us into consuming and being good little mindless cogs—that fills up our lives. The TAZ is a space for all of us to move forward emotionally and spiritually by allowing us to be who we really are and who we really can be. No coercion, no bullshit. Specific improvements to reach closer to the ancient idea of the beat.[53]

In 1993, Geoff White took these ideas further in his influential essay "CyberTribe Rising," in which he posited a global rave culture he called the CyberTribe, which is based on the newly emerging paradigm he dubbed C5I2 (*community*, *consensus*, *cooperation*, *communication*, *cybernetics*, *intelligence*, and *intuition*). According to White, "one way to look at all of this is to view C5I2 as the technology behind Temporary Autonomous Zones, and to see the CyberTribe as a step towards the realization of global TAZ networks."[54]

Sustainability

Raves are ephemeral and temporary in nature, lasting for one evening or, at the most, several days, and the TAZ is temporary by definition. Yet, the rave scene has now been in existence for well over seventeen years and has proven to be more than a temporary phenomenon. Accordingly, ravers are beginning to envision and to articulate the possibility of an alternative culture that is more lasting and sustainable in the long term, and one of the main ways that they seek to accomplish this sustainability is through the emergence of rave communities:

> You know, the party thing's cool, but it was one night and it was over. And that archetype was logged into the history books and soon forgotten. . . . So we were pondering what we could do together that had an actual lasting effect.[55]

> Initially, in the early '90s, the rave scene was a lot about taking drugs and mind expansion and dancing and ecstatic dance and connection with the divine and connection with others, and destruction of ego and self, and oneness, and all that—I think there was an innocence about it then that prevented this taking it further outside of that. There was the sense of it being a discrete experience that you could talk about outside but it wasn't evolved enough at the time to be applying it or taking it beyond

the discrete experience. And it was very innocent. It was really great that way that you could connect with one person one night, but you'd never see them again, which is beautiful in its way but also you could only take that for so long. Like, what's the use of that if that connection isn't lasting? It was kind of magical and beautiful as its own little thing but, okay, what else? And so when I experienced the Rhythm Society later on, the experience I had was that it was a next step, evolutionarily, of something beyond the discrete experience that was being applied more holistically—about spiritual awareness, about self-awareness, about building community, and what community actually meant, what the possibility of community really was, what the potential of being in community really was, and having that be a lasting experience over time, and what that enables.[56]

However, it is one thing to put on a rave, but it is something altogether different to try to create a long-term, sustainable community. Ravers also touched on the challenges and difficulties of this endeavor:

When you try to create something almost serious or fixed, with a sense of outcome, for something that can be as amorphous as an electronic dance culture, it enters a lot of ambiguity that makes it hard for you to establish anything lasting—because we're not living together, because we're not depending on each other for our survival, we're just seeing each other here and there. . . . So I've been working on this vision in various ways, trying to see how we can arrive at it with attention to our economics and how we work with that. Because, if we're an alternative culture, perhaps we're going to draw towards alternative economic structures and maybe we'll be better able to receive it. We'll be able to, through throwing events, provide ourselves with the training for us to work on larger projects, so that by the time we get to that stage where perhaps we're really dependent on each other, we're living on the same geographical space, on land, or trying to create business, that sort of thing, we have the skills. And I think, like any community, what we're going to come up against is all of our shadows, all of our issues that the mother culture has passed down to us, the world karma, and we're going to have to work through all of that. And that's the test right now, I find, is graduating from these adolescents to mature beings that have inherited the benefit of that whole experience and can now take those tools and apply them in a way that will be useful for a long time, without growing cynical, without taking ourselves too seriously, and without losing track of what it was that made us so special to begin with.[57]

Integration into the Real World

As noted earlier, one raver talked about the difference between hippies and ravers:

> *Hippie* was tune in and drop out, you know, leave culture. Try to live in right livelihood, try to live in a good way, but they thought you couldn't do that and be a part of society. But I see rave people trying to do that and be part of society, be part of culture.[58]

This concern with integrating the rave scene back into the mainstream is another important hallmark of rave culture in its efforts to be a viable long-term phenomenon:

> I think that the people that are within the cosm of experiencing the dance culture can remember, maybe, that we're not just an island unto ourselves and that we are connected to a larger world and that, in the end of the day, no matter how high or how amazing the experience we have goes when we're together, it's going to inevitably have to integrate back into the world. And the success to which we are able to do that is going to determine the sustainability of our communities.[59]

> These communities, over a long period of time, will have more economic and social impacts, will have more interlaced networks amongst other communities. Actually, because of the nature of how they were formed, they have an interest in the workings of the world, and are willing and interested in impacting it in positive ways.[60]

Some ravers have even taken this idea to almost humorous extremes; for example:

> I would like to see it the way we see 7-11s now. I would like to see little studios in every town where Friday nights, or whatever it is, you go and do your thing and you make your donation and you go home. Franchised. I want it out there. I want it everywhere. Just like Walgreen's in Cole Valley, you know? I really do. That would be fantastic. . . . Wally's Trance World—Sunday! Sunday! Sunday! . . . That would be awesome. Wouldn't that be fun? Because what that would represent is that this stuff is so enculturated and so integrated that it's not only a lucrative franchise, its reality is not even questioned—of course it's that way.[61]

Humorous though the concept may be, however, it is actually a serious goal shared by many ravers who would "love to see the scene in malls and churches and out on the streets."[62]

Global

Another important hallmark of rave culture is its global nature, not just in the sense that electronic dance music and raves are found in almost every country around the world, but—perhaps more important—because ravers feel themselves to be part of a larger unified planetary network. It begins with the music, which, because it generally has no lyrics, has the capacity to bypass verbal and conceptual distinctions that separate people and, instead, unites them:

> People are literally listening to it [electronic dance music] in every corner of the planet and it's wonderful because it unites a planet in a language that is beyond language. It really isn't about lyric music, it's about a beat, and everybody can dance, so that's what's really great about it. I think that's what gives it hope to unify people in a way that maybe hasn't happened before.[63]

> Dance music is so universal. It transcends language and so many cultural barriers, which is why it is such global music.[64]

Another global aspect is that electronic dance music has created its own network that, to a large degree, functions outside the framework of the mainstream popular music industry. Armed with a few affordable pieces of equipment, a techno aficionado can write a song in his bedroom and, if it's good, it can easily find its way to a local dance floor. If the song blows up on the dance floor in one location, it can quickly spread around the world in a short period of time due to the tight interconnectivity of global rave communication networks. In this way, electronic dance music is a powerful facilitator of planetary connections:

> We want to be connected and this is our wire. Music is our link and always has been, but never in this way, never on the equal level between everything involved. I think it's the true music in the world, it's just going to feel like more of a together place. Closer connections, really. It's hard to specify because it's really large . . . . It will go anywhere and everywhere and it'll make just more and more connections and bring

more things together to make them one. In reality, that's all we really map to, that's all we are, we're all one. I deeply believe in that and see it clearly and live it and breathe it. . . . And music is our link. This is what's going to work for us more and more in the future, more and more and multiplying by every year. And it's going to move really fast.[65]

Beyond the music itself is the global nature of the rave scene, which has spread like wildfire throughout the world. As Jimi Fritz has noted in his study *Rave Culture*:

There are well-developed scenes in almost every country with people of diverse backgrounds raving in every major center in the USA, Canada, Europe, South America, Scandinavia, Japan, Thailand, India, Australia, New Zealand, Russia, South Africa, and many other parts of the world. . . . [Rave culture is] alive and well in Bahrain, China, Chile, Costa Rica, Denmark, Dominican Republic, Ecuador, Iceland, Kazakhstan, Lithuania, Luxembourg, New Zealand, Norway, Panama, Paraguay, Peru, Puerto Rico, Romania, Slovakia, Slovenia, Spain, Taiwan, Turkey, Morocco, Korea, Jamaica, The Ukraine, Cayman Islands, Kenya, Ghana, Zaire, and Zimbabwe. . . .[66]

According to Dave Jurman, senior director of the dance music department for Columbia Records:

The Far East and Japan now have a huge scene. . . . It's very, very big over there. It's growing all over the world. A friend of mine recently went to a rave event in Israel and said it was unbelievable. There are now rave events in unthinkable places. . . . The hot spots right now are England, mainland Europe, followed by Japan and the United States. I should also mention Australia.[67]

Yet it's not simply that rave *events* are happening around the world, but that rave *culture* is happening around the world, and that it is a united culture that is making a big impact. Fritz writes:

The phenomenal growth of rave culture throughout the world over the past decade has been astounding, proving that regardless of cultural conditions or bias, the appeal of rave is truly universal . . . .[68]

Rave culture is an international movement with a unified vision and global sense of community. . . . Rave may well be the biggest pop culture movement in history and it is only recently beginning to move from its underground status to a full-blown social revolution with the potential to positively influence a generation and ultimately change the course of human consciousness. . . .[69]

Some ravers have articulated this potential of global rave culture to spiritually transform the planet even further:

> We as a global dance community . . . are keepers and manifesters of a vision, a vision of a conscious planetary party, a vision of global ceremony. Ceremony means gathering with intention, celebrating our vision of a peaceful, free, and love-filled world where mankind is unified and living in harmony with our planet, Gaia, Earth. . . . When a large portion of the collective consciousness of humanity unites in love, it creates a ripple affect and triggers another large portion of the collective consciousness into the same state. Both personally and collectively we need to recognize how our mental and emotional states create the general psychic atmosphere on this planet. . . . Through sending ecstatic energy that we generate into the [earth's] grid, it automatically channels into the collective consciousness. As we individually activate ourselves as breathing, dancing, channeling vortices of light, we connect as one light. Each conscious party a vortex, a point of light on the globe. If we were to fly from above and imagine all of our brothers and sisters around the globe dancing for planetary peace, then we would see that they've woven a web, a matrix of light that surrounds the globe.[70]

Tribal and Shamanic

While an important element of rave culture is looking to the future, there is also an important element of looking to the past as well. Ravers highly value ancient, indigenous cultures, viewing them as repositories of wisdom and models for living in harmony with the earth and with spirit worlds. At the same time, ravers are not about to give up their high-tech postmodern lifestyle; rather, they are seeking to integrate it with the ancient wisdom of indigenous cultures. One phrase commonly used to characterize this approach is *future primitive*. Another word that is even more widely used is *tribal*, which often appears in the names of crews and events (e.g., Tribal Harmonix, Moontribe, and Gathering of the Tribes).

> *Tribal* is a dominant word because if you are in wonder with music that has rhythm, and a number of you feel the rhythm and you move to the

rhythm at the same time, it's a way of coming together and that's what being tribal and ritualistic is all about.[71]

The dance music experience, ritual, and community are essential, especially when our culture is so devoid of that. . . . They want to be part of a tribe. . . . They're going back to a much more communal, tribal way. It's because they're not happy the other way, they're not healthy the other way. . . . People who are part of this culture are willing to explore spirituality maybe that they weren't allowed to. But they really look toward tribal traditions.[72]

We are each part of an immense tribe of travelers, thousands and thousands huge, spread across the planet and circumnavigating it, now for the first time in the history of mankind. Enabled by communication technology and cheap airfare, we can now have friends scattered across every continent, and keep in touch by phone, fax, and e-mail, connecting and reconnecting in various places as our karma dictates. Perhaps we are the earth's first global tribe.[73]

It's a modern-day tribal society. We're reinventing that experience in a modern-day context.[74]

While most ravers have no direct experience with real tribal cultures, one raver I interviewed actually does, and she discussed the influence it had on her involvement in rave culture, and more specifically, in the Oracle:

I'm from a tribe which is native to Guam. And part of the tribal culture, cultural dances or fire dances, are these really intense amazing staff dances, where they just get so rooted and raw and primal in their dance, and it's totally centered around creating magic. . . . This is hundreds of years old, thousands of years old, just tribal dance, and creating spiritual intent and magic through dance. What I've found through the Oracle and through dance culture is the deeper I go, the more of that wisdom and knowledge comes through, when I'm sharing it with people. I feel like we're tapping into magic from the past to support magic for the present to guide us into magic for the future.[75]

Another word that is widely used by ravers—often in conjunction with *tribal*—is *shamanic*, which references the religious figure in tribal cultures, the shaman who journeys to spiritual worlds by means of an ecstatic trance state, often induced by rhythmic drumming, for the purposes of healing, divination, and community well-being:

This is a tribe; we're all a tribe. This tribe finds itself needing healing, needing magic, needing natural connection. . . . I realized I was playing the role of the shaman, having a tribe, and bringing a tribe on these ceremonial ritual journeys. . . . I facilitate realizations and transformations and healings and all these things are completely shamanic.[76]

There is an element of shamanism involved with the way I like to DJ, the alchemy of blending rhythms together, and the particular style of music that I tend to lean towards. I like people to think of what I'm doing as a tribal thing. Because I see the culture, as it is, as very fragmented and separate, and my attempts musically are to draw some more of that ancient tribal notion into our culture and attempt to shamanically implant those characteristics that tribes have that are valuable in our culture, that they can be revived, that give each individual a deeper sense of value. . . . The real root of shamanism is almost invariably drumming and chanting. And that's where I feel like I kind of channel that element in, is I do tend to play a lot of kind of a rootsy tribal style. That's what I like to make when I'm creating music. So that's my angle is to represent it in an extremely modern world with the highest technology I can have at my fingertips and reaching as far back as I can and finding elements that can apply.[77]

I felt like I really was part of some quasi-religious cult: The shaman DJs in conjunction with nature's energy and the altered states of consciousness of the participants created a religious atmosphere. . . . The roots of raving are really intertwined with ageless tribal rituals of music, dance, trance, and the partaking of mind-expanding sacraments, where reaching a oneness with our inner nature links us to a oneness with the forces of nature around us and in each other. You don't have to watch many National Geographics to see the obvious similarities between parties such as these and the religious ceremonies of more "primitive" cultures. Ritualistic ravings will remain viable because it appeals to the sense of spirit in us that has been viable since the dawn of human consciousness. . . . On Sunday we were a tribe of the Universe, of the basic essence of life and energy, body and mind.[78]

A New Form of Spirituality and Religion

Many ravers see spirituality as a central aspect of rave culture. In fact, some ravers go so far as to view rave culture itself as a new form of spirituality or even a new form of religion. For example, Fritz, in *Rave Culture*, writes, "I have talked to many ravers about this issue and have become convinced that raving does indeed meet all the requirements of a grass roots people's religion."[79] Another raver put it this way:

> What I'm actually participating in here is a movement [that] . . . does everything a traditional religious movement does.[80]

At the same time, however, it is also very different from traditional religious movements. Fritz notes, "For the most part, ravers do not cling to the religious models of the past, preferring instead to create something new. Structure, conformity, and subservience have given way to a more personal and free-form model."[81] One raver articulated his vision of this model:

> What we model is how the openhearted can live together and cooperate while following many spiritual pathways to the same goal. We are ending the age of prophets and priests, and massive, institutional religion. Everyone who is so inclined will have the capacity for sacred knowledge and divine inspiration, without intermediary. Everyone will bring their own individual expression of the divine to share at the feast. We are each of us a full and perfect manifestation of divine presence.[82]

This quotation touches on a number of key features of this model—noninstitutional, nonhierarchical, unmediated, and individualistic. But perhaps the most important feature is its inclusive, postdenominational nature. As a new form of spirituality and religion, rave culture unites people from a wide variety of religious and spiritual paths:

> If you pull all those people off the dance floor and ask each one of them individually exactly what they believe and what their cosmology is about God, you'd find every one of them have a different answer. . . . [But] if you get out on the dance floor, and you're all in that vibe, we suddenly become one regardless of cosmology. And that's what seems to be so transformative is that people aren't hung up on any particular dogma, like religion. It's more about sharing this spiritual nature that we all have with each other, and an understanding that we all do have it.[83]

In a world where religious differences and dogmas have fostered division, hatred, violence, and wars that have killed untold millions, transcending these differences would indeed be a radical and hopeful development.

Music, Dance, and Mixing as Models and Metaphors

Electronic dance music is extremely different from almost any other style of popular music in a number of important ways: It usually has no lyrics, the beat is a central defining feature, its primary intention is to make people dance, and it is composed with an entirely different set of organizational principles. Moreover, most tracks are not meant to stand on their own, but, rather, to be incorporated into a sequence of tracks mixed together seamlessly by a DJ into a set that is itself a larger form of musical expression, a set that also does not stand alone, but is combined with several other elements that create the total dance floor experience at raves. While each of these features of electronic dance music has a largely functional aspect, each can also be considered as a smaller fractal template for the philosophies, worldviews, and codes for living of the larger rave culture. Thus, music, dancing, and mixing each are activities that serve as important models and metaphors for ravers and their culture.

The hallmark of most electronic dance music is the pounding, trance-inducing repetitiveness of the beat, coupled with the soaring visionary textures of the keyboards. The beat keeps one grounded in the body, while the harmonies and melodies transport one to higher realms, producing some of the incredible experiences we have examined at length. Because of the profound nature of these experiences, ravers have articulated a philosophical perspective of the deep transformative power of music, not only on a personal level, but at a universal level as well:

> The feeling that music gave me was higher than anything. . . . And it's the only thing that links me to all my deepest feelings and connections and ideas. Things that words could never say, music can. Music can be anywhere, anytime, in that same form, and fill the entire atmosphere and bring what it needs to bring, and connect people. . . . To me, that's the ultimate bliss . . . music. Everything is music. If we really said what we really wanted to say, if we really said everything that is our deepest feeling within our soul, we'd actually be singing to each other, I think. And I'm only here for that reason. I'm only here to see that. And I can't survive on anything else. That's the only thing that I hope for as far as the future goes. Nothing else can feed me life. As far as I'm concerned, I'm pretty much dead right now until that happens. That's the only thing that's going to bring me to life. And I thank God for music every day. Nothing else that can get me there, absolutely nothing.[84]

This perspective is true for dance as well, particularly because dance is the primary means of entering deeply into the music. To illustrate this perspective, I repeat here part of a quotation I used in chapter 3:

> It's a form of entering a place that you can't [by] just walking around and observing the normal everyday. And it's a form of going inside the music. It's a relationship that you have with the music. And, once you come in harmony, you're in bliss, really. . . . I think that every beautiful approach inside of life, every gesture can be a musical gesture. And it is, but it's so on the surface that we don't see it. . . . If you look at the leaves, the way they go in the wind, they're dancing! That's all they're doing, is dancing. It's all anything does that's natural. It's all dancing. . . . If we cut down the bullshit, we'd be dancing. That's what I see.[85]

The picture that emerges from this perspective is of a universe made up of music, where everything is dancing:

> We start to feel that the earth is dancing with us, and trees and the wind and the sky. . . . One of the senses I get when I'm dancing, when I'm most in that flowing place, is that sense of *I am the Creator*. . . . At those times, I'm really glimpsing how spirit is . . . that spirit is this endlessly moving, creating, playful energy that the dance has made very apparent to me.[86]

This picture of a dancing universe made up of music strongly echoes Hindu cosmology, in which one of the primary deities, Shiva, is often depicted as Nataraja, the Lord of the Dance, dancing in a ring of fire to maintain the cosmic harmony of a universe in motion. In the sonic theology of Nada Brahman, music and sound are understood as being synonymous with God and, thus, music is seen as a particularly effective path to experience and unite with the divine. In these formulations, dance and music are recognized as sacred practices that lead to understanding one's true nature, the true nature of the universe, one's place within it, and ultimately to union with God.

In addition to music and dance, the practice of DJ mixing also has important philosophical implications for ravers, particularly as a metaphor for how to follow a spiritual path and live one's life in an artful and harmonious manner. Essentially, what a DJ does is to take a number of tracks, each of which has its own distinctive feeling and structural components (i.e., rhythm, tempo, melody, harmony, timbre, instrumentation, etc.) and blend them together so that the transitions are seamless and the entire set is an integrated whole. In order to accomplish this task, a DJ must utilize the similarities between the tracks, through techniques like beat matching and key matching and, at the same time, must also utilize the differences between the tracks to create a sense of dynamics and forward momentum. This means that the DJ must devote a great deal of time and energy to finding the appropriate tracks and to acquiring an intimate knowledge of each one. These same skills are precisely what is required of the postmodern spiritual seeker in cobbling together a coherent spiritual path from a variety of disparate sources. One must devote a great deal of time and energy to find the appropriate traditions, teachings, and practices, and to acquire an intimate knowledge of each of them. Then, one must learn to deftly use the similarities and differences to blend them together seamlessly into a larger spiritual path that forms an integrated whole. And just as a good DJ must practice her skills for countless hours before she becomes technically proficient and must DJ live countless times before she learns the deeper artistry of how to craft a great set, a dedicated spiritual seeker must likewise put in countless hours of practice and study, and must work to learn the deeper artistry of how to craft a fulfilling spiritual path. The same metaphor can also be applied to the larger path of leading one's whole life, since everybody faces the challenge of mixing together the separate sectors of work, family, community, spirituality, recreation, and so forth into an integrated whole. In this way, the art of mixing can be seen as the ultimate postmodern practice—sampling, cutting, and pasting pieces from a melange of different contexts into a new configuration of coherent meaning, an important skill to have in the ever-increasing complexities of our contemporary world!

There is another postmodern aspect to DJ mixing as a metaphor, and that has to do with its highly technological nature. In contrast to the hippie counterculture, which viewed technology with suspicion, in some cases even as something inherently evil, rave culture embraces technology and sees it as a key component of our future evolution. Accordingly, notes Scott Hutson:

> The DJ is . . . a mixed symbol of human and machine. By spinning 'tribal' beats on sophisticated equipment, the DJ synthesizes our desire to be spiritual with our rootedness and dependence on the material. The

DJ thus serves as a model of the place of machines in the world and a model for how the soul can be integrated with them.[87]

In his groundbreaking book *More Brilliant Than the Sun*, Kodwo Eshun has developed some of the most innovative thinking on this theme, essentially arguing that the machine sounds and beats of electronic music are reprogramming human consciousness to a new evolutionary paradigm in which humans are rapidly becoming the technologically advanced alien other so widely referenced in UFO imagery that is also very popular in rave culture. To conclude this chapter, here is a taste of his unique writing style, which he calls *sonic fiction*, the intersection between science fiction and sound, and which he sees as reflecting the groundbreaking styles of electronic music:

It [the music] alienates itself from the human; it arrives from the future. Alien Music is a synthetic recombinator, an applied art technology for amplifying the rates of becoming alien. . . . Machines *don't* distance you from your emotions, in fact quite the opposite. Sound machines make you feel *more* intensely, along a broader band of emotional spectra than ever before in the 20th Century. Sonically speaking, the posthuman era is not one of disembodiment but the exact reverse: it's a *hyperembodiment*, via the Technics SL 1200. . . . You are willingly mutated by intimate machines, abducted by audio into the populations of your bodies. Sound machines throw you onto the shores of the skin you're in. The hypersensual cyborg experiences herself as a galaxy of audiotactile sensations. You are not censors but sensors, not aesthetes but kinaesthetes. You are sensationalists. You are the newest mutants incubated in womb-speakers. Your mother, your first sound. The bedroom, the party, the dancefloor, the rave: these are the labs where the 21st C nervous systems assemble themselves, the matrices of the Futurhythmachinic Discontinuum. The future is a much better guide to the present than the past.[88]

Earthdance, Laytonville, CA, 2004. Photograph courtesy of Shawn "Skoi" Lass (Archivist@oracle.com).

CHAPTER 6
LIVING LABORATORIES:
RAVE COMMUNITIES AND
NETWORKS

Perhaps the most important laboratory is one not mentioned by Kodwo Eshun, in *More Brilliant Than the Sun* (see chapter 5)—namely, the emerging communities in which ravers are attempting to integrate the rave experience into the nitty-gritty details of their daily lives. Rave communities provide a working context in which this integration can take place—through a supportive network of like-minded fellow travelers, through ongoing events and activities informed by rave culture, through organizational structures that are more concrete and lasting, and through a sense of ongoing spiritual and religious fellowship:

> It's more a part of my life than I thought it could be before. It's taken a whole other realm of meaning that's beyond music—the sense of building community, having an impact in the world, how do you live the lessons of community outside and spread the gospel. . . . To me, while the rave scene, while the music and everything is very, very important, what I've come out of the experience having is it was an enabler to create community and to explore what community really is. We all know that music is a great way to bring people together, but in this case, it feels like it's not the end-all and be-all, it's not where the experience ends. It's just a catalyst to create the experience to make the spark happen and then

there's all the stuff that happens beyond that when you stick with the connections that you make. . . .[1]

This is no longer a new experience for me in certain ways and it's come to the point where I'm helping create the reality I want to create with that medium of dance culture—being a part of collectives, being a part of communities and networks where people strive towards some sort of goal with it all, whether it be creating change or creating a more spiritual sense of community. And we have a very unique culture in that we're not quite a dance scene, in the sense that we're not just a scene, we're a community. And as far as communitarian movements, we're not quite your average community because we're based in this common ground of partying together.[2]

I think that's where community becomes a strong force in the process because, whereas the drug became the binding catalyst for this unified experience, in the new form I sense it's the community, the group of people that have done the work, that have created the increasing closeness, the sympathetic resonance, that when you come together and create, they actually are creating a field. . . . New seeds have been brought to the table that whole communities are emerging around and new manifestations. . . . I've always said that when the economics crashes, it will actually be the community that stands. . . . And I think they will have the transformational significance that was at the root of the original rave scene. . . . The real evolving communities, you can see it in the individuals in the community, that they're growing, they're becoming stronger. These communities, over a long period of time, will have more economic and social impacts, will have more interlaced networks amongst other communities. That they actually, because of the nature of how they were formed, they have an interest in the workings of the world, and are willing and interested in impacting it in positive ways.[3]

There are a wide variety of rave communities, and each one has its own distinct flavor and modus operandi. Although there are rave communities throughout the United States and the entire planet, in particular, the West Coast seems to be one of the most fertile areas; here a significant number have emerged, taken hold, and thrived. As ravers note,

I think a lot of it has to do with the West Coast is such a hot spot for kids in America. It seems like if they've got any kind of light in them, they want to head for the West Coast.[4]

I always look at the energy of the West Coast as having a bit more of the Goddess energy. There's just more space, there's a lot more nature, and the vibration is in the people.[5]

And, within the West Coast, the San Francisco Bay Area seems to have the greatest density of rave crews and communities. For example, in addition to the Rhythm Society, I am personally familiar with several well-established like-minded underground rave communities (Cloud Factory, False Profit, Friends n Family, Koinonea, Opel, Pacific Sound, Radiant Atmospheres, Raise the Frequency, and Vibrant) and there are probably dozens beyond these. Moreover, not only are there a significant number of West Coast rave communities, but they also seem to be connecting with each other more in the last few years. This is happening in a number of ways, but perhaps the most significant of these is the intentional creation of larger networks of rave communities at events such as Burning Man, Earthdance, Gathering of the Tribes, and the Storm Sessions. I will examine these networks in more detail shortly, but for now I will begin with some specific West Coast rave communities that illustrate a wide range of different approaches and models. This survey is not meant to be exhaustive or even representative, but simply to give a sense of a few important rave communities and their unique characteristics.

The Rhythm Society

I start with the Rhythm Society because it is the community with which I am most familiar and whose events I have attended the most consistently over the years. The St. John's Divine Rhythm Society held its first All Night Dance Celebration (ANDC) in spring of 1996 at the Episcopal Church of St. John the Divine in San Francisco's Mission District. This ANDC and subsequent events at the church took place with the cooperation and blessing of the church's leadership, and not only were several members of the congregation in attendance, but several of them were members of the Rhythm Society as well. The vision of these events has been articulated in a specific statement that has remained consistent over the years: "The Rhythm Society comes together in dance and celebration to encourage spiritual and personal growth, community, and primary religious experience. We welcome people of all faiths or no faith at all. WE ARE ONE IN THE DANCE!"[6] All Rhythm Society events are by invitation only, and the only way to get an invitation is from a member of the Rhythm Society; they are not commercial raves open to the public. Moreover, the doors close at a certain time, usually somewhere from 10:00 P.M. to midnight, and once you leave, you cannot return. This is because, as I noted earlier, as the Rhythm Society states on its invitations, "a foundational element of our divine celebrations is the creation of a ritual safe 'container' in space and time."[7] I have already described an ANDC in some detail in this volume's introduction, so I will not repeat that information here except to say that all ANDCs have a theme, an opening and closing ceremony, and altars, thus reflecting the Rhythm Society's strong spiritual orientation. In 2002, a series of events led to a rift between the Rhythm Society and St. John's Church, and this separation was formalized in the winter solstice ANDC, which was held at another venue for the first time. Since then, the Rhythm Society has dropped St. John's from its name, and subsequent events have been held at other locations. Needless to say, this has been a huge shift in the history and direction of the Rhythm Society.

The overall vision of the Rhythm Society (RS) as a community has also been articulated into the following statement:

> The Rhythm Society has a twofold purpose:
>
> First, we create space for direct, experiential forms of spiritual practice. Recognizing that divine rhythm is everywhere, the Rhythm Society celebrates spirit through music, dance, meditation, and play. Familiar traditions express our identity; new explorations evolve it. The Rhythm Society encourages each person to develop their own spiritual path.
>
> Second, we cultivate community in which we can play out the daily life implications of insights gained from primary religious experience. Our spiritual, social, and business meetings call upon us to balance our individual desires with the goal of harmony among ourselves, our neighbors, and the world.[8]

Rhythm Society Friends meetings take place once a month and are consistently well attended. In a conversation with one of the founders, it became clear to me that one of the Rhythm Society's models is the Quaker Society of Friends. A person can only become a member of the Friends through the sponsorship of a Friend and then attending a meeting and other RS events. After a year or so, if the person is interested, she can advance to become a voting member. There is also a smaller council with key decision-making responsibilities, as well as a number of committees that focus on particular concerns, such as communications, development, membership, events, and so forth. The RS Friends, the council, the committees, their meetings, and their decision-making process are run on a consensus model and, to my continuing amazement, it appears to be a model that works very well. Given its strong spiritual and religious orientation, it is no coincidence that the RS has been associated with a church and, since the split with St. John's, the RS has decided to move in the direction of not only incorporating as a nonprofit organization, but also one that falls under the designation of both "religious organization" and "'church"!

In addition to the four seasonal ANDCs, generally held on solstices and equinoxes, there are also a number of other ongoing RS events and activities. Each summer, there is a weekend long campout rave at a remote location in Mendocino County. This campout includes two nights of dancing to electronic music, shared meals, and other organized activities. However, one of its main pleasures is the opportunity for RS members to socialize with each other throughout the weekend in a relaxed way in a natural setting. Along similar lines, there is an annual weekend-long retreat, also usually held in a remote location north of San Francisco, but with indoor facilities and lodging. In addition to the opportunities for socializing, the retreat activities revolve more around workshops and discussion groups on a variety of subjects, including dance, spiritual and ceremonial practice, and community building. The RS has a group camp, Blyss Abyss, at the Burning Man festival each year, that takes a lot of time and energy to prepare and that serves as a central focus for RS members and is a place to spend time together. In the Bay Area, there are occasional Friday Night Gatherings, or FNGs, which are organized around a variety of themes or activities and generally last a couple of hours. Some FNGs have featured spiritual and ceremonial practice, talks and discussions, and various explorations in movement and dance. There are two weekly evening meditation groups, one in San Francisco and one in the East Bay. There is an RS choir that meets regularly for members to sing together. There are occasional "supper club" gatherings in which RS members have potluck dinners at a member's house or apartment, and these may also feature videos/DVDs or talks/discussions. Beyond all of these semiformal activities, there are also countless additional spontaneous activities constantly taking place, such as organizing a group of people to go see a movie, or attend a musical event, party, or political rally, and so on.

In addition, the RS has a thriving online community as well, with members posting on their confidential chat board messages on a wide variety of topics, ranging from the profound to the trivial, the universal to the personal—including successful calls for help with a number of different matters. Finally, many RS members live together in group households and are involved in each other's lives on a daily basis.

The sum total of all of this activity is a tight-knit group of people who have created a very strong sense of community and, in the process, created a context where the rave experience can be integrated into their lives. RS members touched on this in no uncertain terms:

> I have a couple of spiritual communities, but the Rhythm Society is my primary one right now. It's where I put most of my energy. Definitely, it's a spiritual community. People can have these transcendent spiritual experiences, but I think without a context to understand them in, they can get lost, they can get forgotten. They're seeds and they don't really grow into the flower, unless you have some place to plant them. Like in the Rhythm Society, we have two meditation groups that meet weekly. And we have monthly get-together events where we talk about spiritual topics. We've had Huston Smith come and talk, we've done Sufi dancing, we've had a shamanic drumdown visioning ceremony, we've done lots of things like that where people come and participate and there's a lot of discussion on spiritual topics. There's a lot of people in the group who meditate or teach meditation or what have you. So I think what it gives everybody is a context to share these spiritual experiences in. It's also a spiritual community that is intentionally trying to live in a heart-focused way. So I think it's very important to have that context. . . .
>
> I think it makes me a better person. I have the opportunity to take that spiritual experience, that experience of love and a way to be with people, out into the world with me. And I think other people in the RS have that same opportunity, too; we provide for each other. And also the Rhythm Society networks extend past just our all-night dances. People are always helping each other out. If you want to buy real estate, you've got a friend in the RS who's a real estate agent. If you need a doctor or psychologist, one of your friends is a psychologist or can refer you to somebody. So we're supporting each other in that way, in a day-to-day way. But I also think what happens is people come through the RS and they come to our events and they go back out in the world and they do their thing. There's people who run shelters for kids and there's people who run recycling programs and there's people who work at a job

wherever, like me at a financial institution. And we just go out and we bring that light into the world.[9]

A good friend of mine invited me to go to a meeting, actually, and I went. And I noticed that it was not just people who dance, but that it was a full-on community. And that they had issues of finances and planning, you know, back then they were minor issues, but they did. It was a community. It was a real, live, honest-to-God community that met over quarterly to dance. And I just thought, *My God, this is too unreal.* It was my dream being manifest in this real Gothic cathedral. It blew me away. . . .

It's a spiritual community. I think it's as close to a spiritual community as I have right now. I'm not in any church. I feel like that is a container for me to express spirit. I feel like there are a lot of people in there I have great spiritual conversations with. I can name five people right now who, the way they dance, that's my spiritual community, when we're dancing and we're having the same experience and getting playful. And I can tell who they are on the dance floor—they resonate the same way, they dance the same way I do. Yes, that's my spiritual community. It would be harder for me to say that about the RS as a whole. I mean, it's a community, and there's the spiritual component of that community. I don't think the community holds my spirituality the way that spiritual expression does. It's very experiential and there's a lot of talk on the list and there's a lot of times when we're not dancing together. That's friendship, that's connection, that's community, that's a very strong community, but I would not be able to say that I find a spiritual community with everyone. But I do like the resonance.[10]

Yes, absolutely, spiritual community. And I think community around common interests. I don't know if you call doing self-exploration work a spiritual practice—some would call it a psychological practice, so I think that there are different realms you can exist within. Because I know that not everybody in the Rhythm Society's spiritual community considers it a spiritual community for themselves. They consider it a social community, an incredibly powerful social community for themselves. But I think there are different levels that allow for however someone needs to be, experiencing whatever they need to be experiencing to have that. But, for me, it's a spiritual community. As well as other things. . . . I think being in community with like-minded people is a facilitator and a support network.[11]

Moontribe

Moontribe is one of the original Southern California rave communities and it has been throwing the epic Full Moon Gatherings at various locations out in the Mojave Desert for over twelve years. Inspired by the seminal outdoor Full Moon parties put on by the Wicked crew in the San Francisco Bay Area in the early 1990s, a core group of Los Angeles ravers threw the first Moontribe full moon desert party in June of 1993, and things took off from there, growing from a small, intimate event to large gatherings of several thousand people. I have already described some of the distinctive features of these gatherings: the hand-holding circles, chanting *om*, watching the sunrise, and so on. According to one of the founding members of Moontribe,

> The full moon parties were . . . profound for me because I was going in knowing what I was doing. We would facilitate energy circles where the entire party would be holding hands and dancing together, giving each other energy and love. It was wonderful to see all these different people coming together through music, dance, and psychedelics. We had some very profound group experiences.[12]

And these profound group experiences led to a growing sense of community, not just out in the desert, but also back in Los Angeles, where people lived. As Moontribe veterans note,

> It pretty much created a community, a network, or group of networks of people.[13]

> It was very spiritually important to people. People came out and the energy they took back into the city from the events would keep them going. Friendly people, acceptance. . . . Within the Full Moon Gathering, definitely there's smaller groups of friends and everything, there's probably maybe twenty, thirty of my closer friends that are sort of our community. We hang out a lot, spend a lot of time together. But certainly the Full Moon Gathering became a place where people could go and have a sense of community, which I think is sorely missing in Western capitalistic society in general and particularly in a place like L.A., where it's absolutely almost a void. I mean, I barely even talk to my neighbors here. And get a sense of belonging. The community's the big thing, people you can turn to for help. There's definitely people who look to the community to help them with finding places to live, work.

I certainly don't think I'd be as successful doing what I do . . . without this network of people. It's largely due to the fact that these are all good people.[14]

However, as the Full Moon Gatherings grew in size, they also experienced growing pains:

We had gotten to this size at our three-year anniversary where it was just like three or four thousand people or something crazy like that. And it was really starting to get a little out of control. And we didn't have any security. And we all recognized it was just a matter of time before someone gets hurt. Someone's going to drive home and get into an accident, or something bad was going to happen. And so we talked about it and we basically decided to take it farther underground. There would only be a handful of directions that would go out and you would have to caravan with somebody and follow them to get to the party, which greatly reduced the size back down to maybe a couple hundred people. We got a lot of flak about that in the larger southern California scene down here. But I mean, the party, we had basically lost control. Kids were showing up on amphetamines, doing nitrous, all this kind of stuff that we really weren't about, all this negative sort of gross stuff. So we were just like, "well, we're not going to lose this" and we took it more underground.[15]

Some of these concerns turned out to be prescient:

The Moontribe had a really huge trauma when a kid died about four years ago now. And it's a mystery exactly how he died, what happened, whether he was high on something or not, or tripped and fell, or jumped. But that was a big turning point and sort of a moment of people really having to start looking at what they were doing in a little bit more serious way. Then the Moontribe went on a more infrequent schedule after that, instead of every month regularly, which had been completely like clockwork, no matter rain, shine. They missed only one full moon out of seven of eight years up to that point. And then they kind of broke down to doing it every three months. But they've been through waves where it would get really large for a while and really chaotic, and then they'd have to shrink it down and get really exclusive and elitist in how they organized, and have the directions and the caravans. And it's gone through a few cycles of that kind of expansion, contraction, expansion, contraction.[16]

Despite accusations of elitism, however, the end result of these contractions is that Moontribe has been able to continue with its core identity and "vibe" intact. "We survived," notes one member,

> And we just had our ten-year anniversary this summer. And I don't think we would have survived nearly that long if we hadn't done that, not even close. . . . It still does have that vibe today.[17]

A similar process has taken place over the years with Moontribe's organizational structure as well:

> There was always a core collective, sort of loose around the fringes, but with about a dozen central people that were pretty much always involved to one degree or another. And then of course, there'd be lots of huge rows and soap opera dramas, and people would break off of it and it would reform. But there's always been that sort of a core collective. And sometimes it's been very precisely defined. And other times, it's been loose. And then there was a point where actually, after Pablo died, they tried to have the council, which was the inner, inner core, and then a collective, which was people that were into generally helping out, volunteering and doing whatever needed to be done. Then there was the so-called community. And they were going to try to have regular community meetings, where the broader community could give input to the decisions of the council. And they did that for a while, but it kind of petered out.[18]

In this regard, Moontribe is an interesting example of a rave community because of its longevity, having now been in existence for over twelve years. Moontribe folks have had an opportunity to form lasting bonds over that time and grow up and go through various life changes together:

> A lot of the people that go I would say are in their thirties now, as opposed to their twenties, which was ten years ago, obviously. Everyone's got jobs, kids. . . . I've made lifetime friendships that have come from this event and we're still involved. Maybe we're not hanging out dancing in the desert [every full moon] anymore but we're having dinner parties or going to our friends' daughter's three-year-old birthday. It's looking very unexciting and unadventuresome but those bonds were definitely formed in that time. . . . It really changes the way you look at things and gives you hope about people. So there's a bunch of people that, they basically met, and they're married and have kids now and are

very happy, and they all met out there boogying on the dance floor. I mean, that's why we're all still friends, it was such a bonding experience that it's still there.[19]

And, interestingly, the tribe's ten-year anniversary party was such a great event that the Full Moon Gatherings seem to be going through a bit of a renewal, which seems to indicate that Moontribe may well continue to be a model of longevity for rave communities into the future:

> That's probably the best event I've been to in three or four years. . . . The party itself was just wonderful. Lots of happy smiling people . . . just a really nice special time. So yeah, I think it [the vibe] really has been preserved. . . . There's been a little bit of momentum, I think, from that ten-year event because it was such a good party. I know this past month, they had a really good one and I think they're talking about throwing another one.[20]

The Oracle

While Moontribe is an example of longevity in a rave community, the Oracle in Seattle is an example of how a newly formed rave community can make a big impact in a short time. The three founders of the Oracle had already had extensive experience in two of Seattle's more popular and influential rave crews in the late 1990s—Seelie Court and Starseed—and were drawn to join forces to create something new together. A generous contribution from a donor/investor enabled them to focus full time on developing their vision for a number of months:

> So we got to quit our jobs and, for four months, just focus on how we were going to create an intentional, consistent lifelong process together. And we set a commitment together and decided to go as deep as we possibly could.[21]

This process generated the inspiration to create a tarot deck that would be the basis of a series of gatherings:

> It led to this new model, which was . . . to set in motion a series that always changed its theme but that was mysterious. You knew what the possibilities were but you didn't know what the exact outcome was going to be. . . . How could we do this where we're really capturing an energy and focusing it in a way to step up the level of inspiration each time we

do it? And we came up with the Oracle Gatherings, and each of the twenty-three archetypes were born in a two-day period.[22]

As I've described earlier in chapter 4, each event is based on an archetype represented by an Oracle card drawn at the closing ceremony of the previous event. This archetype is creatively expressed not only in the decorations, but also especially in the distinctive midnight ritual theater performance. The sequence of events, the Oracle's website tells us, is usually as follows:

> The evening is opened with a ceremony, yoga, and meditation, as well as special workshops such as contact dance, butoh, etc. Musicians then begin with up to two rooms of up-tempo and down-tempo music. At the peak of the night, we offer the Oracle Ritual based on the archetype of the event, which usually lasts from twenty to forty minutes. Musicians in both rooms continue throughout the night with other community performances until the closing ceremony."[23]

The first Oracle Gathering was held in June 2001 and was attended by several hundred people. Although there was some initial resistance to the tarot-based archetypes and ritual theater performances, this resistance faded as the Oracle found its audience, and attendance has more than doubled in the ensuing three years. In that time, the Oracle has become a well-established and influential rave event and community in Seattle and the larger Northwest region. In addition to all-night events in the city, the Oracle has also held weekend-long campout events in more remote locations, and these have featured a full slate of workshops and forums throughout the day.

I have already related the story of how, at one of these campout events named for the Mystery School archetype, a member of the Rocky Mountain Mystery School made contact with the Oracle founders and this encounter subsequently led to their close involvement with the school. Here is a bit more about the nature of this involvement:

> We had met with a few other groups that called themselves mystery schools as well that have a very long tradition, and our points of contact have always wanted this kind of fusion between the mystery school and what we were doing, but when we went to this one, that was not in the question. There was no fusion. It was, *This is a unique process.* And they just said, "We would like to supply an ancient foundation for you guys to

build this new system." That this is a unique, separate, and new system that needed to come out. And that's when we knew we were in the right place. . . . What the mystery school we're attending now actually teaches is that all the information is available to every person by themselves. No one needs to go outside themselves to discover anything. You just have to get yourself out of the way of the knowledge. And that's what this process has been for us.[24]

What was really interesting is when we went to the mystery school in August, we brought representations of the Oracle, like our promotional pack, and described it to one of the teachers there, even our seal. And he took it and matched it to their lineage of information and realized they're very, very similar. And our seal actually works with Enochian magic—it's very aligned. And so what we're finding right now, in studying with the mystery school, is so much of what we've already done is totally aligned. And the mystery school is teaching us more about discipline and focus, and how to bring the magic in at an even deeper level. . . . We're going to be helping to create a new program for the mystery school in June and they're going to create a school that's centered around learning how to tune in and express through different forms of art like dance and music and performance, etcetera.[25]

This involvement with the Rocky Mountain Mystery School has now extended well beyond the Oracle's founders into their larger community in the form of ongoing classes, workshops, practices, and ceremonies in Seattle, and it is clear that this work has had a powerful impact in everyone's lives. So, much in the same way that the Quakers' Society of Friends serves as a model for the Rhythm Society, the mystery school serves as a model for the Oracle community.

This model applies to the organizational aspect of the community as well and, as one might expect with a mystery school, it is not a model that is based on consensus. The idea is,

Organize a group of people that's small enough to maintain focus but not big enough to disperse that focus or imbalance the process. And then organize a group outside of that. So, if any of this group out here we lose or have differences with or they have differences with each other, as long as we keep this nucleus focused, it should vibrate out and rectify issues, which has been really successful so far.[26]

We have a table, called the Oracle Round Table, of leaders that come together and talk about how the Oracle needs to grow. But, what happens is all this information comes and the three of us solidify it, take it in, and make decisions. And we're finding, when we had other production companies and it was an open consensus scenario, it worked for a while, but certain things just never quite got done or decided, really. There's a lot of decisions that were never quite made. So we found with this particular scenario that this system works for us.[27]

Interestingly, within the framework of this kind of clearly delineated power structure, community members are strongly encouraged to empower themselves and take an active part in shaping the direction of the Oracle:

One thing I've been finding that I really appreciate about dance culture is, when somebody comes, the process from moving from the side of the wall to the dance floor is almost like a stepping up, a showing up for yourself. So you move to the dance floor, there's a safety of a lot of dancers dancing on their own or with each other there, but it's almost like a development in finding yourself, breaking down by releasing through dance, and moving into a leadership position and showing up. Because, ultimately, we need leaders right now. And everybody is a piece of the puzzle. And so our intention with the Oracle is to create a foundation or space for people to come in and step into the dance floor, show up for themselves, do the transformational work that they need to do, go through the letting go process that they need to, and ultimately find a piece that they see that the Oracle maybe isn't tapping into in any part of their life, and take a leadership position to help move the culture forward. . . . It's helping people discover what their personal power is and what their personal calling is. Because everyone's got a personal vision and the key is discovering how the visions match up together and how they support each other.[28]

As with other rave communities, members of the Oracle community also live together in group households, spend a lot of time with each other in various contexts, and actively participate in an online community forum.

Tribal Harmonix

While the Oracle was becoming an influential rave community in the Seattle area, Tribal Harmonix was doing the same thing north of the border in the Vancouver area and the Sunshine Coast of British Columbia. However, their evolution was more gradual and organic, arising out of community processes already in motion:

Mind Body Love [a peer-based harm-reduction project] went into the party scene and provided knowledge about safer use of drugs and safer sex practices and just provided a grounding point in the gatherings where people could get support. The notion behind this became so apparently needed and so nourishing that very quickly it accumulated its own community. And I found myself living with a household of people in this context of, "We're creating community now. This is what we're doing. We're attracting this community and setting that intention." This began to precipitate into other realms where we were, like, "okay, now we discover that we have something beyond just partying that holds us together. How else can we create relationships so that we have more things we can do together?"

And from that began a potluck series where people would rotate around and friends of friends would get to know each other as we were spreading ourselves into each other's homes and sharing space with each [other] in more intimate settings. Another thing we did was create something called Sunday School, where we took Sundays as a time to gather and school each other in different things that we were interested in or that we had learned about or wanted to investigate. And out of that came dance projects, where we created dance ritual together. We investigated Timothy Leary's eight-circuit model. We explored communication and emotions, our relationships, all kinds of things that just built community.

And all of the sudden, it came through at Earthdance, that we're onto something really powerful, all of our solstices and equinoxes are generating this intentional atmosphere where people are coming out to connect with something more ancient and recognizing that in the modern-day context and putting things towards causes that can help benefit today. And a few of us involved in the Earthdance organizing began to imagine what it would be to create an ongoing organizational form that helps generate more of this kind of community building, helps to become more of service in the larger context than just for ourselves. And this is where Tribal Harmonix was conceived. . . .[29]

In addition to Earthdance, there were other outside influences that helped shape Tribal Harmonix as well:

[In 1996] several people from the Vancouver area that were doing underground-related events traveled to Burning Man for the first year that they'd been. And when they came back, they started to bring a very artistic level into their events that was also inspirational. That's roughly around the time that the harm reduction stuff started taking off in response to a lot of need for it. . . . And the response was creating slightly more intentional events, where people got to feel more nurtured and feel more a sense of family.

The second year we went down to the Gathering of the Tribes, there were twenty of us, up from four the first year. And in our own community, we had gone through a process of fundraising to get to Gathering of the Tribes that brought us together as a collective, as we had to work together to fundraise our way. And the traveling experience was like a rite of passage where we took our community on the road and introduced it to other communities, and received feedback on our own community that we have something that's special. And we came back with the information that we learned. And so we began entering into this whole other way of acting as a community.[30]

The group has articulated its vision for this way of actingon its website:

Tribal Harmonix is an umbrella organization that promotes the growth of sustainable community and tribal culture through dance, music, celebration, creative expression, and education. Our mandate is to encourage new ways of thinking by supporting gatherings, workshops, and special events that raise consciousness of environmental, social, political, spiritual, and youth issues.[31]

I have already described my experience at Intention, Tribal Harmonix's annual New Year's retreat held over five days on the Sunshine Coast, but here I include a veteran Northwest raver's description:

The thing that makes those gatherings special is they're really not just parties. They're really more about workshops and sharing and learning and that goes on for many days and then there's a party at the end for New Year's. . . . It's all these workshops and all this learning that went on that was really memorable and powerful and empowering and awesome. I think Tribal Harmonix, they do it the best of anything I've seen. . . .

The Tribal Harmonix crew, those people are completely open. Their doors are all open. They pretty much are all living their lives actively in the mission of the path. They're very integrated with each other. So they're really working on community building and increasing the collective energy. It's a very collective level. They've really moved beyond the individual. Up there it's like the tribe comes together. We're not bringing all these individual elements—it's the tribe. Those gatherings, you'll totally see somebody sitting in the middle of the dance floor doing yoga all night. There's massage sessions on the side, Reiki healing going on here and there. It's almost completely in excess, the spiritual practices that are going on around there. It's like they've really taken the cork off the bottle and the genie's completely out, so you get your complete fill with people being in spirit at those kinds of things.[32]

The model for this community is clearly tribal in nature and the spiritual orientation is very earth-based. In this regard, they also reflect classic concerns of alternative culture in the Pacific Northwest—environmentalism, sustainability, permaculture, and bioregionalism. Like other rave communities, many Tribal Harmonix folks also live together in group households, both in the Vancouver and Sunshine Coast areas, spend a lot of time together in various contexts, and actively participate in an online community forum.

Earthdance

The vision for Earthdance began in 1996, when Chris Deckker, a member of the electronic tribal trance band Medicine Drum had the idea to synchronize dance floors at raves throughout the world in a global meditation for peace that would also raise money to benefit Tibetan causes. At the Dalai Lama's suggestion, the scope of these causes was expanded beyond Tibet to include charities that benefit children, indigenous peoples, international relief and development, the environment, and peace, and, through 2003, Earthdance events have raised a cumulative total of more than one million dollars. According to the Earthdance website:

> What began in 1997, with 22 cities in 18 countries has now expanded to over 130 cities in 50 countries. Rising out of the global electronic music scene, Earthdance has now grown to include a diverse cross-section of musical genres including world music, jazz, conscious hip-hop, folk and reggae.
>
> Earthdance has shown how the potent combination of music, dance and technology can be harnessed for positive and humanitarian aims. For one night all around the globe, people join together to dance as one global community, united with a common vision for peace and humanitarian aims.[33]

Some of the participating cities in 2004 included Vancouver, Los Angeles, San Diego, Calgary, Albuquerque, Colorado Springs, Madison, Chicago, Detroit, Ann Arbor, Pittsburgh, Asheville (NC), Sarasota, Miami, Toronto, Ottowa, New York, Mexico City, Rio de Janeiro, Buenos Aires, Santiago, Johannesburg, Capetown, London, Manchester, Amsterdam, Cologne, Vienna, Budapest, Sarajevo, Madras, Delhi, Beijing, Sydney, Melbourne, and several cities in Japan. Each city has its own sequence of activities and musical lineup, but they all unite at a prearranged time for the synchronized global meditation for peace.

I was in the Pacific Northwest at this time, so I attended the Vancouver satellite version put on by Tribal Harmonix at a beautiful beachfront location in Stanley Park, and it was a fantastic event. At 4:00 P.M., a couple hundred people joined hands and formed a large circle for the global meditation. This prayer circle was amazing in and of itself, but it was made more powerful by the knowledge that we were connected to thousands of people across the planet doing exactly the same thing. Live drumming followed and then DJs spun electronic dance music as the dance floor went off with high energy and a palpably great vibe. The central hub event, held on the Hog Farm's land in Laytonville, California, was attended by thousands of people, and featured several stages of music and performance, along with an area for activist and nonprofit organizations, a speakers forum organized by Gathering of the Tribes, a children's area, and a film festival. The success of Earthdance demonstrates that global rave culture is more than just a theoretical construct, and is truly an interconnected planetary network that can be mobilized as a force for good in the world.

Gathering of the Tribes

While Earthdance has done a lot to facilitate the planetary network of global rave culture, Gathering of the Tribes (GoTT) has focused more on linking up different rave communities on the West Coast of the United States and Canada. The inspiration for GoTT came from tours undertaken by Moontribe in which they discovered a number of sister rave communities and felt it was important to link them all up:

> Gathering of the Tribes had the idea of getting together all these tribes up and down the West Coast for gatherings to put all our heads together and see ourselves as a unified whole and work parallel themes. They've been doing a couple of gatherings a year.[34]

Here is GoTT's mission statement and self-description:

> Gathering of the Tribes unites and supports dance music collectives and others in support of the dance movement by cultivating networks and promoting activism, education, sustainability, and the art and culture of the dance music underground.
>
> The Gathering of the Tribes is an annual conference and festival uniting artists' collectives from across North America and Europe. Founded in 1999, Gathering of the Tribes (GoTT) began as a networking and unity building resource for organizers and artists within the electronic dance music culture. Five years later, GoTT has emerged as a meeting ground for artists, activists, organizers and visionaries from across the progressive spectrum. Using a unique blend of interactive workshops, visual art displays and live performance, Gathering of the Tribes provides participants with a space for dialogue and expression, and the information and resources necessary for building progressive change.[35]

In 2004, GoTT decided to go beyond their annual conference and festival and work within the context of larger intertribal gatherings attended by different rave communities. One big project was to organize the speakers forum at Earthdance's central hub event in northern California. In addition, they also organized a forum at Burning Man, which I was fortunate to be able to attend, along with members of False Profit, Moontribe, the Oracle, Rhythm Society, Tribal Harmonix, and other rave communities. It provided a great opportunity for rave communities not only to feel they are part of a larger network and vision, but also to make connections, learn from each other's experience, and perhaps even to collaborate on future projects. Similar endeavors have been undertaken by other rave groups, such as the Storm Sessions, organized by the Cloud Factory Collective in Oakland the last three years, which feature workshops and forums that bring together a number of rave communities from up and down the West Coast.

In general, there has been a notable increase in this type of larger networking activity in the last several years, perhaps indicating that rave communities have moved into a new developmental phase, a significant point acknowledged by a number of ravers:

> A new model is emerging. And a lot of new models are emerging out of that. You go to a different place and you can see, wow, that's happening

too, but it's totally different, you know, how they organize themselves and everything. Before, it was like raves had a formula to it, you have these speakers, you put these flyers up and you have a party, but now, it's mutating in such a way that it's actually a group of people that are dynamically creating how the container emerges and what it looks like. And we're only into the phase now where those containers are at a velocity where a community can move. When it starts moving and interacting with other communities and those inspirations cause other inspirations, you'll start seeing a lot more stuff happening.[36]

There are people in this community that are doing it, in other communities that are doing it, and everyone is doing it in a slightly different way but with the same goal in mind and that is having a positive impact on the self and the world, starting with the self, the self-loving and the self-awareness and the self-actualization and the consciousness. And then applying that and creating a support network of people that are all working toward creating a better world, and stepping outside of the paradigms that we are looking at now that are not working, and creating something different. It's a different movement, but I think the movement of the '60s was a similar revolution. It's happening much more quietly here, but I see it happening. How things are going is not working, so let's be exploring the different ways that we can be creating goodness in the world and beauty and love and compassion and tolerance and unity.[37]

CONCLUSION: RAVE NEW WORLD

It is early October 2004 as I write the conclusion to this book. I have just spent my Saturday at the inaugural San Francisco Love Parade, a satellite version of the original Berlin event that local organizers have brought to San Francisco in the hopes of starting an annual tradition in the United States. Beginning at 2:00 P.M., a succession of thirty "floats," each with its own high-quality sound system blasting electronic dance music and accompanied by an entourage of colorful dancers, wound its way south along the Embarcadero and past SBC Park (home of the San Francsico Giants), eventually ending in a one-square-block area just south of the stadium. Here, each sound system continued to play music to an enormous crowd of enthusiastic dancers until 9:00 P.M., after which everyone dispersed to a large number of "after-parties" throughout the city that continued on into the morning. It was a fantastic event that had a great "vibe" and was very well attended. *San Francisco Examiner* columnist P. J. Corkery seemed to "get" the vibe in writing the following description and, in reading his account, it is important to keep in mind that he is a mainstream journalist, not a raver or an alternative culture aficionado:

> On Saturday, the Love Parade, a magical pavement-burning street dance that originated in Berlin, stepped off in the Embarcadero. About 15,000 passed by, all dancing to electronic music played by DJs on floats. . . . It was less a march than it was a pulsing mile-long membrane full of bouncing molecules thumping and sliding down the Embarcadero. Watchers

on the sidewalks were absorbed into the being. Haven't seen anything like it since the Summer of Love [in San Francisco in 1967]. A be-in gone bio-molecular. So new, so spontaneous, and so San Francisco.[1]

It has been more than seventeen years since the rave scene first burst into public view in the Summer of Love in England in 1988, and the continuing emergence of magical new rave events like the San Francisco Love Parade proves that, despite the occasional pronouncements by naysayers that "the rave scene is dead," it is actually very much alive and thriving. In fact, in the eight years since I conducted my initial research on the rave scene, rave culture has matured and evolved and produced a number of significant new developments, including this new incarnation of the Love Parade and several others that I have examined in this study. For example, Earthdance, Gathering of the Tribes, the Oracle, the Rhythm Society, the Storm Sessions, the Street Parade, and Tribal Harmonix have all come into existence and had a strong impact during this time. The Moontribe celebrated its twelve-year anniversary, and has gone through both a near death and a rebirth during this time. Burning Man has increased dramatically in attendance, from fewer than twenty thousand people to more than thirty thousand, and has become much more widely known in mainstream culture during this time. The Street Parade has grown exponentially in size to one million attendees during this time. Less spectacular, but perhaps more important, there has been a marked increase in the number of raves that incorporate opening and closing ceremonies, altars, spiritual themes and practices, and workshops and educational forums during this time.

In looking at all of these developments, what stands out for me is not so much the quantitative growth, but rather, the qualitative growth of the rave scene. Using statistics, one could make a strong case either way as to whether the rave scene is getting bigger or smaller. However, based on the new research I conducted for this book, there is no doubt whatsoever that the rave scene, particularly the "intentional" rave scene, is one of the most fertile breeding grounds for cutting-edge explorations in spirituality and community. Taken together as a whole, these phenomena suggest that rave culture is growing out of its infancy and beginning to enter a new developmental stage. And even though members of mainstream society may view ravers as "freaks" and the rave scene as a "fringe" group—entertaining, perhaps, but ultimately irrelevant to their concerns—paradoxically,

I believe this new developmental stage of rave culture is actually pointing the way toward the new forms of religion and spirituality best suited for the complexities of life in the twenty-first century.

We have all seen the devastating effects of religious divisions for thousands of years, and hatred, violence, and war continue to rage unchecked across the planet in this new millennium. Everyone yearns for a connection with the sacred, but many of the religious institutions that are supposed to provide us with that connection do so in such a way that perpetuates the divisions that are at the root of these crises. So how do we connect with the sacred in a way that unites us rather than divides us? How do we connect with the sacred in a way that allows each of us to follow our own distinctive spiritual path and still find a sense of fellowship and community with others whose path may be different? How do we connect with the sacred in such a way that elements from all the diverse resources available to us in this postmodern global world—a hodgepodge of religious and spiritual traditions, artistic expressions, popular culture, advanced technology, planetary communication networks, and so forth—can be combined together into an integrated whole that has depth, power, elegance, and longevity? While no one individual or group or approach can provide definitive answers to these large and important questions, I do see that rave culture is out on the front lines exploring this new territory with energy and passion and vision—and not just in a theoretical sense, but by actually creating experimental new forms and putting them into practice and seeing how they work. To put it simply, global rave culture is a significant new spiritual and religious phenomenon, both in and of itself, and as a template for the complex dynamics of other new spiritual and religious phenomena in the twenty-first century. In this conclusion, I would like to highlight several important themes that have emerged in the course of this study.

The first and most important point I would like to make is simply to acknowledge the tremendous power of electronic dance music (in a rave context) to trigger profound, life-changing religious experiences. In the course of my interviews, I was truly amazed at the testimonies of ravers describing these deep experiential states and their deep spiritual implications. In the modern secular Western world where such experiences rarely occur even within the framework of traditional religions, these testimonies clearly point to a significant religious phenomenon, one that thousands of people are participating in on a regular basis. Although there is an almost universal connection between music and religion, most of us tend to think of this connection in terms of sacred music in a formal religious context—church choirs, Jewish cantors, Hindu kirtans, Buddhist chanting, and so forth. But in rave culture we see an example of an entirely new form of music emerging in a seemingly nonreligious context that, through the sheer power of the experiential states it triggers, leads people inexorably into the realm of spirituality and religion. In this regard, it is also an example that seems to confirm the 'history of religions' notion that the human encounter with the numinous, the religious experience, is primary and serves as the foundation for subsequent developments that lead to the organized external forms that we call religion. It is also an example of one of the key features of new spiritual and religious phenomenon emerging in the twenty-first century that I have noted in the introduction: Because of the intensity of transmission, experience has become more important than content.

Second, rave culture is an exceptional example of the lofty ideal of "unity in diversity" being put into practice, both on the dance floor at raves and in rave culture in general. Time and again, ravers spoke of how the powerful peak experience on the dance floor broke down traditional boundaries of race, class, ethnicity, nationality, religion, age, gender, sexual orientation, and so forth, bringing everyone together in an ecstatic unity that transcended these differences. This is especially significant in terms of spirituality and religion, because it demonstrates that even this historically difficult Pandora's box of divisions can be transcended. This revelatory experience has given ravers a precious taste of unity in diversity actually manifested in the real world, and has provided the impetus to try to figure out how to implement it in a more practical, ongoing way. Some of the intentional rave communities I have examined in this study are compelling examples of this process, providing a context for people of different backgrounds and orientations to come together in unity in their daily lives outside of the dance floor and the rave. In many cases, there is also a strong, conscious spiritual component to these community functions, and again, one that transcends religious differences. Beyond these communities are the larger networks that have been forged throughout the West Coast, the United States as a whole, and the entire world, and these are also compelling examples of transcending traditional divisions in a larger unity. In particular, the global nature of rave culture demonstrates that geographic, ethnic, and nationalistic divisions can be transcended, and this is no small feat! Of course, I don't wish to naively romanticize or idealize rave culture, as it is clearly a primarily white, upper-middle-class, Western youth phenomenon. Nevertheless, this critique in no way diminishes the significance of the real accomplishments that have been achieved by rave culture in showing how a new spiritual and religious phenomenon can unite people so powerfully that historically crippling divisions are easily overcome.

Third, in conducting new research for this book, I was struck by how the intentional rave communities have truly matured and evolved and grown into the next developmental stage. They have created forms that allow ravers to integrate the rave experience into the context of their daily lives; they have created forms that allow ravers to experience an ongoing sense of community and spiritual fellowship; they have created organizational forms that are more substantial and long lasting, and that can be integrated more easily and harmoniously into mainstream society; they have created forms that bring these communities together in larger networks to strengthen connections, pool information and resources, benefit worthwhile causes, and have a positive impact in the real world in a variety of ways. Here again, I don't wish to naively romanticize or idealize rave culture; many rave communities are superficial, flaky, and unreliable, rife with debilitating soap-opera melodramas, bogged down in inefficient and ineffective group structures and processes, and lacking a "bigger vision." However, I have been very favorably impressed by the communities I examined in this study and feel they serve as exemplary models for growth and development that is intelligent and grounded, and has depth and integrity. In the course of the time I have spent with them, they have filled me with hope and optimism for the future evolution of rave culture and its ability to be a positive influence on mainstream society by demonstrating the viability of peaceful, loving, spiritually oriented alternative communities.

Finally, I have also been struck by the way the intentional rave scene has increasingly focused on the spiritual and ceremonial aspects of what it does, the increasing awareness and acknowledgment that raves and rave culture are a legitimate source of spirituality and a new form of religion, and the continuing efforts to push the cutting edge of exploration and evolution forward in this area. As I have noted, there has been a marked increase in the number of raves that incorporate opening and closing ceremonies, altars, spiritual themes and practices, and workshops.

All of the intentional communities in this study have an underlying spiritual orientation, and most have some kind of mission statement explicitly recognizing the spiritual and religious nature of their work. Virtually every one of the ravers I interviewed not only acknowledged the spiritual and religious significance of raves and rave culture in their lives, but also were extremely eloquent in articulating both the specific details and the larger framework. Many ravers have used the spiritual breakthrough they have experienced in raves as a stimulus to explore more traditional forms of spirituality and religion. Many ravers are also conducting experiments in working with the sacred energies generated through trance dancing to electronic music by exploring more structured forms in which to focus and direct those energies. In some cases, this involves taking components from traditional ceremonial, spiritual, and religious practices, and using them in a rave-influenced context.

In light of this increasing awareness and acknowledgment of raves and rave culture as a legitimate source of spirituality and a new form of religion, I will end with an excerpt from an essay by raver Gregory Sams, "Dance Culture—A New Church," that expresses this understanding:

> Every weekend . . . half a million or more people gather in places of worship and joyfully celebrate their humanity and love for one another. . . .
> The church I am speaking about has no central organization and no published doctrine. There is no one to worship in this church but God in whatever form the churchgoers perceive the universal concept. This new church takes many forms, and gatherings can be located in empty warehouses, purpose-built venues, open fields, on the beach or wherever circumstances lead. . . .
> The church goes by many names and here I will simply call it the New Party. I do this because the new devotees often refer to "going to a party" when they are planning their worship, though nothing in the history of partying has ever been the same. The celebration is of life, love, and harmonies. . . . Indeed, through these parties, today's generation is re-inventing the community, a valuable social tool that has become an increasingly endangered tradition over the last few decades.
> Central to the new church is the new music, techno. . . . It is essential to the ritual of the dance and the nature of the party that it supports. It is pure music that works with rhythms and beats, made by musicians who work with computers as well as instruments, sampled sounds, and dedicated new technology. . . . It is music to take your mind where you like, with an absence of complex lyrics or story lines. It is music to dance

through the night with. . . . The closest thing to the preacher . . . is today's DJ, who draws people to a party because of his or her skill at getting the music right—being the vibrant pulse of the party, moving with it and being moved by it. . . . Dance is the ritual—a celebratory and traditional form of worship. . . .

As with some religions, there is a sacrament often taken at these parties, in the form of specific drugs—substances the same as or very like those taken at some of the earliest religious ceremonies recorded from different faiths. . . . Many celebrants will take no drugs at all and just partake of the spirit that is tangibly present. . . . It is a church of personal enlightenment and revelations that are shared and compared. . . . And it is first-hand experience. . . . Participants . . . see God in every aspect of creation . . . and particularly in their fellow human beings. . . .

The new church, party, call it what you like, is evolution happening—meeting the needs of our society and filling some of the gaps that the old generation traditionally complain about. It has happened quietly enough on the fringes of society and without the benefit of PR companies or listings in events guides. The church has managed to grow large with a low profile. It is a church that takes great joy in the wondrousness of being—of life itself. . . . It would seem appropriate that, at a time when the planet itself is threatened, a community should develop that is able to glimpse and thereby respect the glory of the universal spirit in everything it infuses.[2]

APPENDIX: THE INTERVIEWEES

2003

James Frazier was born in 1974 and lives in Whidbey Island, Washington, with his wife Rainie Sunshine and their two children. He is a DJ, an organizer of special events, a permaculturist, and the cofounder and manager of a small investment management company. The interview was conducted in a hotel room in Aptos, California.

Kevin Gervais was born in 1981 and lives in Portland, Oregon. He works as an emergency communications operator for the City of Portland and is also in a Ph.D. program in urban studies at Portland State University. The interview was conducted in a coffeehouse in Portland.

Isis Indriya was born in Guam in 1978, where she lived until moving to Seattle in 1996, where she currently resides with her husband, Osiris. She is one of the cofounders and core leaders of Seelie Court, a Seattle-based rave production crew. She is also one of the cofounders and core leaders of the Oracle gatherings in Seattle, as well as a performer, teacher, and clothing designer. The interview was conducted at her home in Seattle.

Osiris Indriya was born David James Kaiser in 1978 in Bellevue, Washington, and currently lives in Seattle with his wife, Isis. He is one of the cofounders and core leaders of the Oracle gatherings in Seattle. He is also the director of the Theurgy Foundation, a nonprofit organization that promotes conscious creation and healthful living through projects like Living Paradise, a living foods restaurant and center in Seattle. Osiris is a graphic and web designer, as well as a musician, producer, composer, and DJ. The interview was conducted at his home in Seattle.

Jason Keehn, a.k.a. Cinnamon Twist, was born in 1961 and lives in Los Angeles, California, where he designs and runs biotech conferences for Infocast. An influential thinker in West Coast rave culture, he is the author of several books, including *Children of the Moon*, *Guerillas of Harmony*, and *Totally Toroidal: Adventures in the Higher Meaning of Donuts*. He has also produced many dance events, including the Learning Parties 1–13, ShivaShakti, and Tribal Donut. The interview was conducted at a café in Santa Monica, California.

John Kelley was born and raised in Los Angeles, where he continues to reside. Now in his early thirties, he became a primary DJ for the Moontribe in 1993 and a core member soon thereafter. He has gone on to attain great success as a DJ, with the release of numerous mixed CDs and both national and international tours to his credit. He is also the cofounder of Ball of Waxx, an electronic music production group. The interview was conducted at his home in Los Angeles.

Michael Manahan was born in 1966 and lives in Seattle with his wife and son. He was one of the cofounders and core leaders of Starseed, a now defunct Seattle-based rave production crew. He is currently one of the cofounders and core leaders of the Oracle gatherings in Seattle. He is also a DJ, composer, producer, and musician, and runs Starborne Soundsystem. The interviews were conducted at a house in Seattle and in a café in San Francisco.

Manoj Mathew was born in 1968 and lives in Portland, Oregon, where he has been a key force in the Portland area rave scene as a promoter and a DJ for over thirteen years. Some of the events and crews he has been involved with include the Ahau Collective, Circle of Friends, Jedi Knights, One Love, One Tribe, the Tribe, and Uplift. The interview was conducted at a café in Portland.

Shams Samuel Shirley was born in 1961 and lives in Oakland, California, with his two daughters. He is a graphic artist and web designer. He is also a Raphaelite healer in the Sufi Healing Order, a shamanic ceremonialist, and a Shotokan karate blackbelt and instructor. The interview was conducted at his home.

Natasha Singer was born in Minneapolis, Minnesota, in 1964, where she was raised on a steady diet of old funk, soul, and disco records. A resident of San Francisco for many years, she works as a writer in a Silicon Valley startup company. She is also a DJ who is building a business that leverages good beats for the greater social good. The interview was conducted at her home.

Rainie Sunshine was born in 1978 and lives in south Whidbey Island with her husband, James Frazier, and their two children. The interview was conducted at a hotel in Aptos, California.

Shannon Titus lives in Oakland, California, and works as a high-tech marketing executive. Now in her late thirties, she is also a DJ who spins at various underground events. The interview was conducted at her home.

Sobey Wing was born in 1972 and lives in Gibsons, on the Sunshine Coast of British Columbia. He is a cofounder and core leader of Tribal Harmonix and an organizer of Earthdance Vancouver. He has been involved in various projects in ecoeducation, youth empowerment through the arts, positive playgrounds, and harm reduction, and works at Urban Shaman in Vancouver, British Columbia. The interview was conducted at a home in Vancouver.

1997

Bahar Badizadegan was born and raised in Iran, spent her adolescence in Los Angeles, lived in the San Francisco Bay Area for a number of years, and currently resides in New York City. She is in her twenties and works for a record store. She has been involved with various electronic music genres for several years. The interview was conducted at a coffeehouse in San Francisco.

Joel Dinolt was born and raised in Detroit and now lives in San Francisco. He is in his twenties, is a guitarist in a band, and has been involved with the rave scene for eleven years. The interview was conducted at a coffeehouse in San Francisco.

Jim Dunn was born in 1970, raised in a small town in Indiana, and now lives in San Francisco. He has been involved with the rave scene for nine years and has been a DJ for many rave events. The interview was conducted in Golden Gate Park in San Francisco.

Charlotte Kaufman was born and raised in Chicago and now lives in San Francisco. She was exposed to house music as a teenager and has been involved with the electronic dance music world ever since. Now in her thirties, she is a respected DJ known as the Baroness who spins at numerous raves and clubs and has released two CDs. The interview was conducted at a coffeehouse in San Francisco.

Gus Lanzas was born and raised in Nicaragua, moved to the the San Francisco Bay Area in 1982, and currently lives in San Francisco. He is in his twenties and has been involved with the rave scene for twelve years. He works in multimedia technology and composes electronic dance music. The interview was conducted at a coffeehouse in San Francisco.

Chris Lum grew up in southern California and moved to San Francisco in 1993. He is twenty-nine years old and works at a record store. He went to his first rave in 1990 and has been involved in the rave scene since then, as both a participant and a DJ. The interview was conducted at a restaurant in San Francisco.

Alaura O'Dell was born and raised in London and, as a member of the band Psychic TV, was strongly involved with the original British acid house and rave scenes in the mid-1980s. Now in her thirties, she resides in Occidental, California, and has her own business conducting travel tours with a spiritual and geomantic orientation. The interview took place in her home.

Sabrina Page was born and raised in New Jersey and now lives in Fairfax, California. Born in 1948, she has been involved with various dance communities for over ten years and is a DJ who spins twice a week in San Rafael, California. The interview was conducted at her home.

James Romero was raised in various locations in California and has lived in the San Francisco Bay Area for eight years. Now in his forties, he became involved with the rave scene since moving to San Francisco and is himself a DJ. The interview was conducted in his home.

Tiffany Scott was born and raised in Los Angeles and has lived in San Francisco since 1994. Now in her twenties, she was involved with the rave scene in Los Angeles since its early days in the late 1980s and has continued her involvement in San Francisco. She is a graduate student who also works for XLR8R, an electronic dance music magazine. The interview took place in a coffeehouse in San Francisco.

Jeff Taylor was born and raised in the San Francisco Bay Area and lives in San Francisco. Now in his twenties, he has been involved with the rave scene since the early 1990s. He works in the computer industry and composes his own electronic dance music. The interview was conducted in his home.

Vince Thomas lives in San Francisco and works for the computer industry. Now in his thirties, he has been involved with the rave scene since the late 1980s, including organizing large raves and ongoing weekly events in clubs. He is also a key figure in the local electronic dance music label Zoe Magik. The interview took place in his home.

NOTES

Part I

1. Tiffany Scott, interview with the author, San Francisco, July 24, 1997.
2. Jeff Taylor, interview with the author, San Francisco, July 24, 1997.
3. Vince Thomas, interview with the author, San Francisco, February 2, 1996.
4. Alaura O'Dell, interview with the author, Occidental, California, July 13, 1997.
5. Jim Dunn, interview with the author, San Francisco, July 25, 1997.
6. Charles H. Long, "Popular Religion," in *The Encyclopedia of Religion*, ed. Mircea Eliade (New York: Macmillan, 1987), 18:447; emphasis added.
7. Ibid., 18:444.
8. Catherine L. Albanese, *America: Religions and Religion*, 2d ed. (Belmont, Calif.: Wadsworth, 1992), 463–500.
9. Catherine L. Albanese, ed., introduction to *American Spiritualities: A Reader*, ed. Catherine L. Albanese (Bloomington: Indiana University Press, 2001), 11.
10. For more information on my theoretical and methodological approaches in this study, please see the introduction to part 2.
11. James Romero, interview with the author, San Francisco, July 7, 1997.

Chapter 1

1. Harvey Tyler, "History of Rave," April 1995; available online at http://www.breaks.com/Journey/intro.html
2. Chris Torella, Dino&Terry, and 2 Hillbillies, "Explorer's Guide to House, 2nd Edition," *Streetsound*, August 1993, 16.
3. Kai Fikentscher, "Feel the Groove: An Examination of the Interaction between House Music DJs and Dancers," paper presented at the annual meeting of the Society for Ethnomusicology (Los Angeles, October 19, 1995), 4.
4. Ibid., 6–7.
5. Ibid., 6.
6. Frankie Knuckles, quoted in Fikentscher, "Feel the Groove," 6.
7. Greg Raver-Lampman, "Controlling Drugs," *AlterNet*, accessed October 4, 2004, available online at http://www.alternet.org/drugreporter/16165/

8. Johnny Walker, quoted in Matthew Collin, *Altered State: The Story of Ecstasy Culture and Acid House* (London: Serpent's Tail, 1997), 53.

9. Adam Heath, quoted in Collin, *Altered State*, 52.

10. Muff Fitzgerald, quoted in Tyler, "History of Rave."

11. See, for example, Sarah Thornton, "Moral Panic, the Media and British Rave Culture," in *Microphone Fiends: Youth Music and Youth Culture*, ed. Tricia Rose and Andrew Ross (New York: Routledge, 1994), 176–92.

12. Tyler, "History of Rave."

13. Alaura O'Dell, interview with the author, Occidental, California, July 13, 1997.

14. Tyler, "History of Rave."

Chapter 2

1. For the first and most influential articulation of the significance of the year 2012 in the Mayan calendar and cosmology, see José Arguelles, *The Mayan Factor: Path Beyond Technology* (Santa Fe, N.M.: Bear, 1987). For McKenna's first formulation of his time wave theory, see Dennis McKenna and Terence McKenna, *The Invisible Landscape: Mind, Hallucinogens, and the I Ching* (New York: Seabury, 1975).

2. In fact, many people enjoy the chill-out mode so much that the chill-out party has emerged as a distinct event unto itself. At a chill-out party there is no uptempo dance music, only downtempo or ambient music; the entire space is decorated in a chill room style, and the focus is more on the relaxed, intimate interactions of a chill room than on high-energy trance dancing. While most chill-out parties are small, indoor affairs, one of the most successful and influential chill-out parties has been the Big Chill, an outdoor festival held each summer in England that draws thousands of people.

3. Since the time I wrote this chapter, 1015 Folsom has taken over the booking of their Friday and Saturday night events from Spundae and Martel and Nabiel, who have moved on to other clubs.

4. Jason Keehn, interview with the author, Santa Monica, California, November 30, 2003.

5. John Kelley, interview with the author, Los Angeles, December 1, 2003.

6. Kevin Gervais, interview with the author, Portland, Oregon, November 8, 2003.

7. Michael Manahan, interview with the author, San Francisco, November 20, 2003.

8. Michael Manahan, interview with the author, Seattle, November 10, 2003.

9. Keehn interview.

10. Rainie Sunshine, interview with the author, Aptos, California, October 28, 2003.

11. Sobey, interview with the author, Vancouver, British Columbia, November 9, 2003.

12. Gervais interview.

13. For more on Burning Man, see the introduction to this volume.

14. James Frazier, interview with the author, Aptos, California, October 28, 2003.

15. Manahan interview, November 20, 2003.

16. Frazier interview.

Part II

1. Charles H. Long, "Popular Religion," in *The Encyclopedia of Religion*, ed. Mircea Eliade (New York: Macmillan, 1987), 18:447.

2. Ibid.

3. William James, *The Varieties of Religious Experience: A Study in Human Nature* (London: Collins, 1968).

4. Joachim Wach, *The Comparative Study of Religions* (New York: Columbia University Press, 1958), 18.

5. Gerardus Van der Leeuw, quoted in Eric J. Sharpe, *Comparative Religion: A History* (La Salle, Ill.: Open Court, 1986), 231.

6. Robin Sylvan, *Traces of the Spirit: The Religious Dimensions of Popular Music* (New York: New York University Press, 2002), 18–44.

7. Ibid, 42–43.

8. Steven Friedson, *Dancing Prophets: Musical Experience in Tumbuka Healing* (Chicago: University of Chicago Press, 1996), 168.

9. Judith Becker, *Deep Listeners: Music, Emotion, and Trancing* (Bloomington: Indiana University Press, 2004), 1.

10. Ibid, 147.

11. Ibid, 1, 29, 54, 66, 67, 116, 155.

12. Ibid, 1, 66.

13. Ibid, 54, 66, 67.

14. Ibid, 127.

15. William Benzon, *Beethoven's Anvil: Music in Mind and Culture* (New York: Basic Books, 2001), 44, 86, 157.

16. Walter J. Freeman, "A Neurobiological Role of Music in Social Bonding," in *The Origins of Music*, eds. Steven Brown, Bjorn Merker, and Nils L. Wallin (Cambridge, Mass.: MIT Press, 2000), 422.

17. Andrew Newberg, *Why God Won't Go Away: Brain Science and the Biology of Belief* (New York: Ballantine Books, 2001), 86–87.

18. Benzon, 81.

Chapter 3

1. James Frazier, interview with the author, Aptos, California, October 28, 2003.

2. Jason Keehn, interview with the author, Santa Monica, California, November 30, 2003.

3. Michael Manahan, interview with the author, Seattle, November 10, 2003.

4. Isis Indriya, interview with the author, Seattle, November 10, 2003.

5. Shannon Titus, interview with the author, Oakland, California, November 24, 2003.

6. John Kelley, interview with the author, Los Angeles, December 1, 2003.

7. Jimi Fritz, *Rave Culture: An Insider's View* (Victoria, British Columbia: SmallFry, 1999), 76.

8. Ibid., 5.

9. Lloyd Morgan, quoted in Fritz, *Rave Culture*, 82.

10. Chris Lum, interview with the author, San Francisco, July 10, 1997.

11. Leandre (no last name given), quoted in Fritz, *Rave Culture*, 83.

12. Alex Martyshev, quoted in Fritz, *Rave Culture*, 84.

13. Vix (no last name given), quoted in Fritz, *Rave Culture*, 86.

14. Simon Reynolds, *Generation Ecstasy: Into the World of Techno and Rave Culture* (New York: Little, Brown, 1998) 84–85.

15. Charlotte Kaufman, interview with the author, San Francisco, July 23, 1997.

16. Gus Lanzas, interview with the author, San Francisco, July 16, 1997.

17. Jeff Taylor, interview with the author, San Francisco, July 24, 1997.

18. Tiffany Scott, interview with the author, San Francisco, July 24, 1997.

19. James Romero, interview with the author, San Francisco, July 7, 1997.

20. Joel Dinolt, interview with the author, San Francisco, July 16, 1997.

21. Sabrina Page, interview with the author, Fairfax, California, July 14, 1997.

22. Kaufman interview.

23. Lum interview.

24. Vince Thomas, interview with the author, San Francisco, February 2, 1996.

25. Ibid.

26. Jim Dunn, interview with the author, San Francisco, July 25, 1997.

27. Bahar Badizadegan, interview with the author, San Francisco, August 2, 1997.

28. Scott interview.

29. Lum interview.

30. Sam Shirley, interview with the author, Oakland, California, November 3, 2003.

31. Natasha Singer, interview with the author, San Francisco, November 5, 2003.
32. Titus interview.
33. Dunn interview.
34. Scott interview.
35. Sobey Wing, interview with the author, Vancouver, British Columbia, November 9, 2003.
36. Titus interview.
37. Taylor interview.
38. Shirley interview.
39. Keehn interview.
40. Kelley interview.
41. Michael Manahan, interview with the author, San Francisco, November 20, 2003.
42. Rainie Sunshine, interview with the author, Aptos, California, October 28, 2003.
43. Wing interview.
44. Titus interview.
45. Manoj Mathew, interview with the author, Portland, Oregon, November 11, 2003.
46. Singer interview.
47. Keehn interview.
48. Manahan interview, November 20, 2003.
49. Kevin Gervais, interview with the author, Portland, Oregon, November 8, 2003.
50. Kelley interview.
51. "Inner Rave: Enlightenment By Dancing," accessed July 3, 2004, available online at http://www.innerrave.org/
52. Romero interview.
53. Keehn interview.
54. Frazier interview.
55. Gervais interview.
56. Page interview.
57. Wing interview.
58. Taylor interview.
59. Singer interview.
60. Page interview.
61. Badizadegan interview.
62. Shirley interview.
63. Gervais interview.
64. Shirley interview.
65. Gervais interview.
66. Singer interview.
67. Lanzas interview.
68. Kaufman interview.
69. Thomas interview.
70. Dinolt interview.
71. Lanzas interview.
72. Dinolt interview.
73. Romero interview.
74. Wing interview.
75. Page interview.
76. Romero interview.
77. Titus interview.
78. Singer interview.
79. Dinolt interview.
80. Lanzas interview.
81. Page interview.
82. Titus interview.
83. Shirley interview.
84. Singer interview.

85. Titus interview.
86. Page interview.
87. Shirley interview.
88. Singer interview.
89. Keehn interview.
90. Frazier interview.
91. Romero interview.
92. Mathew interview.
93. Keehn interview.
94. Page interview.
95. Keehn interview.
96. Frazier interview.
97. Sunshine interview.
98. Shirley interview.
99. Singer interview.
100. Page interview.
101. Frazier interview.
102. Page interview.
103. Wing interview.
104. Titus interview.
105. Shirley interview.
106. Wing interview.
107. Frazier interview.
108. Page interview.
109. Singer interview.
110. Manahan interview, November 20, 2003.
111. Frazier interview.
112. Shirley interview.
113. Robin Sylvan, *Traces of the Spirit: The Religious Dimensions of Popular Music* (New York: New York University Press, 2002).
114. For more on the continuity between West African musicoreligious practices and sensibilities in African American musics, see Samuel A. Floyd, *The Power of Black Music: Interpreting Its History from Africa to the United States* (New York: Oxford University Press, 1995); Charles Keil, *Urban Blues* (Chicago: University of Chicago Press, 1966); Portia Maultsby, "Africanisms in African-American Music," in *Africanisms in American Culture*, ed. James Holloway (Bloomington: Indiana University Press, 1990); Portia Maultsby, "West African Influences and Retentions in U.S. Black Music: A Sociocultural Study," in *More Than Dancing*, ed. Irene V. Jackson (Westport, Conn.: Greenwood, 1985); Paul Oliver, *Savannah Syncopators: African Retentions in the Blues* (New York: Stein and Day, 1970); John Storm Roberts, *Black Music of Two Worlds* (New York: Praeger, 1972); Eileen Southern, *The Music of Black Americans* (New York: W. W. Norton, 1983); Michael Ventura, "Hear That Long Snake Moan," *Whole Earth Review*, spring–summer 1987, 28–43, 82–93; Richard Waterman, "African Influences on Music of the Americas," in *Acculturation in the Americas*, ed. Sol Tax (Chicago: University of Chicago Press, 1952); Olly Wilson, "The Significance of the Relationship Between Afro-American Music and West African Music," *Black Perspective in Music* 2, no. 1 (1974): 3–22; and Olly Wilson, "The Association of Movement and Music as a Manifestation of a Black Conceptual Approach to Music-Making," in Jackson, ed., *More Than Dancing*.
115. Frazier interview.
116. Thomas interview.
117. Shirley interview.
118. Frazier interview.
119. Kaufman interview.
120. Titus interview.
121. Page interview.
122. Singer interview.

123. Titus interview.
124. Indriya interview.
125. Keehn interview.
126. Frazier interview.
127. Gervais interview.
128. Shirley interview.
129. Scott interview.
130. Taylor interview.
131. Dunn interview.

Chapter 4

1. Sam Shirley, interview with the author, Oakland, California, November 3, 2003.
2. For example, see Catherine Bell, *Ritual Theory, Ritual Practice* (New York: Oxford University Press, 1992), 88–93.
3. Jonathan Z. Smith, *Imagining Religion: From Babylon to Jonestown* (Chicago: University of Chicago Press, 1982), 54–55.
4. Isis Indriya, interview with the author, Seattle, November 10, 2003.
5. James Romero, interview with the author, San Francisco, July 7, 1997.
6. Chris Lum, interview with the author, San Francisco, July 10, 1997.
7. Jim Dunn, interview with the author, San Francisco, July 25, 1997.
8. Vince Thomas, interview with the author, San Francisco, February 2, 1996.
9. Victor Turner, *The Ritual Process: Structure and Anti-Structure* (Chicago: Aldine, 1969).
10. For the classic formulation of rites of passage, see Arnold Van Gennep, *The Rites of Passage* (Chicago: University of Chicago Press, 1960). Van Gennep's work strongly influenced Turner.
11. Smith, *Imagining Religion*, 54–55.
12. Lum interview.
13. Ibid.
14. Tiffany Scott, interview with the author, San Francisco, July 24, 1997.
15. Shirley interview.
16. Dunn interview.
17. Alaura O'Dell, interview with the author, Occidental, California, July 13, 1997.
18. Jeff Taylor, interview with the author, San Francisco, July 24, 1997.
19. Romero interview.
20. Shirley interview.
21. Natasha Singer, interview with the author, San Francisco, November 5, 2003.
22. Sobey Wing, interview with the author, Vancouver, British Columbia, November 9, 2003.
23. Shirley interview.
24. Singer interview.
25. Jason Keehn, interview with the author, Santa Monica, California, November 30, 2003.
26. Shirley interview.
27. Singer interview.
28. Shirley interview.
29. Manoj Mathew, interview with the author, Portland, Oregon, November 11, 2003.
30. Keehn interview.
31. John Kelley, interview with the author, Los Angeles, December 1, 2003.
32. Shirley interview.
33. Ibid.
34. Ibid.
35. Ibid.
36. Scott interview.
37. James Frazier, interview with the author, Aptos, California, October 28, 2003.
38. Sabrina Page, interview with the author, Fairfax, California, July 14, 1997.
39. Joel Dinolt, interview with the author, San Francisco, July 16, 1997.

40. Page interview.
41. Gus Lanzas, interview with the author, San Francisco, July 16, 1997.
42. Gilbert Rouget, *Music and Trance: A Theory of the Relations between Music and Possession* (Chicago: University of Chicago Press, 1985), 84.
43. Charlotte Kaufman, interview with the author, San Francisco, July 23, 1997.
44. Rouget, *Music and Trance*, 101.
45. Lanzas interview.
46. Page interview.
47. Frazier interview.
48. Michael Manahan, interview with the author, San Francisco, November 20, 2003.
49. Frazier interview.
50. Kelley interview.
51. Frazier interview.
52. Manoj interview.
53. Ibid.
54. Shannon Titus, interview with the author, Oakland, California, November 24, 2003.
55. Ibid.
56. Shirley interview.
57. Keehn interview.
58. Ibid.
59. Ibid.
60. Ibid.
61. Kevin Gervais, interview with the author, Portland, Oregon, November 8, 2003.
62. Scott interview.
63. Isis Indriya interview.
64. Shirley interview.
65. Bob [no last name], "Rave Mass," in *The Spirit of Raving: Archives, Hyperreal,* November 28, 1995, available online at http://www.hyperreal.com/raves/spirit/culture/Rave_Mass.html
66. Lee [no last name], "Rave Mass."
67. Singer interview.
68. Isis Indriya interview.
69. Isis and Osiris Indriya, interview with the author, Seattle, November 10, 2003.
70. Ibid.
71. Isis Indriya interview.
72. Romero interview.
73. Wing interview.
74. Keehn interview.
75. Singer interview.
76. Isis Indriya interview.
77. Keehn interview.
78. Singer interview.
79. Shirley interview.
80. Ibid.
81. Wing interview.
82. Keehn interview.

Chapter 5

1. Charles H. Long, "Popular Religion," in *The Encyclopedia of Religion*, ed. Mircea Eliade (New York: Macmillan, 1987), 18:444.
2. Chris Lum, interview with the author, San Francisco, July 10, 1997.
3. Kevin Gervais, interview with the author, Portland, Oregon, November 8, 2003.
4. Natasha Singer, interview with the author, San Francisco, November 5, 2003.
5. Jeff Taylor, interview with the author, San Francisco, July 24, 1997.

6. Jim Dunn, interview with the author, San Francisco, July 25, 1997.
7. Gus Lanzas, interview with the author, San Francisco, July 16, 1997.
8. Alaura O'Dell, interview with the author, Occidental, California, July 13, 1997.
9. Vince Thomas, interview with the author, San Francisco, February 2, 1996.
10. Sabrina Page, interview with the author, Fairfax, California, July 14, 1997.
11. Charlotte Kaufman, interview with the author, San Francisco, July 23, 1997.
12. Lanzas interview.
13. Dunn interview.
14. James Romero, interview with the author, San Francisco, July 7, 1997.
15. Lanzas interview.
16. Shannon Titus, interview with the author, Oakland, California, November 24, 2003.
17. Joel Dinolt, interview with the author, San Francisco, July 16, 1997.
18. Singer interview.
19. Titus interview.
20. Isis Indriya, interview with the author, Seattle, November 10, 2003.
21. Osiris Indriya, interview with the author, Seattle, November 10, 2003.
22. Taylor interview.
23. Tiffany Scott, interview with the author, San Francisco, July 24, 1997.
24. Romero interview.
25. Titus interview.
26. Manoj Mathew, interview with the author, Portland, Oregon, November 11, 2003.
27. Jason Keehn, interview with the author, Santa Monica, California, November 30, 2003.
28. Titus interview.
29. For example, Section 609 of the Child Abduction Protection Act of 2003, also referred to as the Illicit Drug Anti-Proliferation Act of 2003, broadly expands the federal "crackhouse statute" (21 U.S.C. 856), which prohibits opening or maintaining a building for the purpose of manufacturing, distributing, or using a controlled substance. Instead of restricting the application of the crackhouse statute to ongoing, continuous drug operations, Section 609 expands the provisions, making them applicable to temporary, one-time, and outdoor events. Civil provisions have also been added which lower the burden of proof required to punish innocent business owners. This legislation was introduced in a conference committee as an attachment to Senate bill 151, widely referred to as the Amber Alert bill, legislation about child abduction that has nothing to do with drug policy issues. It is a reworking of the controversial Rave Act bill proposed by Senator Joseph Biden in 2002—legislation clearly targeting the rave community.
30. The Electronic Music Defense and Education Fund's mission is "[t]o raise and provide funds for legal assistance to innocent professionals in the electronic dance music business who are targeted by law enforcement in the expanding campaign against 'club drugs.' In addition to providing funds for legal efforts to protect the industry, EM:DEF will serve as a spokes-agency for the electronic dance music industry—providing an independent voice on behalf of industry professionals, while allowing professionals to avoid public association which could result in retaliation by law enforcement." See "About EM:DEF: Mission Statement," accessed August 21, 2004, available online at http://www.emdef.org/aboutemdef.html

    The San Francisco Late Night Coalition is "a broad-based group composed of promoters, activists, dj's, musicians, artists, community members and club owners. Our goal is to protect, preserve and promote San Francisco's late-night culture. We work to encourage understanding and awareness of the regulations and issues surrounding after-hours entertainment in San Francisco, and to provide a voice for the rights and the passions of this diverse community. We are an integral part of the cultural fabric of San Francisco, and make significant contributions to the economy and artistic diversity of this city." See "SFLNC Mission Statement," accessed August 21, 2004, available online at http://www.sflnc.com/index/mission/
31. James Frazier, interview with the author, Aptos, California, October 28, 2003.
32. Gervais interview.
33. Mathew interview.
34. Sobey Wing, interview with the author, Vancouver, British Columbia, November 9, 2003.
35. Thomas interview.

36. Dinolt interview.
37. Titus interview.
38. Dinolt interview.
39. Sam Shirley, interview with the author, Oakland, California, November 3, 2003.
40. Keehn interview.
41. There is some debate as to its origins, but the *peace, love,* and *unity* parts are widely attributed to New York DJ Frankie Bones, one of the pioneers of the U.S. rave scene, who helped organize the influential Storm Raves. A short time later, the *respect* part was added, variously attributed to Brian Behlendorf, Laura LaGassa, and Geoff White. LaGassa wrote an influential essay that put the four words together (see http://www.hyperreal.org/raves/spirit/plur/PLUR.html online), and then Rishad Quazi coined the acronym. For more on this history, see http://www.hyperreal.org/raves/spirit/plur/Origin_of_PLUR.html online.
42. Gervais interview.
43. Titus interview.
44. Shirley interview.
45. Singer interview.
46. Mathew interview.
47. Shirley interview.
48. Michael Manahan, interview with the author, San Francisco, November 20, 2003.
49. Titus interview.
50. Shirley interview.
51. John Kelley, interview with the author, Los Angeles, December 1, 2003.
52. Hakim Bey, *T.A.Z.: The Temporary Autonomous Zone, Ontological Anarchy, Poetic Terrorism* (Brooklyn, N.Y.: Autonomedia, 1985), 101.
53. Mark Kelsey, "Experimental Protocol and Meditation," *fUSION Anomaly: Temporary Autonomous Zones,* accessed August 24, 2004, available online at http://fusionanomaly.net/taz.html
54. Geoff White, "CyberTribe Rising," in *Guerillas of Harmony: Communiques from the Dance Underground,* ed. Cinnamon Twist (Los Angeles: Tribal Donut, 1999), 86.
55. Manahan interview.
56. Titus interview.
57. Wing interview.
58. Shirley interview.
59. Wing interview.
60. Mathew interview.
61. Singer interview.
62. Manahan interview.
63. Romero interview.
64. Dave Jurman, senior director of the Dance Music department, Columbia Records/SONY, quoted in Jimi Fritz, *Rave Culture: An Insider's View* (Victoria, British Columbia: SmallFry, 1999), 252.
65. Bahar Badizadegan, interview with the author, San Francisco, August 2, 1997.
66. Fritz, *Rave Culture,* 38, 252.
67. Jurman, quoted in Fritz, *Rave Culture,* 252–53.
68. Fritz, *Rave Culture,* 236.
69. Ibid., 38.
70. Leyolah Antara and Nathan Kaye, "Connected Consciousness in Motion: The Power of Ceremony for Creating Positive Social Change," in Twist, ed., *Guerillas of Harmony,* 100–106.
71. Badizadegan interview.
72. Scott interview.
73. Consortium of Collective Consciousness, "Traveler Reality," *Earth: The Origin of Things,* accessed August 26, 2004, available online at http://www.ccc.ac/2001/index.htm
74. Manoj interview.
75. Isis Indriya interview.
76. Frazier interview.
77. Manahan interview.

78. Lee Fogel, "FMM—The Legend Continues," in *The Spirit of Raving: Archives, Hyperreal*, March 28, 1994, available online at http://hyperreal.org/raves/spirit/testimonials/FMR-SantaCruz-CA.html

79. Fritz, *Rave Culture*, 179. I should be clear that Fritz is not a religious studies scholar and that his assertion is not based on scholarly criteria. However, according to anthropologist of religion Tim Olaveson, "Scholars of rave, post-rave, and other dance cultures have recently suggested that these movements may be viewed as NRMs [new religious movements]. My own research on the central Canadian rave scene supports these conclusions to a limited extent . . . . Rave is just the latest example in the process of sociocultural revitalization that underlies the development of all religions and the health and regeneration of cultures throughout human history." See Olaveson, "Rave as New Religious Movement?" in *Rave Culture and Religion*, ed. Graham St. John (London: Routledge, 2004), 100. For those interested in scholarly perspectives on these and other religious aspects of rave culture, I strongly recommend St. John's book, which serves as an excellent complement to this study. I have herein chosen not to quote many other scholars, preferring to let ravers speak for themselves.

80. Gervais interview.

81. Fritz, 181.

82. Sam Shirley, personal communication with the author, January 15, 2004.

83. Romero interview.

84. Badizadegan interview.

85. Ibid.

86. Page interview.

87. Scott Hutson, "Technoshamanism: Spiritual Healing in the Rave Subculture," *Popular Music and Society* 23, no. 3 (Fall 1999): 71.

88. Kodwo Eshun, *More Brilliant Than the Sun: Adventures in Sonic Fiction* (London: Quartet, 1998).

Chapter 6

1. Shannon Titus, interview with the author, Oakland, California, November 24, 2003.

2. Sobey Wing, interview with the author, Vancouver, British Columbia, November 9, 2003.

3. Manoj Mathew, interview with the author, Portland, Oregon, November 11, 2003.

4. Michael Manahan, interview with the author, San Francisco, California, November 20, 2003.

5. Mathew interview.

6. From the invitation to the Rhythm Society's All Night Dance Celebration, *Ripples*, December 31, 2000.

7. Ibid.

8. The Rhythm Society, "Rhythm Society: Vision Statement," accessed September 25, 2004, available online at http://rhythm.org/vision.html

9. Sam Shirley, interview with the author, Oakland, California, November 3, 2003.

10. Natasha Singer, interview with the author, San Francisco, California, November 5, 2003.

11. Titus interview.

12. Gena Womack, quoted in Jimi Fritz, *Rave Culture: An Insider's View* (Victoria, British Columbia: SmallFry, 1999), 175.

13. Jason Keehn, interview with the author, Santa Monica, California, November 30, 2003.

14. John Kelley, interview with the author, Los Angeles, December 1, 2003.

15. Ibid.

16. Keehn interview.

17. Kelley interview.

18. Keehn interview.

19. Kelley interview.

20. Ibid.

21. Isis Indriya, interview with the author, Seattle, November 10, 2003.

22. Michael Manahan, interview with the author, Seattle, November 11, 2003; Manahan interview, November 20, 2003.

23. Oracle Gatherings, "The Experience," accessed September 25, 2004, available online at http://www.oraclegatherings.com

24. Osiris Indriya, interview with the author, Seattle, November 10, 2003.

25. Isis Indriya interview.

26. Manahan interview, November 11, 2003.

27. Isis Indriya interview.

28. Ibid.

29. Wing interview.

30. Ibid.

31. Tribal Harmonix, "Mission," accessed September 26, 2004, available online at http://www.tribalharmonix.org/mission.php

32. James Frazier, interview with the author, Aptos, California, October 28, 2003.

33. Earthdance, "About: History," accessed September 27, 2004, available online at http://www.earthdance.org/

34. Frazier interview.

35. Gathering of the Tribes, "Mission Statement: About," accessed September 27, 2004, available online at http://www.gottribes.org/mission.html

36. Mathew interview.

37. Titus interview.

Conclusion

1. P. J. Corkery, "Big Bucks, Big Names, Big Love Parade," *San Francisco Examiner*, accessed October 4, 2004, available online at http://www.examiner.com/article/index.cfm/i/100404c_pj

2. Gregory Sams, "Dance Culture—A New Church," in *Uncommon Sense* (online book, 1998), available at http://www.chaos-works.com/ch27.html

BIBLIOGRAPHY

Albanese, Catherine L. *America: Religions and Religion*, 3d ed. Belmont, CA: Wadsworth, 1998.
———. "Religion and Popular American Culture: An Introductory Essay." *Journal of the American Academy of Religion* 54, no. 4 (1996): 733–42.
———, ed. *American Spiritualities: A Reader*. Bloomington: Indiana University Press, 2001.
Amoaku, W. Komla. "Toward a Definition of Traditional African Music: A Look at the Ewe of Ghana." In *More Than Drumming: Essays on African and Afro-Latin American Music and Musicians*, ed. Irene V. Jackson, 31–40. Westport, CT: Greenwood, 1985.
Becker, Judith. *Deep Listeners: Music, Emotion, and Trancing*. Bloomington: Indiana University Press, 2004.
Bell, Catherine. *Ritual: Perspectives and Dimensions*. New York: Oxford University Press, 1997.
———. *Ritual Theory, Ritual Practice*. New York: Oxford University Press, 1992.
Benzon, William. *Beethoven's Anvil: Music in Mind and Culture*. New York: Basic Books, 2004.
Bey, Hakim. *T.A.Z.: The Temporary Autonomous Zone, Ontological Anarchy, Poetic Terrorism*. Brooklyn, NY: Autonomedia, 1985.
Blacking, John. *"A Commonsense View of all Music": Reflections on Percy Grainger's Contribution to Ethnomusicology and Music Education*. Cambridge: Cambridge University Press, 1987.
———. *How Musical Is Man?* Seattle: University of Washington Press, 1973.
Bohlman, Philip P. "Is All Music Religious?" *Criterion* 28, no. 2 (1989): 19–24.
Boiles, Charles Lafayette. *Man, Magic, and Musical Occasions*. Columbus, OH: Collegiate, 1978.
Bourguignon, Erika, ed. *Religion, Altered States of Consciousness, and Social Change*. Columbus: Ohio State University Press, 1973.
Boyd, Jenny. *Musicians In Tune: Seventy-Five Contemporary Musicians Discuss the Creative Process*. New York: Simon and Schuster, 1992.
Brewster, Bill, and Frank Broughton. *Last Night a DJ Saved My Life: The History of the Disc Jockey*. New York: Grove, 2000.
Bussmann, Jane. *Once in a Lifetime: The Crazy Days of Acid House and Afterwards*. London: Virgin, 1998.
Chernoff, John Miller. *African Rhythm and African Sensibility: Aesthetics and Social Action in African Musical Idioms*. Chicago: University of Chicago Press, 1979.
Coakley, Sarah, ed. *Religion and the Body*. Cambridge: Cambridge University Press, 1997.
Collin, Matthew. *Altered State: The Story of Ecstasy Culture and Acid House*. London: Serpent's Tail, 1997.

Crafts, Susan D., Daniel Cavicchi, Charles Keil, and the Music in Daily Life Project. *My Music*. Hanover, NH: Wesleyan University Press, 1993.

D'Aquili, Eugene G., and Charles D. Laughlin Jr. "The Neurobiology of Myth and Ritual." In *The Spectrum of Ritual: A Biogenetic Structural Analysis*, eds. Eugene G. d'Aquili, Charles D. Laughlin Jr., and John McManus, 152–82. New York: Columbia University Press, 1979.

Epstein, Jonathon S., ed. *Adolescents and Their Music: If It's Too Loud, You're Too Old*. New York: Garland, 1994.

Eshun, Kodwo. *More Brilliant Than the Sun: Adventures in Sonic Fiction*. London: Quartet, 1998.

Fikentscher, Kai. *"You Better Work!": Underground Dance Music in New York City*. Hanover, NH: Wesleyan University Press, 2000.

——. "Feel the Groove: An Examination of the Interaction between House Music DJs and Dancers." Paper presented at the annual meeting of the Society for Ethnomusicology, Los Angeles, October 19, 1995.

Floyd, Samuel A. *The Power of Black Music: Interpreting Its History from Africa to the United States*. New York: Oxford University Press, 1995.

Freeman, Walter J. "A Neurological Role of Music in Social Bonding." In *The Origins of Music*, eds. Steven Brown, Bjorn Mesker, and Nils L. Wattin, 411–24. Cambridge, MA. MIT Press, 2000.

Friedson, Steven M. *Dancing Prophets: Musical Experience in Tumbuka Healing*. Chicago: University of Chicago Press, 1996.

Fritz, Jimi. *Rave Culture: An Insider's View*. Victoria, B.C.: SmallFry, 1999.

Gilbert, Jeremy, and Ewan Pearson. *Discographies: Dance Music, Culture and the Politics of Sound*. London: Routledge, 1999.

Greeley, Andrew. *God in Popular Culture*. Chicago: Thomas More, 1988.

Grimes, Ronald. *Beginnings in Ritual Studies*. Lanham, MD: University Press of America, 1982.

Hutson, Scott. "Technoshamanism: Spiritual Healing in the Rave Subculture." *Popular Music and Society* 23, no. 3 (1999): 53–77.

James, William. *The Varieties of Religious Experience: A Study in Human Nature*. London: Collins, 1968.

Kempster, Chris, ed. *History of House*. London: Sanctuary, 1996.

Leppert, Richard. *The Sight of Sound: Music, Representation, and the History of the Body*. Berkeley and Los Angeles: University of California Press, 1993.

Lex, Barbara. "The Neurobiology of Ritual Trance." In *The Spectrum of Ritual: A Biogenetic Structural Analysis*, ed. Eugene G. d'Aquili, Charles D. Laughlin Jr., and John McManus, 117–51. New York: Columbia University Press, 1979.

Lidov, David. "Mind and Body in Music." *Semiotica* 66, nos. 1–3 (1987): 69–97.

Lippy, Charles H. *Being Religious, American Style: A History of Popular Religiosity in the United States*. Westport, CT: Praeger, 1994.

Long, Charles H. "The History of the History of Religions." In *A Reader's Guide to the Great Religions*, ed. Charles J. Adams, 467–75. New York: Free Press, 1977.

——. "A Look at the Chicago Tradition in the History of Religions: Retrospect and Future." In *The History of Religions: Retrospect and Prospect*, ed. Joseph M. Kitagawa, 87–104. New York: Macmillan, 1985.

——. "Popular Religion." In *The Encyclopedia of Religion*, ed. Mircea Eliade, 18: 442–52. New York: Macmillan, 1987.

Ludwig, Arnold. "Altered States of Consciousness." In *Trance and Possession States*, ed. Raymond Prince, 69–95. Montreal: University of Montreal Press, 1968.

McAllester, David P. "Some Thoughts on 'Universals' in World Music." *Ethnomusicology* 15, no. 3 (1971): 379–80.

McLeod, Norma, and Marcia Herndon. *Music as Culture*. Darby, PA: Norwood, 1982.

McNeill, William H. *Keeping Together in Time: Dance and Drill in Human History*. Cambridge, MA: Harvard University Press, 1995.

Manuel, Peter. "Music as Symbol, Music as Simulacrum: Postmodern, Pre-modern, and Modern Aesthetics in Subcultural Popular Musics." *Popular Music* 14, no. 2 (1995): 227–39.

Maultsby, Portia. "Africanisms in African-American Music." In *Africanisms in American Culture*, ed. James Holloway, 185–210. Bloomington: Indiana University Press, 1990.

———. "West African Influences and Retentions in U.S. Black Music: A Sociocultural Study." In *More Than Dancing*, ed. Irene V. Jackson, 25–57. Westport, CT: Greenwood, 1985.

Mazur, Eric Michael, and Kate McCarthy, eds. *God in the Details: American Religion in Everyday Life*. New York: Routledge, 2001.

Nattiez, Jean-Jacques. *Music and Discourse: Toward a Semiology of Music*. Princeton, NJ: Princeton University Press, 1990.

Needham, Rodney. "Percussion and Transition." *Man* 2 (1967): 606–14.

Neher, Andrew. "A Physiological Explanation of Unusual Behavior in Ceremonies Involving Drums." *Human Biology* 34 (1962): 151–60.

Nelson, John Wiley. *Your God Is Alive and Well and Appearing in Popular Culture*. Philadelphia: Westminster, 1976.

Newberg, Andrew. *Why God Won't Go Away: Brain Science and the Biology of Belief*. New York: Ballantine Books, 2001.

Otto, Rudolf. *The Idea of the Holy*. New York: Oxford University Press, 1958.

Parkin, David. "Ritual as Spatial Direction and Bodily Division." In *Understanding Rituals*, ed. Daniel de Coppet, 11–25. London: Routledge, 1992.

Poschardt, Ulf. *DJ Culture*. London: Quartet, 1998.

Reynolds, Simon. *Generation Ecstasy: Into the World of Techno and Rave Culture*. New York: Little, Brown, 1998.

Rose, Tricia, and Andrew Ross, eds. *Microphone Fiends: Youth Music and Youth Culture*. New York: Routledge, 1994.

Rouget, Gilbert. *Music and Trance: A Theory of the Relations between Music and Possession*. Chicago: University of Chicago Press, 1985.

Schechner, Richard. *Performance Theory*. New York: Routledge, 1988.

———. *The Future of Ritual: Writings on Culture and Performance*. London: Routledge, 1993.

Shapiro, Peter, ed. *Modulations: A History of Electronic Music*. New York: Caipirinha Productions, 2000.

Shepherd, William C. "Religion and the Counter Culture—A New Religiosity." *Sociological Inquiry* 42, no. 1 (1972): 3–9.

Silcott, Mireille. *Rave America: New School Dancescapes*. Toronto: ECW, 1999.

Smart, Ninian. *Dimensions of the Sacred: An Anatomy of the World's Beliefs*. Berkeley and Los Angeles: University of California Press, 1996.

Smith, Jonathan Z. *Imagining Religion: From Babylon to Jonestown*. Chicago: University of Chicago Press, 1982.

———. *To Take Place: Toward Theory in Ritual*. Chicago: University of Chicago Press, 1987.

Spencer, Jon Michael. *Theological Music: An Introduction to Theomusicology*. Westport, CT: Greenwood, 1991.

———, ed. *Black Sacred Music: A Journal of Theomusicology* 3, no. 2 (1989).

———, ed. *Black Sacred Music: A Journal of Theomusicology* 5, no. 1 (1991).

———, ed. *Black Sacred Music: A Journal of Theomusicology* 6, no. 1 (1992).

St. John, Graham, ed. *Rave Culture and Religion*. London: Routledge, 2004.

Straw, Will. "Systems of Articulation, Logics of Change: Communities and Scenes in Popular Music." *Cultural Studies* 5, no. 3 (1999): 368–88.

Sylvan, Robin. *Traces of the Spirit: The Religious Dimensions of Popular Music*. New York: New York University Press, 2002.

Thornton, Sarah. *Club Cultures: Music, Media, and Subcultural Capital*. Hanover, NH: Wesleyan University Press, 1996.

Torella, Chris, Dino&Terry, and 2 Hillbillies. "Explorer's Guide to House, 2nd Edition." *Streetsound*, August 1993, 20–25.

Turner, Victor. *The Ritual Process: Structure and Anti-Structure*. Chicago: Aldine, 1969.

Twist, Cinnamon, ed. *Guerillas of Harmony: Communiques from the Dance Underground.* Los Angeles: Tribal Donut, 1999.

Van der Leeuw, Gerardus. *Religion in Essence and Manifestation,* 2 vols. New York: Harper and Row, 1963.

———. *Sacred and Profane Beauty: The Holy in Art.* New York: Holt, Rinehart, and Winston, 1963.

Van Gennep, Arnold. *The Rites of Passage.* Chicago: University of Chicago Press, 1960.

Ventura, Michael. "Hear That Long Snake Moan." *Whole Earth Review,* Spring–Summer 1987, 28–43, 82–93.

Wach, Joachim. *The Comparative Study of Religions.* New York: Columbia University Press, 1958.

———. *The Sociology of Religion.* Chicago: University of Chicago Press, 1944.

———. *Types of Religious Experience: Christian and Non-Christian.* Chicago: University of Chicago Press, 1970.

Wilson, Olly. "The Association of Movement and Music as a Manifestation of a Black Conceptual Approach to Music-Making." In *More Than Dancing,* ed. Irene V. Jackson, 9–23. Westport, CT: Greenwood, 1985.

———. "The Significance of the Relationship between Afro-American Music and West African Music." *Black Perspective in Music* 2, no. 1 (1974): 3–22.

ABOUT THE AUTHOR

Robin Sylvan has a Ph.D. in religious studies and is the founder and director of the Sacred Center, a San Francisco Bay Area nonprofit educational organization dedicated to helping people find their unique spiritual paths within the complexities of a postmodern world. He has taught in both mainstream academic and alternative experiential contexts, including: the California Institute of Integral Studies in San Francisco; the College of Wooster in Wooster, Ohio; Fairhaven College in Bellingham, Washington; the Graduate Theological Union in Berkeley, California; the Ojai Foundation in Ojai, California; and the University of California at Davis. He is the author of *Traces of the Spirit: The Religious Dimensions of Popular Music*, and has been a music aficionado and spiritual explorer for most of his life.

INDEX

9 7 8 0 4 1 5 9 7 0 9 1 4

An environmentally friendly book printed and bound in England by www.printondemand-worldwide.com

PEFC Certified

This product is
from sustainably
managed forests
and controlled
sources

www.pefc.org

PEFC/16-33-415

This book is made of chain-of-custody materials; FSC materials for the cover and PEFC materials for the text pages.

#0392 - 050116 - C0 - 229/152/12 - PB - 9780415970914